Praise for

NOTHING B

THE BLOOD OF

"*Nothing but the Blood of Jesus* is nothing but good. From sin to salvation, Jeremy Myers takes readers step by step through the workings of God's grace to expose the structures of scapegoating and to redeem a humanity fallen victim to the ensuing violence. Channeling René Girard and the biblical authors, Myers aptly shows how the blood of Jesus cleanses us from endless cycles of violence and takes us instead into endless cycles of divine/human forgiveness, grace, and peace for the glory of God and the furtherance of God's kingdom."

–**SHARON BAKER PUTT,** Professor of Theology and Religion, and author of *Executing God*

"I've spent years searching for exactly this book. Myers clearly outlines how sacrifice throughout Scripture is a human practice that God accommodates, and how Jesus changes everything with His death and resurrection! The work and research found in *Nothing But the Blood of Jesus* transforms the traditional way we have understood sacrifice to function in the Ancient Near East and paves the way to a fuller understanding of God's heart for humanity revealed in Jesus."

–**BRUXY CAVEY**, Teaching Pastor at The Meeting House and author of best-selling *The End of Religion* and *(Re)union: The Good News of Jesus for Seekers, Saints, and Sinners*

"When we talk about the cross of Christ and how it is that we find salvation in it, we inevitably begin to use words like sin, law, and sacrifice. But these words are always in danger of collapsing into empty religious cliche. Thankfully, J. D. Myers takes us beyond the realm of cliché and into substantive answers in his book, *Nothing but the Blood of Jesus*. The chief task in atonement theology is to think about the cross in ways that do not project upon

God our own sins of retributive violence. This is what *Nothing but the Blood of Jesus* achieves."

–**BRIAN ZAHND,** Lead Pastor of Word of Life Church in St. Joseph, Missouri, and author of *Sinners in the Hands of a Loving God*

"Building on his previous book, *The Atonement of God*, the work of René Girard, and a solid grounding in the Scriptures, Jeremy Myers shares fresh and challenging insights with us about sin, law, sacrifice, scapegoating, and blood. This book reveals to us how truly precious the blood of Jesus is and the way of escaping the cycle of blame, rivalry, scapegoating, sacrifice, and violence that has plagued humanity since the time of Cain and Abel. *Nothing but the Blood of Jesus* is an important and timely literary contribution to a world desperately in need of the non-violent message of Jesus."

–**WESLEY ROSTOLL,** author of *Seeing the Cross with New Eyes*

"Every Sunday, countless Evangelicals, with their embedded sacrificial mindset, sing of how the blood of Jesus washes away their sins. But what does this really mean? In *Nothing but the Blood of Jesus*, Myers puts forth an answer that may surprise most. With a strict adherence to both the Hebrew and Christian scriptures, the author gently guides his readers through heavy issues like sin, the law, sacrifice, and scapegoating, beautifully concluding his survey with a subversive look at how the blood of Jesus, as we Christians proclaim, indeed saves us."

–**MATTHEW J. DISTEFANO,** regular contributor for Unfundamentalist Christians on Patheos, and author of *From the Blood of Abel*

"Many pastors of mainline churches struggle to explain the cross to their congregations. My churches have often seen themselves as "Christmas and Easter churches," but not "Lent and Good Friday churches." The mainline church needs to reclaim Lent and Good Friday, and to do this, we need to reclaim the cross. Jeremy Myers' book *Nothing but the Blood of Jesus* does just that. Read this book alone or with your community to discover the radically nonviolent love of God that Jesus revealed on the cross."

–**Rev. Adam Ericksen**, Education Coordinator at the Raven Foundation and Minister of Faith Development at Lake Oswego United Church of Christ

"I am not typically impressed by much of the contemporary conservative evangelical scholarship on the violence in the Old Testament and why Jesus had to die and become consumed by that endless stream of human hostility to restore us to a relationship with God.

"Until recently there was only one acceptable view of the atonement among evangelicals which focused exclusively on penal substitutionary atonement. If one strayed a little from that view of the atonement, it often led to heresy accusations and scapegoating among the evangelical faithful. The irony is that in the 2,000-year history of the church there have been multiple views. All are expressions, based on Scripture as to why Jesus had to die.

"Jeremy Myers, in the spirit and similar tradition of N. T. Wright, offers a theological breath of fresh air along with a practical biblical contemporary application to this ancient discussion.

"As one who considers himself a disciple of René Girard, I found the chapters on sacrifice and scapegoating the most meaningful and enriching to my journey to better understand the death of Jesus.

"I highly recommend this book to all readers who want a fresh evangelical perspective on the death of Jesus and who crave not only great scholarship but also outstanding writing."

–**Jeff Burns**, Peace maker, life coach, writer, and bodyboarder
jeffburns.org
findinggodinthewater.com
carolinacoastalcoaching.com

NOTHING BUT THE Blood OF JESUS

HOW THE SACRIFICE OF JESUS SAVES THE WORLD FROM SIN

NOTHING BUT THE

Blood

OF JESUS

HOW THE SACRIFICE OF JESUS SAVES THE WORLD FROM SIN

J. D. MYERS

RP
RedeemingPress.com

NOTHING BUT THE BLOOD OF JESUS
How the Sacrifice of Jesus Saves the World from Sin

Published by Redeeming Press
Dallas, OR 97338
RedeemingPress.com

ISBN: 978-1-939992-46-8 (Paperback)
ISBN: 978-1-939992-47-5 (Mobi Kindle)
ISBN: 978-1-939992-48-2 (ePub)

Learn more about J. D. Myers by visiting RedeemingGod.com

Cover Design by Taylor Myers
TaylorGraceGraphics.com

Other Books by Jeremy Myers

The Atonement of God

The Re-Justification of God: A Study of Romans 9:10-24

Adventures in Fishing (for Men)

Christmas Redemption: Why Christians Should Celebrate a Pagan Holiday

Why You Have Not Committed the Unforgivable Sin

What is Prayer?

The Gospel According to Scripture (Forthcoming)

The Gospel Dictionary (Forthcoming)

Books in the *Close Your Church for Good* Series

Preface: Skeleton Church

Vol. 1: The Death and Resurrection of the Church

Vol. 2: Put Service Back into the Church Service

Vol. 3: Church is More than Bodies, Bucks, & Bricks

Vol. 4: Dying to Religion and Empire

Vol. 5: Cruciform Pastoral Leadership (Forthcoming)

All books are available at Amazon.com

Learn about each title at the end of this book

This book is dedicated to
President Donald J. Trump and Hillary Rodham Clinton.
For those willing and able to see it, you provided an excellent example
of imitative rivalry and scapegoating at work.

It is for freedom from this that Jesus sets us free!

TABLE OF CONTENTS

FOREWORD

"Come now, and let us reason together," says the Lord,
"Though your sins are like scarlet,
they shall be as white as snow;
though they are red like crimson, they shall be as wool."
Isaiah 1:18

"*How does that work? What is the connection?"* she asked sincerely.

I stumbled and stuttered out some platitude and we both knew it.

I retreated to mystery and her brow furrowed.

The question was crucially (literally) important to both of us.

The setting was the University of Nottingham where I was sharing study space with another visiting scholar—a "Reverend Doctor" on sabbatical from her priesthood and seminary post in continental Europe. She repeated the question:

"At the heart of Christian faith is the claim that the cross of Christ two thousand years ago is somehow connected to an experience of salvation today. How does Jesus' death in history past create an existential sense that my sins are forgiven today? I see young Christians who sincerely believe this and even seem to experience it in a profound way. *But how does that work? What's the connection?"*

I knew the question was not rhetorical, but the mix of expectancy and skepticism in her face communicated a backstory of frustration. Indeed, she once sat on a committee vetting her capital city's new bishop. And this was the only question she had hoped to ask the new candidate. The committee refused the question. "Too controversial," they said.

How does it work? What's the connection?

I should know this. I self-identify as a "theologian of the cross." My MA and PhD studies centered on the cross. I've edited and written academic volumes on the cross. I should know this, but I was tongue-tied that day. Paralyzed under the clichés on the tip of my tongue. *Well, Jesus died for us. We're washed in the blood. By his stripes we are healed. Baptized in his death.* What is the connection? How does that work?

"It's a mystery," I repeated. Because it is.

"So we don't know," she pressed. "Christianity makes an unintelligible, magical claim of a connection between Jesus' death and our lives that it cannot explain. And this is the foundation on which the whole edifice stands?"

"Um ..."

I should know this. I used to. When I was a child, it was perfectly clear. What is it I once believed and understood as a child? What is it that we tell children now? I was compelled to spend my remaining time at Nottingham exploring the meaning of the cross through the great saints of the church.

When I bounced the question back to my new scholar friend, her cryptic answer was simply, "I don't know ... but I think basically Nicholas of Cusa got it right"—which sent me scurrying back to the library!

Nicholas was a 15th century Renaissance man—a philosopher, jurist, scientist, diplomat and theologian. In his view, Christ is the perfect image of the Father and the mediator of divine sonship for us all. For Nicholas, the vision of Christ liberates us from our entanglement with sin and assimilates us to God. This vision comes into clearest focus on the cross. One commentator summarized him as follows:

> The supreme manifestation of God's love and splendor is Jesus' death on the cross. In his death, we are taught that God holds back nothing, not even the life of his Son. The Cross reveals God's glory; from the Cross all the secrets of

God are displayed."[1]

Ultimately I boiled it down for myself this way. What does 'the cross' (or 'the blood') mean? The cross is the supreme revelation of God's self-giving, radically forgiving, co-suffering love, and God-in-Christ's decisive victory over Satan, sin and death (I expand this in *A More Christlike God* and condense it in *Jesus Showed Us!*).

Attentive readers will note that I have cleverly sidestepped the original question. *How does that work?* To reconstruct the *how*, one would need to revisit and analyze what the scriptures actually say about *sin* and the *law*, *sacrifice* and *scapegoating*, and how the biblical metonym *'blood'* relates to Christ and our salvation.

Thankfully, this is precisely and concisely what Jeremy Myers has done in *Nothing but the Blood of Jesus.* His exploration of the texts is clear-minded and impressively accessible. Treading where I dared not, he walks us step-by-step through the key Bible texts on each of these critical themes. I especially appreciate how Myers weaves and integrates the best of current scholarship into a cogent study that will lead any thoughtful reader to a fresh vision of Jesus Christ and a renewed love for our cruciform God of self-giving love and redemption.

Brad Jersak (PhD)
Author of *A More Christlike God*
Editor-in-Chief at CWR Magazine
BradJersak.com

[1] Lawrence F. Hundersmarck, "Preaching," Christopher M. Bellitto, Thomas M. Izbicki, and Gerald Christianson (eds.), *Introducing Nicholas of Cusa: A Guide to a Renaissance Man* (Mahwah, NJ: Paulist, 2004), 246.

AUTHOR'S NOTE

Thanks for reading! Before you begin, I wanted to let you know that I really struggled with the organization of this book. I struggled in two main areas.

First, this book contains five main parts which look at five key biblical concepts: sin, law, sacrifice, scapegoat, and blood. The problem with each of these concepts, however, is that to understand any one of them, you must first understand the other four. You cannot really understand the concept of sin unless you first understand the concepts of law, sacrifice, scapegoat, and blood. This is true of all five terms. This means there is really no good place to start.

But books must start somewhere, and since the Bible begins by looking at the problem of sin, I decided to start there as well. What this means is that as you read Part I on Sin, you might not fully understand everything that is being said, and you will notice that I frequently refer you to later sections of the book. Then when you get to these later chapters, they will help inform your understanding of the concepts already discussed. Since all five concepts are so intricately connected in this way, by the time you get to the end of the book and have the full picture of all five ideas, hopefully the big picture will be clear.

So please do not get frustrated in the early chapters. Don't give up too soon! Persevere, and the further you go, the more sense it will make.

The second note regarding the organization of this book is in regards to the five chapters of Scripture verse studies that conclude each major Part of the book. Part I on Sin concludes with a chapter titled "Scriptures on Sin."

Parts II, III, IV, and V all have similar closing chapters. You will notice as you read these chapters that many of the passages discussed in one chapter will also be discussed in a later chapter. For example, verses out of Hebrews 9–10 are mentioned in all five chapters.

At one stage in writing this book, I attempted to combine all five of these chapters into one chapter which was placed at the very end of the book, so that I wasn't discussing Hebrews 9–10 in five different places, but only in one place, and you could read the entire study of these verses all at once. But this led to numerous problems, not least of which was the length of this final chapter. It was incredibly long! Furthermore, since this long chapter was at the end of the book, you would not have received immediate application on the five topics discussed in this book about how these topics helped our understanding of Scripture. It seemed better to put a shorter chapter at the end of each Part of the book so that immediately after reading about one of the five concepts, you could see how this concept helped and informed your understanding of the Bible.

So I ended up with what you have before you: five individual chapters on key Scriptures. Though there are some repeated studies, this approach has the benefit of adding a new layer of meaning and significance upon a text as you come to understand new terms within in. Think of it like one of those human anatomy books which contains several transparent pages which, when turned, gives you a new look at the physiology of the human body. That is what will happen as you read this book. As you understand each of the five key terms in this book, you will gain new insight and understanding into various key Scripture passages so that when you reach the end of the book, you will see the entirety of these texts in a whole new light.

Now that you understand the method to my madness in organizing this book, let us begin by diving into sin … Not literally, of course!

CHAPTER 1

HOW PRECIOUS IS THE FLOW?

Have you ever stopped to listen to what we Christians say and sing about the blood of Jesus?

Try to imagine what you would think about a group of people who regularly sang songs about founts of blood, washing in blood, and needing blood to be made whole? Imagine you are walking through a forest on a dark night and as you stumbled along, off in the distance you saw the light of a fire with people dancing around it. As you drew closer, you heard them singing the following song:

What can wash away my sin?
Nothing but this bloody sacrifice.
What can make me whole again?
Nothing but this bloody sacrifice.

O precious is the flow that makes me white as snow;
No other fount I know; nothing but this bloody sacrifice.

I imagine that if you heard people singing this in the woods on a dark night, you would turn around and head the other direction. What if, however, you kept going, and as you drew closer, the song changed to this one:

Have you been to the altar for the cleansing power?
Are you washed in the blood of this man?
Are you fully trusting in his grace this hour?
Are you washed in the blood of this man?

Are you washed in the blood,
In the soul cleansing blood of this man?
Are your garments spotless? Are they white as snow?
Are you washed in the blood of this man?

As your skin crawled with the implications of that song, the people then began to sing about plunging one another beneath a fountain of blood.

There is a fountain filled with blood drawn from our victim's veins;
And sinners plunged beneath that flood lose all their guilty stains.

I think that instead of happily join this group of blood-crazed murderers, you would likely get out of the woods as fast as possible and then call the local police to report what you had heard. I can see the newspaper headline now: "Lone Hiker Discovers Ghastly Cult Bathing in the Blood of a Human Sacrifice." When read outside of their Christian context, that is indeed what these songs bring to mind, is it not? These sorts of songs sound more like a gruesome and gory scene from a Freddy Krueger movie than from something to be joyfully celebrated. Yet when the words of the three songs above are sung as originally written so that they talk about the blood of Jesus Christ as the Lamb of God, we Christians happily sing them with gusto, and think that nothing is amiss.

Why is that?

ARGUING WITH MYSELF

If you have been brought up in the church as I have, you may not have ever stopped to consider what the songs we sing sound like to an outside observer. Just listen to yourself sing sometimes, especially around Easter, and ask yourself what the "uninitiated" might be hearing. I myself have done this, and here is how the conversation went in my head:

Me: What is this about washing in the blood of the Lamb? This sounds like some sort of ancient pagan ritual where the worshipers splashed blood on themselves as they went into the temple to worship their pagan god. Is this really what God wants from us? To bathe in the blood of Jesus. To swim in rivers of blood? To dance around fountains of blood? What's the deal with all this blood?

Myself: Don't take it all so literally! It's only symbolic. It's figurative. Nobody actually bathes in blood or dances in fountains of blood.

Me: I know that! But then why sing about it? Symbolic language must symbolize something, right? Figurative language points to some figure. So what is it? What does the blood of Jesus symbolize? And before you answer too quickly, if it's only symbolic, are you saying that the death of Jesus was only symbolic? That He only died a figurative death?

Myself: Of course not. That would be heresy. Jesus died a real death in a real body. He shed literal blood. The symbolic part of those songs is in the washing and the bathing. We don't literally wash and bathe in the blood of Jesus. We just symbolically imagine that His blood is cleansing and washing us from our sin.

Me: Okay … so we're symbolically washing in literal blood? That still makes no sense to me.

Myself: *Sigh.* This is why I never debate theology with people who didn't go to Seminary.

Me: What? You're me. I'm you. We went to Seminary together.

Myself: Oh, right. Well, that must be why your theology is so messed up. What did they teach you at Seminary, anyway?

The conversation went on like this for quite some time—several decades, to be honest. During that time, Me, Myself, and I also read scores of books on the death of Jesus and engaged in numerous hours of conversation with other people about this subject. And do you know what I found? The books and the people that were most helpful and illuminating were those who were outside observers (even critics) of Christianity. They responded in horror to the Christian infatuation with the blood of Jesus. They view our songs and sermons about His blood in a way that is similar to how you or I might view a cultish sacrificial ritual deep in the woods on a dark night. It seems excessively gruesome and quite alarming to hear people celebrate the bloodletting of someone else.

To such critics, no answer we give, no verse we quote, no explanation we provide can ever do away with the fact that Christianity seems to worship a bloodthirsty deity who required the death of others in order to forgive sins and cleanse people of their iniquity. They complain that God is a cosmic child abuser who tortured His own Son in a twisted display of justice. They criticize God as being less loving and forgiving than regular humans, who can forgive others without the need for death and bloodshed. They point out that the Bible contains more commands for blood sacrifice and warfare against the enemies of God than any other religious book in history, including the Muslim Qur'an. They charge that no matter how much we claim that our God is loving and kind, He is really a God of bloody sacrifice, warfare, violence, and death.

CRITICIZING CHRISTIANS

I imagine you have heard some of the criticisms mentioned before. Most Christians have. And when confronted with these sorts of criticisms, we Christians typically make the situation worse by quoting Scripture. Forgetting that none of these critics consider Scripture to be authoritative, we sometimes think that a few Bible verses will solve the debate. We point out that since all have sinned and the wages of sin is death, everyone must die (Rom 3:23; 6:23). But God loves us, we say, and so He decided to pay the penalty for our sin Himself, which He did by sending Jesus, His own Son, to die in our place on the cross (John 3:16; Rom 6:10; 2 Cor 5:21; 1 Pet 3:18). After all, without the shedding of blood there is no forgiveness of sins (Heb 9:22). We say that someone must die for the sins of the world, and it was either us or God. Since God loves us, He took the bullet on our behalf and sent Jesus to die on the cross for the sins of the whole world.

When the non-Christian response to our "biblical answer" is less receptive than we would like, we shrug our shoulders and quote another verse. We say, "The message of the cross is foolishness to those who are perishing" (1 Cor 1:18), and then head off to our Bible studies and Sunday services where we continue to talk and sing about the blood of Jesus while avoiding or ignoring the hard questions that the watching world is asking.

But if we stick around, the follow-up questions to our "biblical answer" get even harder to explain. For example, if we say that the death of Jesus was necessary to forgive sins, people want to know why Jesus had to die in such a gruesome and bloody way. If we say that the wages of sin is death and so God needed death as payment for sin, people want to know why God set it up this way in the first place (Isn't He God? Can't He do what He wants?) and even then, what would have been wrong with just letting Jesus die from old age? Did Jesus really need to get tortured to a bloody death on the cross? And if we argue that God needed the blood of an innocent victim in order to remove the stain of sin from the world, the critic wants to know how killing an innocent victim is not a sin itself, and how the blood of such a victim can actually do anything for the sin of all people throughout all time. And these questions keep coming, harder and harder at every turn.

DON'T ASK HOW IT WORKS?

Due to the number of difficult questions surrounding the death of Jesus and His blood shed for us, it might simply be best to accept that the death of Jesus *did something* to help restore our relationship with God, even if we cannot understand what it was. For many, rather than agonize over seemingly unanswerable questions, it is preferable to recognize that since we are not God and cannot really understand the nature or the depth of our sin or the character and breadth of His righteousness, we will never be able to understand exactly *what* Jesus did on the cross or *how* His death accomplished it. In other words, it is enough, for many, to simply know that Jesus accomplished *something,* even if we cannot know what it was or how He did it. If this seems like a cop-out, do not worry; this is the approach that C. S. Lewis argued for in his book, *Mere Christianity:*

> The central Christian belief is that Christ's death has somehow put us right with God and given us a fresh start. Theories as to how it did this are another matter. A good many different theories have been held as to how it works …
>
> Theories about Christ's death are not Christianity: they are explanations about how it works. Christians would not all agree as to how important these theories are …
>
> But I think they will all agree that the thing itself is infinitely more important than any explanations that theologians have produced. I think they would probably admit that no explanation will ever be quite adequate to the reality. But as I said in the preface to this book, I am only a layman, and at this point we are getting into deep water. I can only tell you, for what it is worth, how I, personally, look at the matter. On my view the theories are not themselves the thing you are asked to accept …
>
> We believe that the death of Christ is just that point in history at which something absolutely unimaginable from outside shows through into our own world. And if we cannot picture even the atoms of which our own world is built, of course we are not going to be able to picture this. Indeed, if we found that we could fully understand it, that very fact would show it was not what it professes to be—the inconceivable, the uncreated, the thing from beyond nature, striking down into nature like lightning. You may ask what good it will be to us if we do not understand it. But that is easily answered. A man can eat his dinner without understanding exactly how food nourishes him. A man can accept what Christ has done without knowing how it works: indeed, he certainly would not know how it works until he has accepted it. We are told that Christ was killed for us, that His death has washed out our sins, and that by dying He disabled death itself. That is the formula. That is Christianity. That is what has to be believed. Any theories we build up as to how Christ's death

> did all this are, in my view, quite secondary: mere plans or diagrams to be left alone if they do not help us, and, even if they do help us, not to be confused with the thing itself.[2]

If you are one who rarely asks "Why?" or "How?" something works, then the answer of C. S. Lewis regarding the death of Jesus might be enough for you. Yet as much as I love and admire C. S. Lewis (he is my favorite author), his answer is not enough for me. Prior to attending Bible College and Seminary my educational background was in engineering. I chose that field because my entire life has been consumed with pursuing answers to the question "How?" *How* does this work? *How* can it be improved? *How* can it be explained? *How* can it be fixed? While numerous people like C. S. Lewis are content with simply knowing *that* something works, I am never content unless I know *how.*

Nor is the answer of C. S. Lewis enough for the average critic of Christianity. Critics of Christianity will not accept Lewis' logic on the death of Jesus. They will not simply jump with blind faith into worshiping a deity who, to them, appears to be bloodthirsty, vindictive, and cruel. They will not simply accept and follow Jesus because Lewis says we don't need to know *why* Jesus died or *how* His blood works to save us from our sin. For many, including myself, the *how* is the critical question. If the *how* is not answered, then we cannot know *why* Jesus died, and therefore, *what* God is like. And if we cannot know what God is like, then we cannot know whether or not He is worthy of our worship.

For if the Christian God truly is bloodthirsty, vindictive, and cruel, it is more of an act of pure worship to reject such a God than it is to worship Him in blind faith. Why? Because people become like the God they worship. If God is bloodthirsty and vindictive, and if God cannot love and forgive unless He receives payment with blood, then this is also how His followers will live and act toward others. Rather than live in love and forgiveness toward others, we will cry out for the death of our enemies, and

[2] C. S. Lewis, *Mere Christianity* (New York: HarperCollins, 1952), 53-55.

will demand that "justice" be obtained through the price of bloody vengeance upon all who oppose us. And sadly, this is exactly how some Christians behave, as they pray for bombs to fall on Muslims and for Gays to go to hell.

The watching world sees this behavior by Christians, and understands that such behavior is nothing more than a logical extension of our theological belief in a God who demands blood payment for the forgiveness of sins. But we Christians don't know where to turn. Though we recognize, and even condemn, the bad behavior of some groups within Christianity, and though we see how certain passages from a bloody Bible and certain ideas from traditional theology can lead these Christians to think that calling for the death of their enemies in truly within God's will, few Christians have actually found a way out of the dilemma posed by the blood of Jesus.

We cannot, after all, deny the righteous justice of God. Nor can we deny the reality of human sin. And we definitely cannot deny that Jesus bled and died. But as long as we fail to adequately explain *how* all of these truths fit together, the Gospel message will never be good news to a dying world. Christianity needs better answers to the questions the world is asking, and this failure to explain *how the blood of Jesus saves us from our sin* is one of the main reasons so many people have abandoned Christianity over the last few decades.

A BETTER ANSWER

My hope is that the book you now hold in your hands provides a better answer. This book shows how God can be both just and the justifier of those who believe. It shows how sin truly is the problem of the world, and how the death of Jesus—even the violent and bloody death of Jesus on the cross—provides the solution and the answer for sin that the world is looking for. This book also shows how the non-Christian rejection of a bloody and violent deity is right in line with what Jesus revealed about God. In other words, when the world rejects a bloodthirsty god as being unworthy of our worship, they are not following Satan into error and evil, but are instead following Jesus into what He revealed to us about God. Much to our shock and chagrin, the non-Christian who follows his or her own heart into love for all people might be doing a better job worshiping the God revealed in Jesus Christ than the Christian who quotes Scripture and prays to God for the death of our enemies.

I understand that what I have just written might be a shocking statement to some. But it is not a statement I make lightly. It comes as the result of decades of research, study, reading, writing, and prayerful consideration of the biblical text. It also comes more recently from spending time outside the institutional church with so-called "non-Christians."

When I first read *Mere Christianity* about thirty years ago, while I fully agreed that *how* the death of Jesus works was not nearly as important as the truth *that* it works, I intended to do my best in learning *how*. This is, after all, *how* my mind is wired. So I embarked on my investigation. I read and studied everything I could about the death of Jesus, the atonement, and the gospel. I studied Scripture constantly. I attended Bible College and Seminary. I pastored churches, preached sermons, taught Bible studies, and wrote books. I engaged in conversations about these topics with numerous different people from dozens of different backgrounds, beliefs, and perspectives.

Through it all, I followed a trail of breadcrumbs left by Scripture and the illuminating Holy Spirit so that every few months, I uncovered another piece of the theological puzzle. Many of these pieces were shocking or surprising, challenging everything I thought I knew. Some of the truths I learned were utterly inspiring, opening up whole new vistas of theological research and inquiry, and helping me see God in a whole new light. In the process of digging through the pages of Scripture for an understanding of how the death of Jesus saves the world from sin, I discovered a God I never knew existed, as well as some truths about Scripture, sin, and humanity that I never would have found in any other way. The quest for *how* led to some surprising discoveries about the *who*, the *what*, and the *why*.

If you are like me and want to know the *how* of things, the best approach would be to retrace with me the slow and steady slog through theological research of the last thirty years. But that would take too long and be too boring. It would read like the snippet of conversation I had with myself earlier in this chapter. Besides, I spent many of those years in theological missteps, exegetical rabbit trails, and, like Winnie the Pooh, retracing my own steps around and around in the snowy woods searching for a mythical beast of my own imagination.

So rather than take you on that long and circuitous journey, let me instead give you some of the central signposts which will point you in the right direction. This book contains those signposts. The ideas of this book are not everything I learned or discovered in the past thirty years of research, but they do explain where I am at now and what I have discovered. This book contains my best explanation *so far* for *how* the death of Jesus saves the world from sin.

And just as a preview, do you know what I have discovered *so far*? I have discovered that the blood of Jesus is more precious than I ever imagined. I have discovered that the blood of Jesus reveals certain truths to humanity that could never have been revealed to us in any other way. I have discovered that there is very good reason for the Bible to emphasize blood so much, that there is good reason for the New Testament writers to focus our attention on His blood shed for us. I have discovered that it was not just Jesus' death, and not just Jesus' blood, but that it was necessary for His blood to be shed *violently*.

I have discovered some truths that nothing but the blood of Jesus could have revealed to us. I have discovered how the blood of Jesus rescues and delivers us from sin like nothing else ever could. Once we understand how the blood of Jesus rescues the world from sin, we see why it was necessary for Jesus to suffer and die on the cross as He did, and how the entire bloody spectacle of the cross reveals a God who is more deeply in love with us than we ever before imagined. In the end, we see that there truly is something special about the blood of Jesus. The blood of Jesus truly does lead us to worship God and follow Him in love and forgiveness for the world.

If you join me in this journey by reading this book, you will discover the meaning of five words. These five words are *Sin, Law, Sacrifice, Scapegoat,* and *Blood.* If you understand these five terms, you will better understand the work of Jesus on the cross and how His death rescues us from sin. But as indicated above, these five words are not the only things I have discovered over the last several decades of research. As you learn about these five words, there are many related words that you might have questions about as well. Words such as *salvation, wrath, forgiveness, justice, Kingdom of God, grace, world, satan,* and *gospel* are also within the sphere of terms one might need to learn in the quest for understanding the crucifixion of Jesus. If you would like to learn more about these other words, all of them are found in my online theology course, *The Gospel Dictionary,* from which the ideas for this book were pulled. While this book only looks at five words, *The Gospel Dictionary* course looks at 52 key words of the gospel, all of which further support the themes of this present volume and provide greater understanding about what God has done for us in Jesus Christ and how we are to live in response. Understanding these 52 key words of the Gospel truly help make the Gospel "good news" again. Learn more about this course, and my other online theology courses, by visiting RedeemingGod.com/courses.

So are you ready to learn how the death of Jesus rescues the world from sin? If so, the journey begins with a look at everybody's favorite subject: sin. But don't skip the chapter because you think you already know everything about sin (maybe from personal experience). When it comes to sin, the phrase made famous by Inigo Montoya in *The Princess Bride* is quite appropriate: "You keep using that word. I do not think it means what you think it means."

PART I: SIN

In her book, *The Crucifixion,* Fleming Rutledge includes a chapter about sin. The first line of her chapter says, "Who is going to read a whole chapter about sin?"[3] I laughed when I read this, because this book you are now reading contains not one, but two chapters on sin. So maybe I should ask, "Who is going to read *two* whole chapters about sin?" Not only that, these two chapters on sin form the lead chapters of my book. At least Fleming Rutledge was considerate enough to hold off on sin until chapter four. I am leading right off with it.

But the reason is because of what I state in the opening lines of the first chapter on sin: Most people (including most Christians) simply don't understand sin. If we don't understand what Scripture teaches about sin, we really cannot understand much else in Scripture either. So let us turn to Scripture to see what it actually teaches about sin.

[3] Fleming Rutledge, *Crucifixion: Understanding the Death of Jesus Christ* (Grand Rapids: Eerdmans, 2015), 167.

CHAPTER 2

DEFINING SIN

Most Christians would agree that the greatest problem of humanity is sin. If it weren't for sin, all of life would be wonderful and beautiful. Without sin, there would be peace and love everywhere. Without sin, there would be no war, theft, abuse, lust, anger, greed, hatred, jealousy, or any of the other human behaviors that damage relationships and ruin lives. Just imagine for a moment what life would be like without sin. It would be paradise! Many even argue that things like sickness, death, and natural disasters can be traced back to the presence of sin in this world. So if everything damaging and destructive comes from sin, then yes, it is not an exaggeration to say that sin is the greatest problem of humanity.

Of course, if sin is the problem, then what is the solution? The simple answer is "Jesus," but what does this mean? How is it that Jesus is the solution to the problem of sin? And did Jesus provide a solution for sin during His entire life, or just through the events of His death and resurrection? Such questions have been debated for almost 2000 years.

Isn't this strange? What good is a solution to a problem if nobody can agree on exactly what the solution is? How can the average Christian ever hope to find a "cure" for the problem of sin in their life if the average pastor or Bible scholar cannot even agree on how Jesus provided the solution? The answers of "He showed us how to live" or "He died on the cross for our sin," while temporarily satisfactory to some, do not actually do anything to provide an answer. Lots of people in history have provided good examples of how to live, and lots of people were crucified by the Roman Empire. What makes the life and death of Jesus any better?

When we start to dig deeper, the answers become less and less satisfactory. Some will say, for example, that God needed payment for sin, and only the death of a perfect and sinless sacrifice would suffice. Upon hearing this explanation, the critical thinker starts to wonder about what kind of being this God is, who makes human beings with certain desires and weaknesses, and then gives them rules He knows they cannot keep, so that He must punish and kill them when they cannot keep His rules and cannot repay Him for the crimes they committed. But it gets even worse. This deity then demands human sacrifice for the crimes committed against Him, which might be okay if the crime in question was murder, but according to some, God requires death even for things like lying (Acts 5:1-11), stealing (Josh 7:10-26), eating the wrong meat (1 Sam 2:16-17, 24-25), picking up sticks on Saturday (Num 15:32-33), or trying to protect God's holy vessels in the wrong way (2 Sam 6:6-7).

Even when the argument comes around to Jesus, the typical explanations offered for why Jesus had to die usually only add to the confusion about how the death of Jesus is actually a solution to the great human problem of sin. Saying that Jesus had to die does not help us understand why God required death in the first place, nor why Jesus had to die in such a gruesome and painful way, nor how the death of Jesus actually does anything about the sin of the world, or how His death is applied individually to each human being. And despite the fact that these questions have been argued and debated for many centuries, little agreement has been found on the answers. Though everybody agrees that sin is the problem and Jesus is the solution, very few agree on exactly *how* Jesus is the solution.

The primary reason for this failure to understand how Jesus is the solution to sin is due to the fact that few have sought to understand sin itself. Though everybody agrees that the problem is sin, few have actually stopped to consider the question, "What is sin?" The reason few ask this question is because it is assumed that everybody knows what sin is. But if we don't understand the human problem of sin, we will never be able to properly understand or come to agreement about the solution to the problem of sin.

If you and I are baking a cake, and we both agree that the batter tastes "off," but we do not discuss what exactly is "off" about the taste and instead both start to throw ingredients into the batter in attempt to fix it, the chances are good that the cake will not get better but worse. To correct cake batter that tastes "off," we must first have a conversation about what seems to be wrong or what ingredient is missing. Only then can we begin to take corrective action to find a solution and bake a good cake.

This is the same approach we must take when it comes to Jesus as the solution to the problem of sin. It does no good to start talking about how Jesus is the solution until we first understand what sin is and why it is a human problem. It is for this reason that this book begins with a discussion about sin. We must first understand sin before we can understand how the blood of Jesus saves us from it.

Do not be tempted to skip over this chapter. Though sin is the greatest human problem, I have found that most people don't really understand what sin is. People often have a religious view of sin that does not bear much resemblance to the biblical explanation of what sin is and why it is so serious. For this reason, in an attempt to understand sin, it might be best to clear the air and first talk about what sin is *not.*

WHAT SIN IS (NOT)

When it comes to defining the word *sin,* people think of sin in a variety of ways. Some define it as those things we do which separate us from God. Others understand sin to consist of thoughts or actions that break the commands of God. Many think of sin as a burden we carry (think of the burden on the back of Pilgrim in John Bunyan's *Pilgrim's Progress*), or a debt that must be repaid to God.[4] All such views of sin see it as some sort of crime that is committed against God, and therefore as something for which God's honor must be restored or offended righteousness renewed. But such

[4] Gary Anderson, *Sin: A History* (New Haven, CT: Yale University Press, 2009).

views of sin cannot be defended biblically or theologically.[5]

So what is sin?

To answer that question, it might be best to go back in time and understand how people of the Old Testament era viewed sin. The people we read about in the Hebrew Scriptures tended to view sin the way we modern people view bacteria. Sin was an invisible substance which polluted everything it came into contact with. This is why there were clean and unclean animals and locations, and why a person could become contaminated by coming into contact with someone or something that was unclean. Since ancient people did not know about germs and bacteria, they believed that they became sick as a result of being infected by sin, and the laws and commands which guided their life were about avoiding the contamination of sin. Once this ancient view of sin is understood, many of the Hebrew commands and teachings about sin make a lot more sense. They tried to avoid being contaminated by sin the same way we try to avoid being contaminated by germs, bacteria, and viruses.

Our modern failure to understand this ancient view of sin causes us to read the commands and laws of God in a backward sense. We believe that such commands were intended to keep people from sinning. We believe that when people broke God's commands, they sinned. We believe the sacrificial system was intended to cleanse them from the sin that had come upon them as a result of disobeying God. But this is not a correct way of viewing the actual mindset of the ancient person. Breaking the laws and commands of God did not introduce or invite sin into a person's life. No, instead, breaking the laws and commands of God brought a person or community into contact with sin that was already present.

Once again, consider our modern view of bacteria and germs. Germs exist. Everything has bacteria. You are surrounded by viruses all the time. To avoid getting sick, we perform certain actions to reduce the potential damage from germs and bacteria. We wash our hands regularly. We cook our

[5] Mark E. Biddle, *Missing the Mark: Sin and Its Consequences in Biblical Theology* (Nashville: Abingdon, 2005), vii-viii.

food thoroughly. We avoid buildings or rooms in which sick people live. We also avoid people who do not practice good hygiene. When certain buildings become too contaminated with mold and bacteria, we might burn it down. If we fail to do these sorts of things, we are not creating germs and bacteria, but are instead simply coming into contact with germs that are already there or are creating an environment in which they can thrive and do more damage to those of us who are healthy.

Our modern view of bacteria and germs is very close to how ancient Israelites viewed sin. Sin was viewed as an invisible substance that coated almost everything, and if you came into contact with it, it would pollute you and cause sickness or even death. They believed that sin was contagious, that the pollution of sin spread as sinful people touched buildings, possessions, tools, animals, and even other people. By disobeying God's laws, they did not "create" sin, but rather brought themselves into contact with sin or created an environment in which sin could thrive and do more damage. When a person came into contact with sin, they became "unclean" and in need of purification. But they could avoid the pollution and contamination of sin by obeying God's commands.

This view of sin helps explain why blood sacrifices were used to purify people and places from sin (see Part V on Blood).[6] Just as we neutralize bacteria with sanitizers and medicine, ancient people used blood to neutralize the contaminating presence of sin. We cringe at such a practice. Killing animals and sprinkling blood all over the place probably only made health conditions worse. But the fact of the matter is that blood sacrifices have numerous psychological, sociological, and spiritual benefits. Blood sacrifice could very often bring mental, social, and spiritual healing. Sacrifices helped ease tension, erase guilt, create peace, and a whole host of other benefits which caused the people to believe that the blood was having a positive effect on cleansing them from sin (see Part II on Sacrifice). There are, of course, better ways to get these benefits than through sacrifice and bloodshed, but all of that is part of the unfolding revelation of God.

[6] Sharon Baker, *Executing God* (Louisville, KY: Westminster John Knox, 2013), 145.

All of this helps explain where the commands of God come from. They come from God's desire that we humans live healthy lives. God wants us to be mentally, emotionally, physically, spiritually, psychologically, and socially healthy. The rules and commands He provides in the Bible help us do that (see Part II on Law). When we fail to follow God's commands, it is not that we "sin against God" but that we end up living in a way which is unhealthy for us and those around us. When we fail to follow God's commands, we live in a way that is less than fully human. God wants us to be fully human, to live as He created us to live. So the rules and commands which God provides in the Bible are intended to guide us toward the fully human life that God wants and desires for us.

When we do not follow God's rules and commands, God does not get upset at us because we "sinned," but He does get upset because we hurt ourselves through sin. The "upsetness" of God over sin is like the "upsetness" of a mother who weeps and cries over a child who just burned their hand on a hot stove after the mother told the child not to touch it. Just as a mother weeps and chides a wailing child over a burned hand, so also God weeps and chides with humanity over our burned lives. "It need not have been this way," He says. "If you had just followed my instructions, all would be well."

With all of this historical and cultural background in mind, we are now ready to take a second stab at answering the question, "What is sin?" Though ancient people believed sin was an invisible substance that coated everything, we need not follow them in this line of thought. The Bible reveals this way of thinking about sin without actually endorsing it. It is not necessary to think of sin as an invisible substance that coats and contaminates everything it touches, and later Old Testament authors moved away from this way of thinking about sin.

However, this does not mean that our modern way of thinking about sin is necessarily correct either. We tend to think about sin as the breaking of God's commands so that a debt or burden of sin is created between God and man. We think of sin as a violation or act of disobedience to God's instructions. Yet since most of the commands of God were given within the context of viewing sin as an invisible, contaminating substance, it therefore logically follows that the commands were not given to keep people from disobeying God, but rather to keep people from becoming polluted by sin. In other words, many of the commands and laws of God were given, not because they reflect the morality and righteousness of God, but because such prohibitions and instructions kept people away from the people, places, things, and activities that would bring them into contact with the polluting power of sin.

So if sin is not actually an invisible substance, then obeying the commands of God will not necessarily keep us from sin any more than breaking them causes us to come into contact with sin. Therefore, just as the ancients were not correct in thinking about sin as an invisible substance that coated and contaminated everything it touched, so also, we moderns are not exactly correct in thinking that sin is simply when we break or disobey a command of God. Both ideas fall short of what the Bible truly reveals about sin.

In fact, once we understand the true nature of sin, we also come to see that seeking to obey some of God's commands can actually lead us into greater sin! I know this sounds shocking, but this is one of the points Jesus Himself frequently made during His life and ministry. Obeying God's laws without an understanding of why God gave the law can actually lead to sin rather than to righteous living.

The Sabbath day controversies of Jesus are a perfect example. In Luke 6:1-11, Jesus and His disciples engage in various activities on the Sabbath that many religious leaders considered sinful. But Jesus points out to them that the only reason they believe such actions are sinful on the Sabbath is because they misunderstood the reason for the Sabbath and the context in which the Sabbath laws were given. Jesus goes on to show them why the Sabbath was given and what the Sabbath is for. As part of this explanation, He reveals that by attempting to obey the Sabbath laws without a proper understanding of why these laws were given, they were actually violating the Sabbath rather than keeping it. In trying to obey the law, they end up breaking the law.

The author of Hebrews also takes up this theme. Hebrews 9:15 contains the truth that Jesus came as a Mediator of a new covenant, so that His death might accomplish the redemption of the transgressions that were committed under the first covenant. We will look at this passage in more detail later in this book, but note for now that the word used for "transgressions" in Hebrews 9:15 (translated as "sin" by some) is not the normal word for "sin" in the New Testament. The word used here is the Greek word *parabasis,* which means "to overstep or go beyond the boundaries." The word "trespass" might be a good translation. While this word is closely connected with sin in the New Testament, it is used primarily in the context of how humans use religious tradition to disobey the laws of God while claiming to obey the law. In other words, *parabasis* takes place when someone explains and applies the law of God in a way that ends up doing the exact opposite of what the law says. *Parabasis* is a religious sin that occurs when we use the law to defend sinful behaviors that accomplish the exact opposite of what the law originally intended. How this occurs will be discussed further in Part II about the Law.

For now, we can say along with Paul that the law is holy, righteous, and good (Rom 7:12), and when practiced with a proper understanding in the proper context, the law serves to lead people into healthy lives and healthy relationships. But the law was not God's ideal way of leading people into right living, and the failure of the law is best seen when those who claim to know and follow it best are those who actually engage in sin the most, and especially the sin of using the law to justify our own sin. We religious people are experts at judging and condemning the sins in others while ignoring the even greater sins that are in our own lives (Matt 7:5). But we will never see our own sin until we first understand it.

To properly understand and define sin, and its relationship to God's righteousness and God's laws, it is best to see that the entire story of inspired Scripture is seeking to unfold or unveil the truth about sin in a way that allows us humans to finally understand what sin truly is so that we can do something about it. When we seek to understand what all of Scripture unveils about sin, it is then that we discover the shocking truth about it. We see that sin has been crouching at our door and most of us have completely ignored or missed its presence, and as a result, many of us have been devoured and overcome by sin *while thinking* that we are following and obeying God.

This big picture overview of what the Bible reveals about sin will be laid out in this chapter and the next, but now that we have briefly seen that sin is not best understood as an invisible substance coating all things nor simply as the breaking of God's commands, it is time to turn instead to a biblical understanding of what sin actually is.

WHAT SIN IS

Maybe it is best to begin with a simple definition. Sometimes sin is defined as "missing the mark" or "missing the point."[7] This definition is not wrong, as long as the question is asked, "Missing the mark *of what*?" You might have heard that the word "sin" was used in archery contests where any arrow that missed the bullseye was called "sin." Even if this is true (I could not confirm it), the question remains, "What is the target we are shooting for?" Many Christians assume that the target we are shooting for is the holiness of God, and therefore, to "miss the mark" is to fall short of the holiness of God, to fail to live up to the level of His holiness.

Romans 3:23 is often quoted in connection with the understanding that "sin" is falling short of the glory of God, for this is, after all, what Paul states. However, what exactly is "the glory of God" and how does one fall short of it? If the "glory of God" is understood to be God's holiness and righteousness, then sin is whenever we fail to live as holy as God. But is God's glory best defined as God's holiness? Though Scripture does call humans to be holy as God is holy (cf. 1 Pet 1:15-16), how are humans to be "holy"? Let us consider this last question first.

[7] Gerhard Kittel, Ed., Geoffrey W. Bromiley, Transl., *Theological Dictionary of the New Testament* (Grand Rapids: Eerdmans, 1964), I:271.

In Scripture, to be "holy" is not predominantly defined as following a set of religious rules about how to live like God. Holiness is not a religious, moral law code, as most of us in the modern western world have come to understand it. Instead, biblical holiness is a way of maintaining peace and order within human interactions and relationships. Holiness is to have "wholeness" in our lives and relationships. The commands of God to mankind, therefore, were not given for the purpose of keeping God happy by obeying His rules until we get to heaven. God did not give commands to humanity because He simply cannot love us or be with us unless we conform to His righteous standards. No, the commands of God to mankind were for the purpose of keeping mankind happy and healthy on God's earth so that we can rule and reign upon this earth as He intended.

What then is "the glory of God" in humanity? The glory of God in humanity is not accomplished when we deny our humanity to become more like God, but instead when we understand who God made us to be on this earth, and then accept this God-given role. Yes, holiness is accomplished through becoming and doing what God desires. Yet what is it that God desires? He desires that we live as His emissaries, ambassadors, caretakers, and image-bearers on earth. This means that humans become "holy" not by *denying* our role as humans on this earth, but by *embracing* it and living as much like human beings as we possibly can. God created us to be humans, and God wants us to be humans. Therefore, human holiness (and therefore a reflection of God's glory) is not accomplished through escaping this world, but by living fully as the human beings God wants in this world. The glory of God is best seen when humans live as the images of God on earth, just as He created us to be.

This understanding of how God is glorified in this world and what holiness means for humans helps us better understand sin, and especially sin as "missing the mark" or "falling short." While it is true that our target, or goal, is holiness that reflects the glory of God, this holiness is accomplished when human beings live fully as humans. Holiness and the glory of God on the earth are best accomplished when we humans live in right relationship with one another and with all of God's creation. And if this is holiness, then we now know what sin is as well.

Sin is not when we fail to live like God, but when we fail to live like humans. Sin does not keep us from becoming godly; it keeps us from becoming human. Yes, God gave humanity laws to keep, but these laws were not provided so that we could become more like God, but so that we could become more like the humans God wanted on this earth. Maybe an example from Genesis would be helpful.

THE BEGINNING OF SIN

In the beginning, God gave three basic commands to humans. He wanted us to live in relationship with each other, to enjoy His creation, and to take care of the plants and animals of this earth (Gen 1:26-30). The laws that God provided later provided further guidance about these initial commands, but the general thrust was still the same. The laws of God were not primarily directed toward achieving the holiness of God in our lives, but toward the interrelatedness of mankind in creation. When we live this way on earth, we function as the image of God on earth, reflecting and revealing His glory to all.

In such a setting, sin is anything that fails to accomplish our God-given role as His glorious image-bearers on earth. Sin is not a failure to become like God, but a failure to become like the humans God wants us to be. And since God wanted us to live in relationships with each other, to enjoy His creation, and to take care of the plants and animals, sin occurs when we fail to do any (or all) of these things. Anything that negatively affects our relationships with one another and with God's creation diminishes God's glory in us on earth. Sin has to do with alienation from God, from creation, and from one another.[8] It breaks our relationships, hinders our fellowship, and ruins our dominion over the earth.

The progressive revelation about sin in the Bible clearly reveals this. Af-

[8] John Walton, *The Lost World of Adam and Eve* (Downers Grove: IVP, 2015), 141.

ter Adam and Eve eat from the Tree of the Knowledge of Good and Evil, this failure to live up to our calling as humans is exactly what the following chapters reveal. Sin is first mentioned in the Bible, not when Adam and Eve eat the forbidden fruit, but when Cain becomes angry at his brother Abel and enters into rivalry with him. God warns Cain that sin is crouching at his door, seeking to devour him (Gen 4:7). This does not mean that eating fruit from the Tree of Knowledge was not wrong; it was. Adam and Eve disobeyed God when they ate the forbidden fruit. But the account carefully avoids calling their action "sinful" because the text wants to reveal the true nature and character of sin. The Genesis account shows us that sin is not best defined as disobeying God's rules, but instead as failing to live up to our God-given role as human beings. The rules sometimes help us live better as humans, but the goal is not simply to follow the rules, but instead to become and live as the humans that God desires.

The first command of God in Scripture is for humans to live in relationship with one another, and the first sin mentioned in the Bible is when Cain enters into an envious rivalry with his brother, thereby damaging their relationship. But Genesis is not done revealing the sinister nature of sin. By taking a careful look at the events in Genesis 1–4, we see something much more important (and misunderstood) about sin.[9]

In Genesis 1, God performs seven key activities and then invites the humans He created to imitate Him in doing these things as well (See my online study of Genesis for more). God's goal for humanity was that we would live as His image on this earth. We are to be the image of God in the earthly temple of God, and we do this in seven main ways. Yet by the time Adam eats from the tree in Genesis 3:7, he has failed to imitate God in all seven ways. As a result, Adam becomes afraid of God, and goes into hiding. God, however, acts as if nothing happened. In Genesis 3:8-10, God shows up in the Garden for His daily walk with Adam. In the verses that follow, God tells Adam and Eve that while there will be natural consequences for

[9] The following paragraphs contain a summary of some of the ideas taught in my "One Verse Podcast." If you want to subscribe to the podcast to learn more about these ideas, please visit RedeemingGod.com/subscribe-to-podcast/

their decision, they do not need to be afraid of Him. He only loves and cares for them and will walk with them through the pain and suffering they brought on themselves.

Through this event, we see that while Adam and Eve were to imitate God, they ended up imitating the serpent by desiring that which they should not have. This desire led them into rivalry with God and with each other, which in turn led to blame, accusation, and the scapegoating of God and one another. Moving into Genesis 4, it is exactly this cycle of imitative desire that leads to rivalry, scapegoating, and ultimately to the violence which God warns Cain against (Gen 4:7). This cycle is what God calls *sin,* and He warns Cain that this sin is crouching at Cain's door and he must protect himself against it lest it rule over him. Tragically, Cain did not heed God's warning, and the desire to gain for himself what Abel had led Cain into rivalry with Abel, and ultimately into murdering him.

So at the very beginning of the Bible, this is how sin is defined and described. When sin is formally presented in Genesis 4:7, it is in the context of imitation leading to rivalry, which introduces blame and accusation, and ends in scapegoating, violence, murder, and death. When *sin* is introduced in the Bible, it is defined as the breakdown of human interrelatedness as a result of rivalry, scapegoating, and murder (see Part IV about the Scapegoat). While it is true that Adam introduced such practices to humanity, the cycle is only fully seen for the first time in Cain. So now we can see that *sin* is first introduced and defined in the Bible as the cycle of imitative desire leading to rivalry, blame, scapegoating, and violence.

When you read about sin in the Bible, this is what you should think of. Sin is not necessarily breaking God's commands, except in the sense that breaking God's commands leads us to perform actions and develop mindsets which then create rivalry, blame, accusation, scapegoating, and violence. Yes, things like lust, greed, theft, and lying are "sinful," but only because such activities lead us to the *main sin* in Scripture, which is the sin of violence against other human beings.

OH! THE INHUMANITY!

When we understand sin as defined above, it is then that we begin to see that *sin* truly is everywhere. Sin taints everything in life. Whether we are talking economics, politics, sports, entertainment, religion, or even our day-to-day relationships, we desire what others have and this desire leads us into rivalry with them. This rivalry leads to blame, accusation, and violence. In the process of blaming and murdering others, we also blame God and make a scapegoat of Him, saying that He gave us no other choice, or that God wants to kill our rivals just as much as we do, and so all we were doing is carrying out His will. All of this is seen in Genesis 4, which leads directly to the death chapter of the Bible (Genesis 5), and then the description in Genesis 6 that violence covered the face of the earth.

We can now see why the basic problem of sin is that it causes us to live as less than human, to fail to live as human beings made in the image of God.[10] Sin is not so much about pride and rebellion or thinking we know better than God, as it is about living in a way that dehumanizes ourselves and others, and seeks to become rivals with others instead of partners in the divinely ordained task of tending to this world. The problem of sin is seen most clearly in the endless cycle of rivalry and violence which leads us to kill our brothers. But more than that, sin is the problem of blame and scapegoating which leads to killing others *in God's name.*

The fact that this violence toward others is committed in the name of God reveals the truly sinister nature of sin. Most people who engage in this envious rivalry with others which often leads to violence and murder, do not believe that they are doing anything wrong, but instead believe they are carrying out God's will. The most sinister thing about sin is that it is often carried out "according to the will of God." Religious laws and regulations are often brought up as a way to defend and justify our hateful and hurtful actions against those we view as our rivals and enemies. And since we believe God is on our side against our enemies, we believe that any violence

[10] Biddle, *Missing the Mark*, 5, 36-37, 63-65.

against our enemies is therefore sanctioned by God. It is for this reason that I said earlier that sometimes, obeying the law of God can actually lead to sinning against God. When we use the law in a way that allows us to engage in rivalry, scapegoating, and violence, we are using the law to justify sin.

This idea is supported by the word for *sin* itself. The common Hebrew and Greek words for *sin* (*chattath* and *hamartia*) carry with them the ideas of violence toward others, but it is not just the violence that springs from rivalry, but is also—maybe *primarily*—the violence against humans which we perform *in the name of God.* In the Bible, *sin* is frequently connected with sacred violence.[11] It has in view the violent killing of our enemies in the name of God. It is the violence of sacrificing animals in the attempt to gain the forgiveness of God, which He has already freely offered. It is the game we play of blaming God for our own violent tendencies toward others by viewing them as God's enemies, when in reality, they are only our enemies. It is also the habit we have of nodding our heads when disaster falls upon others and saying to ourselves, "Yes, this is the judgment of God for they were worse sinners than everyone else." There are, of course, numerous factors and circumstances that contribute to sacred violence and which come from it, all of which might be part of the overall biblical picture of *sin.* Ultimately then, sin can be defined as violence we humans commit in God's name, and everything related to this practice.

The reason sacred violence, or even sacrificial violence, is singled out as the specific type of behavior that God is most concerned with, is because this is the type of behavior we are most blind to. We almost always know when others behave badly toward us, or even when we behave badly toward others. But very rarely do we ever recognize the sinful nature of those times when we behave badly toward others *in God's name.* We believe that such behavior is good, righteous, and divinely ordained. Desire leading to rivalry which results in blame, violence, and death is the cycle of sin which causes nearly all problems in the world and yet which most humans are completely

[11] Robert G. Hamerton-Kelly, *Sacred Violence: Paul's Hermeneutic of the Cross* (Minneapolis: Fortress, 1992), 88, 113.

blind to. This means that we humans are not living the way we are supposed to. Sin is living inhuman lives; lives that do not treat others as human beings made in the image of God, and lives that do not live up to our full potential as human beings in God's image. Sin causes us to live as less than human.

Humans were made first and foremost to live in relationship with each other as we walked with God in our work of tending to His creation. But when we scapegoat and kill others, and do it in God's name, sin has taken over and all relationships between God and mankind have broken down so that none of us are living with each other the way God wanted. Relationships are key to being human, and when we are living as less than human, it surfaces in how we interact with God and with others.

This understanding of *sin* explains why God gives the commands He does in Exodus 20. The first four commandments deal with our relationship with God, while the final six deal with our relationships with one another. Of these final six commandments, five of them deal with murder and covetous desire. The sixth commandment, "You shall not murder" leads directly into the four ways to avoid murdering. At first, it seems the commandments start to list specific things that should not be coveted or desired. The prohibition against adultery refers to not coveting your neighbor's wife. The prohibition against stealing refers to not coveting your neighbor's possessions. The prohibition against bearing false witness refers to not coveting your neighbor's position, power, and prestige. Finally, the tenth commandment just lists a blanket statement about not coveting anything that belongs to your neighbor. So sin is not so much about a failure to follow the rules and obey the commands. The commands were given to help us live as fully human, but it is quite possible to follow and obey all the commands and laws while still behaving like an animal and treating others as less than human. We will look more at the role of the Law in Part II.

All of humanity's problems stem from the rivalry, blame, scapegoating, and violence that surfaced in Genesis 3–4, and which is the major focus of the Ten Commandments. The "human relationship" elements of the Ten

Commandments are focused on curbing desire (covetousness) that leads to rivalry, violence, and murder. This progression of desire and rivalry to violence and murder is also defined as sin by James. He writes in James 1:14-15 that the temptation to sin does not come from God, but comes from our own desires. James writes that "when desire has conceived, it gives birth to sin; and sin, when it is full-grown, brings forth death." Just as revealed in Genesis 4 and Exodus 20, sin is the result of covetous desire, which ultimately leads to violence and murder. This, then, is how to understand *sin* in the Bible. *Sin* is when we fail to live in loving relationships with one another as God intended, and instead allow desire to take us down the path toward envy, rivalry, accusation, violence, and murder. Sin is violence against others, and especially the violence against them that we commit in God's name.

THE REVELATION OF SIN

So the problem of sin is now revealed. Sin isn't really about breaking God's commands as much as it is about engaging in violence (and the things that lead to violence) against other human beings. Sin is not a contaminating substance that covers everything it touches, nor is it a burden we bear or a debt we owe to God. Sin is primarily violence and the things that lead to violence. Sin is the primary human problem because sin is damaging and destructive against humans and all human relationships. Those who sin are both hurt by sin and hurt others with sin. While sin does occur when we break the laws and commands of God, this is only because the commands of God are given to help restrain the violence of sin that brings harm and pain to ourselves and others. This understanding about sin helps explain where the law came from and why sacrifices were used in an attempt to deal with sin. All these issues will be discussed in future chapters.

Before we get to these other related topics, however, it is necessary to take the concepts we have learned in this chapter and apply them to some key texts of Scripture. Since Scripture guides and informs our theology, it is helpful to let Scripture verify the understanding of sin proposed in this chapter. Doing so will also help us better understand Scripture and what it truly teaches about sin. Only in this way will we be able to better understand what the Bible teaches about how the bloody death of Jesus is the solution to the problem of sin. So let us turn to the Bible to see what it says about sin.

CHAPTER 3

SCRIPTURES ON SIN

Understanding sin as the actions and attitudes that lead humans to engage in rivalry, blame, scapegoating, and violence helps us understand numerous Scripture about sin. This is especially true when it comes to the numerous New Testament texts which explain that Jesus came to save us from our sin. This chapter will look at some of these texts. We cannot look at *all* the texts, of course; there are simply too many to cover in one chapter of a book. The texts discussed below are representative of all other texts, so that if you understand what they are teaching about sin, you will then be able to understand all the other passages in Scripture which reveal similar truths. But first consider a few insights into why the Bible contains so many passages about sin.

The reason there is so much in the Bible about sin is because sin is the greatest human problem. Since sin is the greatest problem of humanity, the Bible unveils exactly what this problem is and how Jesus is the solution. One reason we fail to understand how Jesus is the solution to the problem of sin is that we fail to grasp what the Bible says about sin. This is tragic, because one primary reason God gave us the Bible is so that we could understand the seriousness of the problem of sin and what He is doing about this problem.

Even more importantly, however, the revelation about sin in Scripture is one of the things that makes the Bible unique among all other religious texts in the world. No other holy book in history so clearly unveils the truth about sin as does the Bible. While Scripture reveals many theological truths to us, the vast majority of these can be found in the writings of other world religions. This is not true regarding the Bible's revelation about sin. What the Bible reveals about sin is not found anywhere else. The Bible's revelation about sin is one line of evidence for the divine origins of the Bible.

Yes, all religious texts warn about the dangers of sin. My "day job" requires me to understand the beliefs and practices of all the world religions, so I am quite familiar with how frequently these religions teach against sin and call on their followers to avoid it. Sadly, when it comes to the purely "religious" view of sin, much of Christianity is not all that different from the other world religions in this regard. But as we saw in the previous chapter, and as we will see in this chapter, the Bible's revelation about sin goes far beyond simply providing a checklist of good and bad behavior for people to adhere to. The Bible reveals what sin actually *is*, and also reveals how the religious checklists of laws, rules, and regulations can actually lead us into greater sin. As a result, this makes the Bible unique.

This chapter seeks to show how the Bible actually defines sin as suggested in the previous chapter. We learned that sin is not simply breaking God's commands, but is actually defined as the human tendency to engage in rivalry with other human beings, which then leads to accusation, blame, scapegoating, and violence. The prohibitions of God are all directed toward stopping this never-ending cycle into rivalry, blame, scapegoating, and violence. The texts we look at in this chapter will reveal this truth more clearly.

Before we begin looking at these texts, however, I want to clarify two truths. First, God is not angry at us for our sin. While sin is a serious thing, God is not concerned about sin simply because it is sin. That is, God doesn't tell us to stay away from sin because sin offends, hurts, or angers Him. Purely from God's perspective, sin just isn't that big of a deal. The reason God is concerned about sin and wants all humans to stop sinning, is not because God Himself is offended or angered by sin, but because we humans are hurt and damaged by it. Sin is an issue with God, not because it hurts Him, but because it hurts us. God loves us so much, He tells us not to sin because He doesn't want to see us get hurt by it. When God says "Don't" what He is really saying is "Don't hurt yourself."

This leads to the second truth about sin to keep in mind: God does not punish us for our sin. Yes, we may get punished for sin, but this punishment is not from God. Sin carries its own punishment. In fact, the punishment that comes from sin is the pain of sin that God wants to rescue and deliver us from. God doesn't punish us for sin; He works to rescue us from the punishment of sin. God loves us, and doesn't want us to experience the devastating and destructive consequences of sin, and so He warns us against sin.

These twin concepts are essential to keep in mind as we turn to Scripture to look at some key texts about sin. The following texts will reveal that sin is defined by Scripture as human rivalry which leads to accusation, scapegoating, and violence, and that since such activities create great devastation and destruction on humanity, God's work in human history is to rescue, deliver, and save us from the pain and punishment brought on by sin. The first text that reveals this is the flood account in Genesis 6.

GENESIS 6:5, 11, 13

Then the Lord saw that the wickedness of man was great in the earth, and that every intent of the thoughts of his heart was only evil continually.

The earth also was corrupt before God, and the earth was filled with violence.

And God said unto Noah, The end of all flesh is come before me; for the earth is filled with violence through them; and, behold, I will destroy them with the earth.

Ideally, any biblical study of sin would begin with Genesis 4:7, where sin is first mentioned. But we looked at this text in the previous chapter, where we learned that there is good reason for sin to first be connected with Cain's murder of Abel rather than with Adam and Eve eating the forbidden fruit. While the actions of the first couple did introduce sin into the world, sin only came to fruition when Cain murdered his brother, Abel. So at the very beginning, sin is defined and unveiled as sibling rivalry that leads to violence. The related truth is that whenever we engage in violence against another human being, we are engaging in violence against members of our own family (cf. Eph 6:12).

This revelation about sin as rivalry that leads to violence continues in Genesis 4 when Lamech kills a man for harming him. This revelation about sin is fully revealed and exposed in Genesis 6 where sin is clearly equated with human violence, and especially seen in the fact that violence only breeds more violence until it covers the face of the earth. When sin covers the earth, so also does violence, for sin is violence (cf. Gen 6:5, 11, 13). Strangely, God ends up appearing to be the most violent being in the text by sending the flood upon the earth to kill every human except the eight in the ark. A careful reading of the flood account reveals something quite different however, which will be explained in Part IV about the Scapegoat.

The only point to note for now is that sin is equated with violence in the text. Immediately after describing the earth as filled with evil, the text says that the earth was filled with violence (cf. Gen 6:5, 11, 13). So here in Genesis 6, as in Genesis 4, sin is not necessarily related to breaking God's laws and commandments, but instead with the tendency of humans to engage in the escalation of violence with one another. This violence escalated so precipitously in Genesis 6, that it eventually covered the whole earth.

The truth that "sin is violence" is seen throughout the rest of the Old Testament. You can continue on through Genesis and the rest of the Pentateuch, on into the Canaanite Conquest as recorded in Joshua, and further into the way Israel functioned during the time of the Judges and Kings, and see that sin is equated with violence everywhere. Again, since God wants to reveal our sin to us, and since sin is defined as human rivalry and scapegoating that leads to violence, it is no wonder that the Old Testament ranks as one of the bloodiest religious books in human history. The Bible is violent because the Bible reveals our sin to us. If we continued on through the rest of the Old Testament, this is the truth we would see over and over again. So rather than look at more Old Testament texts which endlessly repeat this truth, let us turn to some New Testament texts which shed additional light about the problem of sin and violence.

MATTHEW 1:21

And she will bring forth a Son, and you shall call His name Jesus, for He will save His people from their sins.

Matthew 1:21 is a prophecy spoken by an angel to Joseph about the son that would be born to Mary. The angel tells Joseph that Mary's son will be called "Jesus, for He will save His people from their sins." The name *Jesus* means "the Lord saves," but what does it mean that Jesus will save His people *from their sins*? Very often when people read and teach this verse, they believe that the angel is telling Joseph that Jesus will be able to purchase the forgiveness of sins for people from God so that they can gain eternal life and go to heaven when they die. But this is not what the angel is saying at all.

First of all, God has always forgiven all people of all their sins, no matter what. Jesus did not have to purchase forgiveness from God. God forgives simply because God is a loving forgiver. Second, the word *save* does not mean "gain eternal life so you can go to heaven when you die." It means "deliver." Though many Christians today think that the words "save" and "salvation" refer to going to heaven when you die, there is no instance of the word being used this way in the New Testament. Salvation is not about going to heaven when you die but often has in view some sort of temporal deliverance from the difficulties of this life.[12] So since the angel is not talking about going to heaven, what is the message of the angel?

The meaning of the angel becomes clear when we recognize that the word *sin* refers to the imitative rivalry that exists within all human interaction and how this rivalry often leads to scapegoating, murder, and violence. This is indeed what Jesus came to save us from. Through His life, ministry,

[12] For more on the words "Forgiveness" and "Salvation," see my online course "The Gospel Dictionary" found at RedeemingGod.com/courses.

and teaching, Jesus sought to deliver us from our rivalrous, scapegoating violence which we carry out in the name of God. Jesus showed us that God does not want the death of our enemies, nor does He want the death of anyone. God does not even want the blood of sacrifices in order to forgive sins (See Part III about Sacrifice and Part V about Blood). Furthermore, Jesus showed that rivalry does not have to end in scapegoating and violence, which always and only leads to more scapegoating and violence. Jesus showed us a different way, a way of love and forgiveness.

The sin of rivalrous, scapegoating violence has torn apart the world since Cain first killed Abel. But Jesus came to stop the cycle of violence, and lead us into the way of love. He came to save His people from their sins.

MATTHEW 3:6 (CF. MARK 1:4; LUKE 3:3)

... and were baptized by him in the Jordan, confessing their sins.

The message that the angel declared to Joseph regarding the ministry of Jesus is also the message that John the Baptist preached. John came preaching a baptism of repentance for the forgiveness of sins. Some forms of the Jewish religion had become corrupt at this time, and so the preaching and teaching of John was a call for the people to return to God and follow His ways with a new heart and a pure mind. As seen by the three specific changes John calls people to practice in Luke 3:10-14, the sins were all related to desire, envy, rivalry, false accusation, and violence. Rather than engage in rivalry that stems from greed, the people were to share with one another and to be generous. Rather than falsely accuse or intimidate others through force, they are to be content with what they have. The sins that John called people to turn from are the sins which lead to human violence. Through such a message, John follows in the prophetic tradition of calling on people to turn from their sin, which is specifically described as rivalry, false accusation, and violence.

JOHN 16:8

And when He has come, He will convict the world of sin, and of righteousness, and of judgment.

One of the ministries of the Holy Spirit is to "convict the world of sin" (John 16:8). This does not primarily mean, however, that the Holy Spirit goes around pointing out the bad behaviors and actions of individual people. If this were so, many people would likely feel a whole lot more conviction for the wrong things they do. As it is, many people don't feel all that bad about what they do, which either means that the Holy Spirit is doing a poor job, or that we have misunderstood the convicting work of the Holy Spirit. I think it is likely the latter.

Regarding the Holy Spirit, Jesus elsewhere says that the Spirit moves where He wills (John 3:8), and also that when Jesus is lifted up, He will draw all people to Himself (John 12:32), which presumably happens through the work of the Spirit in the world. It seems that the convicting work of the Holy Spirit does not primarily involve pointing out the individual faults of individual people, but rather with calling the people of this world to abandon the ways of the world and follow the way of the crucified Christ instead. Since this world is founded upon rivalry, accusation, scapegoating, and violence, the Holy Spirit moves over the earth calling people to abandon such practices and instead follow Jesus in self-sacrificial forgiveness.

I believe the Holy Spirit is doing an excellent job in this task. While it is true that the world still engages in a lot of rivalry, scapegoating, and violence, the world is also waking up to the fact that such practices are wrong. In ancient civilizations, it used to be that nobody questioned scapegoating violence. It "worked" to create peace in a society, and as a result of its effectiveness, it was assumed to be fully in line with the will of the gods. But since Jesus revealed the truth about scapegoating violence to us, and since the Holy Spirit has been convicting the world of this sin, it is no longer as effective as it once was and does not create any lasting or significant peace.

The world is starting to recognize that true peace only comes through forgiveness.

Evidence that the Holy Spirit is at work in this way is seen in the fact that even non-Christians are starting to recognize the truth about scapegoating. Though the Bible is unique among ancient religious writings in the way it exposes and unveils the truth about the sin of scapegoating violence, this truth is found in more and more places today as the Spirit convicts the world of sin. Movies and novels often contain the storyline of desire leading to rivalry, which then leads to violence and murder. People all over the world are teaching and writing about the scapegoat victim. Many non-Christians see that when rivalry leads to violence it must be counteracted with peace and reconciliation. As a result of the convicting work of the Holy Spirit, the entire world senses a burden to end violence, restore broken relationships, and heal ruined communities.

Strangely, while the church should be leading the world in such matters, it sometimes seems the world leads the church. Quite often, when the world is exposing scapegoat victims as innocent and crying out for forgiveness and reconciliation, the church retreats into a position of judgment, accusation, blame, and calls for death. But when we recognize that the Spirit also convicts the world of sin, we do not need to be alarmed when the world sees something wrong before we do. Instead, we can be thrilled when we see the world responding to the movement of the Spirit in their midst, and we can join other people in their efforts to end rivalry, violence, and scapegoating. We can, like Paul in the Areopagus, stand up and say, "The One whom you worship without knowing, Him I proclaim to you" (Acts 17:23).

ROMANS 5–7

Therefore, just as through one man sin entered the world, and death through sin, and thus death spread to all men, because all sinned . . . (Rom 5:12)

These three chapters from Romans are key for understanding the biblical concept of sin and are central to understanding Paul's concept of the righteousness of God. Paul begins by explaining that sin entered the world through one man, Adam (Rom 5:12). Though many Christians love to blame Eve for being the one to introduce sin, such a practice only reveals once again our habit of creating a scapegoat of other people. Sin came through Adam. However, as seen previously in this book, sin is not mentioned until it seeks to devour Cain in Genesis 4:7. The death that came through Adam is the death of scapegoating violence that was first practiced by Cain. But the mention of sin in Genesis 4:7 is only there to carefully reveal and define what sin is. The rivalry, scapegoating, and blame all came from Adam's choice to eat from the Tree of the Knowledge of Good and Evil and then blame Eve and blame God for what happened. Sin came through Adam, and its full fruition is seen when Cain killed Abel.

In Romans 5:15-21, Paul explains how the death of Jesus on the cross brought life to the world, in that it showed us a better way, a way of love and forgiveness based on faith in Jesus Christ. Based on these truths, Paul continues in Romans 6 to show how the death of Jesus helps us defeat sin in our daily life. The key to defeating sin, according to Romans 6, is to consider ourselves dead, buried, and resurrected in Jesus Christ. Sin begins with rivalry, but if we are dead, we do not envy. Furthermore, when Jesus returned from the dead, He did not come back in vengeance, wrath, and retaliation, which is how all man-made myths would have ended the story of Jesus. No, Jesus returned with forgiveness and reconciliation. This is how we too should live toward others.

The discussion of the law in Romans 7 shows what we will learn in the next chapter of this book, that the law was intended to curb rivalry and violence, and as such, its intent was good. But because the law was a substitute for relationship, it could never accomplish peace and reconciliation, but only the opposite (see Part II on Law). Paul describes himself as an example of this. In the end, Paul calls upon his readers to choose. We can follow the way of God, which is a way of love and forgiveness, or we can serve the law of sin, which is a law of rivalry, scapegoating, and violence.[13] In the end, Paul's point in Romans 5–7 is that in using the law to achieve the righteousness of God in our lives, we are only led into greater rivalry and sin. Therefore, to truly follow God, we must follow Him into love and forgiveness.

1 CORINTHIANS 15:56

The sting of death is sin, and the strength of sin is the law.

The key phrase to notice in 1 Corinthians 15:56 is that "the strength of sin is the law." As seen in Romans 5–7, the law, though it was given to curb rivalry and violence, actually only increased it. The law was always nothing more than a substitute for what God really wanted, which was a daily relationship with His creatures. But we were terrified of God, and so we chose to be governed by law instead (see Part II on Law). But the law only created more rivalry with each other as we compared our behavior with that of others, made accusations of others based on the law, created scapegoats out of animals, humans, and enemy nations, and then set out to use the law as a means to justify our own violence toward others. What the law instructed was good (Rom 7:12), but it could never accomplish what humans wanted it to do, which was to serve as a substitute for a daily relationship with God. As a substitute for a relationship with God, the law only led to more rivalry, accusation, and religious violence. The law only led to more sin.

2 CORINTHIANS 5:21

For He made Him who knew no sin to be sin for us, that we might become the righteousness of God in Him.

This is an important text in the discussion of sin because Paul writes that

[13] For a good discussion of Romans 5–7, see Robert G. Hamerton-Kelley, *Sacred Violence: Paul's Hermeneutic of the Cross* (Minneapolis: Fortress, 1992), 106-111.

Jesus became sin for us. When we think of sin as some sort of ethereal force which causes people to do bad things or as disobedience to God's commands, this verse makes very little sense. If sin is a spiritual presence or polluting force brought about by disobedience to God, how can it be said in any way that Jesus "became sin"? But when we understand sin as rivalrous, scapegoating violence done in God's name, we see that this is exactly what happened to Jesus on the cross.[14] Every aspect of the passion narratives in the Gospels is designed to reveal that since Jesus was viewed as a rival to both religious Judaism and political Rome, He was chosen as a scapegoat to create peace among the people. Then, as often happens with scapegoats, Jesus was murdered in the name of God. So although Jesus never practiced sin and was completely innocent of all rivalry, scapegoating, and violence, He became sin *for us* (not for God!) so that we would see sin for what it really was. In Jesus, the sin of humanity—the rivalrous, scapegoating violence we commit in God's name—was clearly revealed for all to see. He *became* sin! When we look at Him on the cross, we finally see our sin for what it really is. Through the crucifixion, sin was unveiled before our eyes so that we would see that all scapegoats were wrongly killed, that God was never behind our religious violence, and that God was calling all people to follow Him in loving forgiveness toward one another.

EPHESIANS 2:1-3

And you He made alive, who were dead in trespasses and sins, in which you once walked according to the course of this world, according to the prince of the power of the air, the spirit who now works in the sons of disobedience, among whom also we all once conducted ourselves in the lusts of our flesh, fulfilling the desires of the flesh and of the mind, and were by nature children of wrath, just as the others.

Ephesians 2 is arranged in a "Problem (2:1-3), Solution (2:4-10), Applica-

[14] See Fleming Rutledge, *Crucifixion: Understanding the Death of Jesus Christ* (Grand Rapids: Eerdmans, 2015), 101.

tion (2:11-22)" format. The "Problem," of course, is sin. But what is sin? Well, we know from looking at previous Pauline texts that Paul's definition of sin does not match the way many modern Christians define it. For Paul, "sin" was not primarily an issue of lust, lying, or stealing. Yes, such things are wrong, and can be understood as "sins" or "sinful," but such activities are actually just indicators of the greater problem of sin, which is a problem most humans are ignorant of and blind to.

Paul's explanation of sin here in Ephesians 2 matches what he has described elsewhere. One easy way to see this is to look at the "Application" section of Ephesians 2. The conclusion of his argument in this chapter helps us understand Paul's view of sin. In Ephesians 2:11-22, Paul instructs Christians to recognize that all human hostilities are done away with in Jesus and we can now live at peace with one another as we follow Jesus and build upon the foundation He built. So if this is the application, then the problem of sin in Ephesians 2:1-3 is that we humans live full of accusation, blame, scapegoating, and violence. Worst of all, we blame all such activities on God. Further still, a big part of the problem of sin is that we see no way out and know of no other way to live. All humans live in sin partly because everybody lives this way. We even believe that God lives this way toward us. We know of no other way to live.

So when Paul writes that we are dead in trespasses and sins, he is not primarily referring to breaking the Ten Commandments or violating individual laws, but is instead referring to the human condition which lies behind those Ten Commandments (and all human laws), which is the condition of rivalry, hatred, accusation, scapegoating, and sacred violence. This is the sin that humans are enslaved to (Eph 2:1-3), and this is the sin that Jesus came to rescue us from (Eph 2:4-10), so that we can now live in peace and unity with one another (Eph 2:11-22). The problem of sin which Paul is concerned about in Ephesians 2:1-3 is not the wrongdoing of breaking God's law, but the larger and more systemic issue of human rivalry, accusation, scapegoating, and violence. These are the things that destroy humanity and which Jesus came to deliver us from.

1 TIMOTHY 1:15

This is a faithful saying and worthy of all acceptance, that Christ Jesus came into the world to save sinners, of whom I am chief.

In this text Paul says that "Jesus Christ came into this world to save sinners," and then describes himself as the chief of sinners. It is quite clear from the various passages looked at previously what Paul has in mind when he thinks of sin. It is also clear that Paul cannot be thinking about all the ways he has broken the law of Moses, for when it came to obedience to the Mosaic Law, he was faultless (Php 3:6). So when Paul referred to himself as the chief of sinners, what did he have in mind? He was referring to how, as a religious Jew, he found himself in a rivalry with the early Christians, and out of zeal for God sought to accuse, arrest, and kill these Christians in God's name (cf. Acts 8:1; 9:1; 1 Cor 15:9; Gal 1:23; Php 3:6). On the road to Damascus, Jesus saved Saul from this life of rivalrous, murderous violence in God's name, and called him to become an apostle to the Gentiles so that the message of God's salvation in Jesus could be preached to them as well. Paul had engaged in more rivalry, accusation, scapegoating, and religious violence than anyone he knew, and so he called himself the chief of sinners.

HEBREWS 9:26

He then would have had to suffer often since the foundation of the world; but now, once at the end of the ages, He has appeared to put away sin by the sacrifice of Himself.

The book of Hebrews explains in great detail why Jesus is superior to everything in the Hebrew Scriptures. In chapters 9–10, the author sets out to show how Jesus is superior to the sanctuary and the sacrificial system. As such, we will consider Hebrews 9:23–10:18 in Parts III and V on Sacrifice and Blood, but what Hebrews 9:26 says about sin is also important to briefly consider here. In this text, the author says that Jesus "put away sin by the sacrifice of Himself." It has often been debated *how* Jesus dealt with sin through His own death. The common view is that through His own death, Jesus purchased forgiveness and paid the debt of sin to God. But this passage makes better sense when we recognize that Jesus "put away sin" by refusing to engage in rivalry and violence, and instead revealed the truth about rivalry, scapegoating, and sacred violence by subjecting Himself to this central human sin. He exposed these practices as the lies and chains that held humanity captive and then showed another way for us to follow, which was His way of love and forgiveness. More on how Jesus did this will be discussed later in this book.

1 JOHN 1:7-9

But if we walk in the light as He is in the light, we have fellowship with one another, and the blood of Jesus Christ His Son cleanses us from all sin. If we say that we have no sin, we deceive ourselves, and the truth is not in us. If we confess our sins, He is faithful and just to forgive us our sins and to cleanse us from all unrighteousness.

One important aspect to gaining victory over sin in our lives is to admit and confess our participation in it. This is especially true when it comes to rivalry, accusation, scapegoating, and violence. We humans are mostly blind to how we participate in such behaviors, but before we can change, our eyes must be opened to how we are involved in this cycle of human sin. We must see where we are at rivalry with others, how we have scapegoated others, and how we have called for the death of others in God's name. Unless we see this, we can never be free from it. One of the best ways to see this is to recognize our own participation in shedding the blood of Jesus (see Part V on Blood).

But it is not always easy to see. The religious leaders in the day of Jesus said that if they had been alive in the days of the prophets they would not have persecuted them (Matt 23:30). Yet these same people turned around and killed Jesus. So also we must admit that if we had been alive in the days of Jesus, we very likely would have joined the crowds in crying out for His crucifixion. Even if this is too hard to admit, the fact that Jesus was killed in God's name is a warning to us whenever we seek to condemn, accuse, or kill others in the name of God. If we say that we don't do this to others, then we have deceived ourselves and the truth is not in us. Rivalry, accusation, and scapegoating violence are part of all human existence, and until we see that we are complicit in such practices, Jesus cannot deliver us from them. But once we agree that we are involved in rivalry, scapegoating, and sacred violence toward others, it is then that Jesus can cleanse us from such practices and lead us into fellowship with God and with one another (1 John 1:3; 3:4-5).

1 JOHN 3:4

Whoever commits sin also commits lawlessness,
and sin is lawlessness.

This part of the book has proposed that sin is not simply the activity of breaking God's laws, but is better understood as the central dehumanizing activities of rivalry, accusation, scapegoating, and violence. Some object to this idea by quoting 1 John 3:4. They say that this text gives a clear definition of sin, for it says that "sin is lawlessness." Therefore, they say, sin occurs when we break God's commands. I have briefly addressed this idea in the previous chapter, but let us consider it here as well in the context of 1 John 3.

It is true, of course, that sin is lawlessness, but if we understand sin in only this way, it does not give the full picture (unless we understand the term Law as well, which we will look at in Part II). Further evidence that sin cannot simply be understood as breaking God's law is seen in Paul's statement that when it came to obeying the law, he was blameless (Php 3:6). Yet

Paul also refers to himself as the chief of sinners (1 Tim 1:15). So sin cannot be *mere* lawlessness, for Paul kept the law but was a great sinner.

The law was given to help guide people in the right way to live and the proper way to love (see Part II on Law). But the law was a faulty guide, for someone like Paul (and the Pharisees or Sadducees of Jesus' day) could keep the entire law yet still fail to love others. We must understand the law as pointing not to "the letter of the law," which is legalistic righteousness, but to "the spirit of the law," which is love.

The best way to understand 1 John 3:4, then, is to see it in light of the rest of John's letter, where he calls his readers to live in fellowship with one another. Fellowship is not accomplished through following a lot of rules, but by living in relationship with others. Love leads to fellowship and relationship, but law does not and cannot. One can follow all the laws and still not have fellowship with God or one another. Similarly, while a lack of love reveals itself in lawless and hateful living, one can follow the laws while hating others. In this way, lawlessness is a *symptom* of a lack of love, but law keeping will not lead to love. So yes, sin is lawlessness, for those who sin do break God's law, but this does not mean that those who keep the law are living in loving fellowship with God and others.

SIN IS THE HUMAN PROBLEM

There are many verses in the Bible about sin, but hopefully the ones discussed here show that the main issue with sin is not the breaking of divine commands so that God becomes angry with us. No, God only gave His commands so that our lives might have less pain, heartache, and sorrow. The reason God doesn't want us to sin is because sin hurts us, and as the objects of His love, He doesn't want to see us get hurt. The main way sin hurts us is in how it destroys and ruins our relationship with Him and with one another. It does this through desire, envy, and coveting so that we come into rivalry with God and with each other. This rivalry spins out of control and turns into accusation, blame, scapegoating, violence, and eventually murder. The worst kind of murder is the murder done in God's name, which essentially turns God into a scapegoat as well. This is *sin*, and this is what Jesus came to expose and reveal so that He could save and liberate us from the sin of scapegoating violence.

So we have now seen what the Bible reveals about the human problem of sin. It is a problem that is at the foundation of all human civilization and society, and which all humans are complicit in and guilty of. Sin is the universal tendency to engage in the cycle of rivalry, accusation, scapegoating, and violence. Most humans are completely blind and ignorant of their involvement in such sin, which explains why the Bible spends so much time trying to reveal our sin to us. Sin truly is a terrible human problem, and the Bible seeks to unveil this problem to us.

After we see the problem so clearly exposed before our eyes, the question must then become, "What is the solution? What is the cure for this problem? What is the fix?" Scripture also provides an answer to these questions. Many people, however, wrongly assume that part of God's answer to the problem of sin involves law and the sacrificial system. When you ask many Christians how God worked to stop sin in the world or take care of our sin problem, many will point to the numerous laws in the Bible or to the sacrificial system. According to many, the laws of God were given to tell us what to do and not to do, and the sacrificial system was provided to purchase forgiveness from God for our numerous sins.

But is the law and the sacrificial system truly God's answer to the problem of sin? The next two Parts of this book consider both. Part II will consider the subject of Law in the Bible, and Part III will consider Sacrifice. We will see that while sin is the problem, law and sacrifice did not take care of our sin, but only made the problem worse. We begin to see this by looking at what Scripture says about the law.

PART II: LAW

Are you ready to be shocked? Many people assume that the law is God's solution to the problem of sin. But as we will see in the next two chapters, the law doesn't actually help with sin, but instead, only amplifies the problem. Sometimes, the law only leads into deeper and greater sin! It's a challenging idea, but the following two chapters will show why this is so.

I must also give credit where credit is due. John Sailhamer's book, *The Meaning of the Pentateuch* was quite influential in helping me prepare the content of the following two chapters.[15] It is quite a long book, which delves deeply into some of the more arcane scholarly research about the Mosaic Law, but the overall argument of Sailhamer's book is breathtaking and beautiful to behold. If you want to read more about the understanding of the law as proposed in the next two chapters, I recommend you get a copy of Sailhamer's book and read the extended explanation and arguments for yourself.

[15] John H. Sailhamer, *The Meaning of the Pentateuch: Revelation, Composition, and Interpretation* (Downers Grove: IVP, 2009).

CHAPTER 4

DEFINING LAW

If sin is the universal human problem, then what is the solution? Some say that the solution to sin is found in obedience to the law. The law was given, they say, to both teach us about sin and to keep us from sinning. They argue that if we obey the law, we will not sin. Yet as logical as this seems, Jesus and Paul had a different perspective about the purpose of the law and its effectiveness in keeping us from sin. They both indicated that the law did not solve the problem of sin, but only added to it. We will see how this is so in this chapter and the next. This chapter begins by defining the law, and moves on from there to see the difficulties in trying to use the law as a solution for the problem of sin.

DEFINING THE LAW

The word law means "rule, or commandment." The Greek word for *law* is *nomos*, while the related word, *commandment*, is *entolē*. The words in Greek mean basically the same thing they do in English. In connection with Scripture, of course, the words refer primarily to the rules and commandments given by God to the people of Israel at Mount Sinai. Most of these laws and commandments are found in the Pentateuch, the first five books of the Bible, with a heavy concentration of them in Exodus 20, Leviticus, and Deuteronomy. When all are tallied, there are 613 commandments in the Mosaic Law. There are, of course, numerous other laws, commandments, and instructions in the Bible beyond just the 613 commandments of the Pentateuch, but for our purposes in this chapter, we are going to limit our study to the law given through Moses to the people of Israel as recorded in the Pentateuch.

HOW WE DIVIDE THE LAW

Many Christians have struggled with the role and function of the Mosaic Law in our lives as followers of Jesus. Since there are numerous laws in the Pentateuch which seem not to apply to modern-day Christians, it is quite common to hear the various 613 commandments divided up into three categories, the Ceremonial Law, the Judicial/Civil Law, and the Moral Law. The Ceremonial Law is thought to be those laws that concern the Priestly and Levitical responsibilities within the Temple. The Judicial/Civil Law consists of those laws that concern the operation of Israel as a nation and the governing of the people. The Moral Law consists of the guidelines and laws which are to be applied to all people everywhere throughout time. This three-fold division helps Christians decide which commands we are to keep, and which ones were specific to the nation of Israel and their worship in the Temple. Those who use this threefold division say that Christians are to obey the moral laws, but not the others.

The primary problem with this three-fold division is that it is never found in the Bible or in the Mosaic Law itself. Therefore, the division of the various laws into these three categories often seems quite arbitrary and random. For example, Exodus 23:9-11 instructs the Israelites to not oppress strangers and foreigners living in their land. This clearly seems to be a moral law. Yet the passage goes on to instruct the Israelites that the way to treat foreigners with fairness is to let their fields, vineyards, and olive groves lie fallow every seventh year so that the needy can harvest food from it for their own use. This seems to be a ceremonial law (letting the land have a Sabbath rest), or maybe even a civil law (providing for the needs of the poor). This one example shows that there is no clear way to divide the law, and even when it is divided, the various types of laws are interconnected and dependent upon each other. It seems then that we must either follow all the law or none of it. So what are we to do?

Thankfully, such questions over the role of the Mosaic Law in the life of the Christian are not new. This issue was actually one of the first and primary theological questions within the early church. From the very beginning, there were questions about whether or not Gentile Christians had to obey the Mosaic Law. As Paul went about teaching the Gospel, he constantly faced opposition from a set of Christians who believed that to truly follow Jesus you had to obey the Mosaic Law. Even the Apostle Peter seemed to side with this group for a while (see Gal 2). Eventually, the church met together to make a decision on this question, and they decided that Christians did not need to obey the Mosaic Law, but they did give some instructions to Gentile Christians which would help them live in fellowship and community with Jewish Christians (cf. Acts 15:22-29).[16] Nevertheless, despite this decision by the early church, we Christians still haven't solved this most basic Christian dilemma.

Some Christians try to solve the issue by focusing only on the Ten Commandments, all of which are thought to be part of the Moral Law (with the possible exception of the Sabbath Law, depending on who you ask). Furthermore, the Ten Commandments themselves are conveniently divided up into two categories, with the first four laws concerning our relationship with God, and the final six concerning our relationship with humans. (The numbering of these differs, depending on who you ask, for there are actually 14 imperatives in the Ten Commandments of Exodus 20.) This two-fold division between laws about our relationship with God and laws about our relationship with other humans fits nicely with Jesus' summary of the law in Matthew 22:37-39: "'You shall love the Lord your God with all your heart, with all your soul, and with all your mind.' This is

[16] Yes, the specific issue of the Jerusalem Counsel was circumcision, but since circumcision is the sign of the Mosaic Covenant, for a Gentile to receive Jewish circumcision at that time, was to agree to also follow the entirety of the Jewish Law. Circumcision was a declaration of your intent to "convert" to Judaism and follow the Mosaic Law. So the question of circumcision was not *just* a question of circumcision, but was about the entire Mosaic Law.

the first and great commandment. And the second is like it: 'You shall love your neighbor as yourself.'"

Yet even though "Love God and love others" is a good summary of the law, this statement is still a law, and Christians are not called to live according to the law. Instead, we are invited to live within a relationship based on love. While God does want us to love Him and love others, we cannot do this until we know that we are loved unconditionally. And once we know we are loved by God, love for Him and for others flows naturally from Him through us as we live within that love. This only makes sense, for no relationship can be built on law. True relationships are always and only built on love.

Imagine if you tried to build your marriage on a checklist of responsibilities. How long would such a marriage last? Let us even assume that the "To do" list was a very good list. It included things like saying "I love you" seven times a day, hugging your spouse three times a day, and having sex once per week. On this list, men were instructed to wash the dishes for their wives on Tuesday nights, and wives were instructed to give their husbands a backrub on Fridays. Imagine that this list had 613 such commandments and you were able to do them all. Would you have a "good" marriage relationship? Well, such a marriage might be better than other marriages, but no one would be able to call it a marriage "relationship." It would be a marriage based on a checklist; not a marriage based on love.

This is exactly how to view the law, and in fact, is exactly how the law is presented in Scripture. The law serves as a substitute when a loving relationship is not possible, but no one should ever confuse law keeping with an actual loving relationship. Though the law may teach people the *sorts of things* one might see in a loving relationship, even a comprehensive list of 613 items can never substitute for an actual relationship built on love. Just as laws are needed where there is no relationship, laws are not needed where a relationship of love exists. If people reject love, the only alternative is law. This truth becomes even clearer when we consider the origin of law.

THE ORIGIN OF LAW

To understand why God gave His law to the Israelites, we must begin with the history of lawmaking itself. Almost any law in any country from any era has a history behind how the law became a law. In most cases, a particular law was put into effect because there were people who were behaving in a way that made the law necessary.

A quick internet search about crazy laws in the United States will reveal several laws that are still "on the books" in various regions. There are laws about taking pictures of rabbits in June, bouncing pickles, and underwater whistling. Yet as strange as these laws are, it is likely that the stories behind these laws are even stranger. What were the circumstances that led lawmakers to forbid the practice of underwater whistling? Was there an underwater whistling contest in which someone drowned? For that matter, have you ever tried to whistle underwater? Why would a law forbid something that was next to impossible to do?[17] Similar questions could be asked about any of the crazy laws around the world.

But even when we think about more mundane laws, like the tax code, or campaign finance law, speed limit laws, or the legal drinking age, all of these laws have stories behind how they became laws. And whatever these stories are, almost all of them will have certain things in common. We can pretty much guarantee that the laws were created in order to stop people from doing something or to get them to start doing other things they were not doing.

In most cases, the things that these people should not have been doing (or should have been doing) are matters of common sense, common decency, or the common good. Since people generally lack common sense, common decency, or the desire for the common good, laws are created to keep us all in line and in check. Laws are created and enacted because some peo-

[17] I became curious about this law, and so I looked it up. The state that forbids underwater whistling is Vermont. The law forbids all sorts of underwater noises, whether from people or devices, because such noises may damage or disorient certain types of underwater mammals who use whistling to communicate.

ple do not properly behave. Laws often require us to do things that put other people before ourselves and other goals before our own.

You probably have "household laws" in your own home which portray this quite well. Maybe you have rules about how much time children can spend on the computer, who gets to sit where at mealtime, or what sort of chores need to be done before bedtime. If you think about any one of these rules and how they came into existence, you will likely recall the events and situations that led up to making such a law necessary for the happy existence of your family.

It is likely that you even have some "crazy-sounding" laws which would make absolutely no sense to any other family in history, but which make sense to you and your family because of certain situations that arose. For example, my family has a rule we follow which says this: "Dishes come before Dataseka." Nobody else in the entire world knows what that rule means or how to follow it, but if you were to ask my wife or any of my children what it means, they would know. As one of our family rules, it has a history of how it developed, and it was created to help us live together as a happy family. Nevertheless, it would be pointless for any other family to try to follow this rule, since they do not know what it means nor why and how the rule came about.

It is helpful to think about all biblical laws this way as well. Every law in the Bible is specific to a time and place and people. And every biblical law has a history behind it for why it was enacted and what it accomplished among the people who lived it. Yes, some of these laws, like "Do not murder," are applicable to other times, people, and places, but this is not because all the laws are timeless decrees, but because people are people everywhere. Even if the Bible did not say, "Do not murder," all humans everywhere would naturally come up with this law against murder in order to maintain peace and stability. So even in the case of the Ten Commandments, all biblical "laws" are specific to a time and place and people, and they have a history behind how they were developed so that those people living in that time at that place could maintain peace and stability.

This is partly why it is so hard to understand or put into practice many of the laws we read about in the Bible. Though many of the biblical laws make sense, there are some that do not. Why is it wrong, for example, to mix wool and linen (Deut 22:11)? What is so terrible about cooking meat in milk (Exod 23:19)? And what caused people to think that if a woman was accused of adultery, they could discern her guilt or innocence by making her drink dirt swept up from the tabernacle floor (Num 5:11-31)? People come up with all sorts of fancy theories and explanations for these laws, but we have about as much chance of understanding the reasons behind these laws as you do of understanding what I mean when I say "Dishes come before Dataseka."

What is more, even if I told you what the "Dishes come before Dataseka" law means, and even if I told you the story behind how and why our family developed this law, this still would not mean that it was applicable to you or to your family, let alone applicable to all families everywhere in all places throughout time. That law helps keep the peace in our family, but it would do absolutely nothing for yours.

Once again, the Mosaic Law is similar to this. All the laws in Leviticus, Exodus, Numbers, and Deuteronomy have a history behind them. This history is specific to the people, time, and circumstances in which the laws were created. While some of the laws have universal and timeless application (e.g., "Do not murder"), many of the laws have no such universal application. We don't even know what some of these laws mean, let alone the story behind them, and even if we did know, this would not mean that we could apply these laws to our situation today. In fact, knowing what the laws mean and knowing the story behind them might actually make it clear that we could not and should not attempt to apply those laws to our lives today. The contrary is also true. If we do not know what a law means and we fail to understand the story behind the law, but we try to follow and obey the law anyway, then our attempt at obeying God's laws might actually lead us into sin.

OBEYING THE LAW CAN LEAD TO SIN

Have you ever realized that blind obedience to the law can actually result in sin? When we try to follow laws that were created for a different people, living in different times, from a difficult culture, at a different era, and in a different situation, we may actually end up sinning by following their laws, because doing so might break laws that are part of our own time and culture. For example, you could follow all the laws found in the Bible and still be a slave owner. Today, however, slavery is universally recognized as sinful, and as contrary to the revealed will of God. But those who owned slaves in the past (or even today) are not violating any specific prohibition against slavery in the Bible. So it is possible to obey all the laws and still sin.

But it gets worse than that. Obeying biblical laws may actually cause you to sin. It is entirely possible that the act of obeying the law will actually cause you to sin against God and others humans. This is especially true when we recall that sin is primarily understood in Scripture as the activities, actions, and mindsets that are related to the human cycle of rivalry, accusation, scapegoating, and violence. Paul (as Saul) is the perfect example. In the act of obeying the law, he set out to arrest, accuse, jail, judge, condemn, and kill Christians.

Something similar can happen to us when we set out to obey the law. When our focus is on obeying the law, we tend to use the law to judge and condemn other people (and maybe ourselves) for their failure to obey the law. We then feel that because the law if "from God," that when people disobey God's laws, they become His enemies. This view of other people allows us to treat them as less than human, or as foes to everything good and godly, giving us cause to correct or condemn them. Sometimes this effort to correct or condemn leads into violence or war against these "enemies of God." In this way, our zeal for the law actually leads us into greater sin against other people.

This is especially true when we fail to remember that there is a story behind almost every law. Before a law was created, someone was doing something stupid, dangerous, foolish, or selfish that harmed other people or parts of God's creation. Maybe what they were doing was even dangerous to themselves. The person who was acting in such harmful ways did so because they lacked love. If they had loved God, loved themselves, or loved others the way they should have, they would not have engaged in such unloving behavior. But when love is absent, laws must be created to inform and guide people into proper behavior.

Yet when laws are created as a way to guide people into love, some begin to think that what is obedience to the law is more important than learning to love. It's definitely easier. Imagine a (mostly) fictional scenario where my wife explains to me that she is not feeling loved, and when I ask her to provide examples of what I can do to show love she gives me a list of three suggestions. I can buy her flowers every week, ask her about her day at dinner, and kiss her every night before bed. But if I do those things perfectly every day for the rest of my life, does this then mean that I truly love her? Not necessarily; I can do all those things and still not show love. Worse yet, I can check these items off my list, but then turn around and do unloving things such as not actually listening to her when she tells me about her day, or mechanically kissing her goodnight. In such a situation, she will not feel *more* loved, but less. My strict obedience to the law actually leads me to treat my wife worse than ever before.

This is exactly how it can work with all laws. Laws are initially created to help people learn to show love toward God, themselves, or others, but when obedience to these laws become an end in and of itself, laws can actually lead to worse behavior than ever before. This is especially true when people begin looking for loopholes in the laws which allow them to live selfishly and dangerously while still obeying the letter of the law. In the example above, although I asked my wife about her day, I didn't actually listen to what she said, which only makes her feel worse. It would have been better if I hadn't even asked.

Usually, as these sorts of loopholes are discovered, the human tendency is to close them with even more laws. If my wife complained (rightfully so) that although I asked her about her day I wasn't really listening, the natural human reaction would be to create an additional law to actually listen to what she said. So now we have a fourth law. But the only way to prove that I was actually listening is to summarize or paraphrase back to her what she says. This creates a fifth law. But even still, I could do this without actually caring or showing any interest. So in an attempt to show interest, a sixth law could be created in which I must ask at least three questions in response to what she was saying. Do you see what is happening here? Due to a lack of love on my part, the laws are starting to multiply. But no matter how many laws we add, they will never be able to create genuine love. Yet in an attempt to produce love where there is none, more and more laws become necessary. This is exactly what happens to all laws. When there is no love, 10 laws become 600 laws which become 6000 laws which become 60,000 pages of laws. And with every new law, the reality of genuine love becomes less and less likely.

But it gets worse. Imagine that my wife and I come up with 613 laws that "work" for us. Our marriage is not perfect, and both of us feel that something is missing in our relationship, but at least it works. The laws we created keep us together and keep us smiling (most of the time). Each of these laws has a story and a history behind it which is based on some argument or misunderstanding in our marriage. She likes flowers and I wasn't giving them to her, so we created a rule about buying her flowers every week. This later generates a law that the flowers have to be daisies, roses, and orchids, because these are her favorite flowers.

Later in life, when one of our daughters gets married, she asks us about the secret to a happy marriage. In response, we give her the list of 613 laws. "Follow these," we say, "and you will have a happy marriage." So she gives them to her new husband, and they attempt to follow them. That first week, he brings home an orchid in a pot. "What's this?" she says. "I hate orchids. The room temperature and light has to be just right; they die easily, and you have to water them with a spray bottle. I'm not doing that. Thanks, but no thanks." He counters that he was just following the marriage laws, and asks if she would prefer daisies or roses instead. "No," she says. "I want tulips. Tulips are my favorite flower." But when they consult the marriage laws, there are no tulips to be found, because my wife and I never made a law about tulips. So my daughter sadly decides that if they are going to have a happy marriage, she must give up her love of tulips and learn to love orchids, roses, and daisies.

Do you see what happened? The law was followed, but love was not. In fact, in following the law, the opposite of love occurred. The new husband did not seek to discover what his wife actually wanted, but followed the law in buying flowers that his wife did not want. And for her part, although she preferred tulips, the fact that the law did not mention tulips caused her to think that her love for tulips was wrong. If this pattern continued, the "Marriage Laws" that worked for my wife and I (though not really) will end up destroying the marriage of our daughter.

This is exactly what happens with all other laws as well. If one culture or group of people looks at the laws of another culture or people, whether it is the 10 laws, the 600, the 6000, or the 60,000, and says, "It sort of worked for them; we'll do the same thing," they will end up treating each other more miserably than any other culture. Why? Because they completely bypassed love and went straight to law. Furthermore, the laws of that other people and other culture were created out of an attempt to enforce love in that particular culture for that particular people. Those particular laws only work for them. Different people in different cultures need to develop different laws if they are going to curb the dangerous and selfish behavior of their own people in their own culture at their own time. But if we skip this difficult law-making process and simply adopt the laws of another culture and era, and try to follow these laws in our own culture and era, we may actually end up living in ways that are the opposite of love!

The example between my wife and I is completely fictional. (Well, mostly … but that's a story to save for the marriage book we will never write.) Let me provide an example from real life. In our modern, western culture (as in many others throughout time), we have a law that a man should be married to one woman. No, I am not talking about the definition of marriage. Put that debate aside for now. I am talking about laws against polygamy. The law says that a man should not have two or more wives. There are numerous reasons for this law, one of which is that "the Bible says so," but even without the Bible, people in our culture believe that in general, a man who has two or more wives cannot properly love them both. People tend to believe that it is unfair to the women involved if a man has more than one wife. Furthermore, since our culture is roughly divided 50/50 between men and women, and man who has more than one wife is not acting in love toward all the other men who also desire to have a wife. Why should one man have ten wives while another man has none? So you see? We have developed a law with the intended purpose of creating an atmosphere of love. Whether this law is successful or not is another question.

But note that this law, which says that a man can only have one wife, has not been universally practiced by all people in all times. A couple years ago, I read in a book by Roland Allen about a Native American Sioux tribe in which the men were expected to have as many wives as they could support. It was their custom and law that if a man could support more than one wife, he should. Why? It wasn't that men wanted to have sex with lots of women. No, the primary reason was that many men went off to war with other tribes and died. As a result, the surviving men took multiple wives so that no woman would have to live alone and childless. In an attempt to take care of the women in the tribe (and to replenish the tribal population), it was decided that each man should have as many wives as he could support. He was expected to care for them, provide for them, and protect them. Furthermore, without such polygamy, most of the women likely would have starved.

When European missionaries arrived to preach the Gospel to this particular Native American tribe, they were appalled to discover that the men were taking multiple wives. And though the reasons for polygamy were explained to these missionaries, they considered such explanations to be nothing more than justification for sin. After all, the Bible says that one man should be married to one woman, and anything else was sinful and wrong. So when the chieftain became a Christian, the missionaries told him that as the leader of the tribe, he needed to set an example for the other men, and this meant that the first thing he needed to do as a follower of Jesus was put away all of his wives except one.

So the chieftain went home, and, with a heavy heart, chose the one wife he would keep. Then he hanged the rest.

When he told the missionaries what he had done, they were more horrified than before. But he explained to them that if he had left all of his wives alive while refusing to let them live under his care, they would have starved to death. He thought that killing them was more loving than letting them starve. The missionaries informed him that God would have taken care of his other wives, but now that he had murdered them, he could never be a Christian. So the chieftain went back to his Native American beliefs and ways.

Do you see? Laws that are intended to produce loving actions in one culture with one particular people in a particular set of circumstances, may actually produce unloving actions when applied to another group of people in a different culture with a different set of circumstances. This does not mean we are moral relativists; it means we have to understand the purpose of the law before we seek to obey it.

If we were to blindly follow some of the Mosaic laws simply "because they're in the Bible," we would be led into some horribly unloving behavior. Like making your wife drink muddy water because you think she cheated on you, stoning your children because they're disrespectful, killing a man for picking up sticks on Saturday, or slaughtering bulls and goats because you feel guilty about something you did. All such things are sinful in our culture, yet can be defended from a strict observance of the law. So as you can see, following the biblical law may actually cause us to sin. Once we see this truth that following the law can actually lead to sin, it is then that we discover that Jesus taught it as well.

JESUS VS. THE RELIGION OF LAW

In Jesus' day, the Pharisees and Sadducees were the most scrupulous of law keepers. And while nobody could accuse them of breaking the law, few people would have thought of them as overly loving. Though they loved those who loved them, and loved those who kept the law like they did, nobody thought of the Pharisees when they thought about love. When someone opposed their teaching or broke a law, these religious leaders would not think twice about breaking fellowship with such a person, bringing them before the courts for condemnation, or seeking to have them stoned to death.

This is why Jesus had so many negative encounters with these religious leaders. He lived in love which often required Him to live outside their law. When faced with love or law, Jesus always chose love. Jesus knew that even if love did not fulfill the letter of the law, it always fulfilled the spirit of the law. If love is the purpose of the law, then love never fails to fulfill the spirit of the law. But following biblical law simply "because it's the law" may actually cause you to sin if the modern application of that law no longer comes from or leads to love.

When Jesus healed on the Sabbath, hung out with prostitutes and sinners, or let Himself get touched by lepers, He was breaking the religious interpretation of the law while He simultaneously fulfilled the spirit in which it was intended. The law was intended to lead to love and Jesus, knowing this, showed love to everyone with whom He interacted, even if His actions went against the letter of the law as understood and taught by the religious leaders of His day. We can follow the example of Jesus in this regard when it comes to the question of the Mosaic Law.

For those who are still a bit skeptical, there are several examples from the Mosaic Law which reveal loving actions in their day, but which would nevertheless be hateful and hurtful actions in ours. Several of the laws about women and slaves, for example, were huge movements toward love in the days when the law was given and both women and slaves were treated like property. In many ways, the laws of Moses gave value and dignity to women and slaves that was unprecedented among other people and cultures of that time.

However, if we were to treat women today as the Mosaic Law stipulates they are to be treated, such behavior toward women today would be misogynistic, sexist, cruel, and mean. The law of love as exemplified in Jesus Christ has brought about better treatment of women today than anything the Mosaic Law could accomplish through law keeping.

The same goes for slavery. The Mosaic Law assumes that slavery was a way of life and provided laws based upon this cultural assumption. But today, most people know that slavery is wrong. It is a great evil for one person to own another. But the Bible says nothing of the sort.

When it comes to women and slaves (and many other topics of the Mosaic Law) an attempt to follow the letter of the law would not be a step forward in godliness and Christlikeness, but a huge step backward. And not just backward, but backward into serious sin. Any man who exactly follows what the biblical Mosaic Law says about women or slaves should be arrested and sent to prison.

But this does not mean that the Mosaic Law was necessarily wrong. Though they were a step toward love in Moses' day, they were a step backward in Jesus' day, which is why He didn't exactly follow the law in every case. He didn't allow the woman caught in adultery to be stoned to death. He let His disciples do "work" on the Sabbath so they could eat. He Himself performed work on the Sabbath in healing. He touched "the unclean" lepers and dead people. All of these were loving actions that technically "broke" various aspects of the Mosaic Law.

But did Jesus fulfill the Mosaic Law? Of course He did! How? Because love is the fulfillment of the law. If Jesus had focused on the law instead of on love, He would not have been as loving as He was. Instead, He would have been a religious sinner. This is partly why any Christian today that uses the Mosaic Law as a foundation for their behavior is often viewed as less loving than their unchristian friends and neighbors. The Mosaic Law is less loving than where the rest of culture is at today.

This doesn't mean that the culture has love figured out and we should follow their cues. Of course not. But we must not begin to think that because the law worked for Moses and the Israelites 3500 years ago as they wandered around a desert that it will work for us today. The Mosaic Law wasn't meant to be a universal guideline for all people everywhere throughout time on how to behave. When we use it this way, we end up behaving in ways that are less loving than many of those today who live without the law.

SO WHY DID GOD GIVE THE LAW?

If all of this is true, why didn't God inspire Moses to just write down "Love one another" and leave it at that? Why did Moses write all these laws? Why did God give all these laws to Moses? Why didn't God appear to Moses and say, "Just tell them to love me and love each other and all will be well"? If love fulfills the law and if obeying the law can often be less loving than simply loving without the law, why doesn't the law consist of one command: "Love!"? Why didn't God appear on Mount Sinai and say, "Love Me. Love each other. Now let's go!"?

The truth is that this is exactly what God did say.

Or near enough.

To understand the origin of the law, we need to return to the history of lawmaking again, only this time, we must look specifically at the history of the Mosaic Law. In the next chapter, we will look at some of the key Scriptures on Law, and will begin by considering the origin and backstory of the Mosaic Law.

CHAPTER 5

SCRIPTURES ON LAW

In the beginning, God wanted an intimate one-on-one relationship with each of us. He wanted to speak with us, walk with us, and be with us, as with a friend. But when Adam and Eve ate from the forbidden tree, one of the fallouts from their decision was the destruction of this intimate relationship that God desired to have with us. From God's perspective nothing had changed, for after they had eaten from the Tree, He still showed up in the Garden for His daily walk with them. But for Adam and Eve, everything had changed, because they were now afraid of God. Fear had entered into their relationship with Him. God did not separate Himself from them; but it was they who separated themselves from God when they hid from Him.

From that point onward, God's goal in human history has been to restore the broken fellowship between Himself and humanity, and to show us once again that we have nothing to fear from Him, that He completely loves us and wants to participate in an eternal friendship with us. The rest of the Bible shows some of the steps God has taken to help make this happen. This is partly why God initiated a relationship with Abraham, and also partly why God gave laws to the people of Israel at Mount Sinai. The giving of the Mosaic Law, however, was not not "Plan A." Much like what occurred in the Garden of Eden, God only gave the law to the people of Israel because they were too afraid to enter into a close relationship with Him. We can see how this occurred by looking at why the Mosaic Law was given to the Israelite people.

THE MOSAIC LAW

"'And you shall be to Me a kingdom of priests and a holy nation.' These are the words which you shall speak to the children of Israel. … And let them be ready for the third day. For on the third day the Lord will come down upon Mount Sinai in the sight of all the people. … When the trumpet sounds long, they shall come near the mountain"
(Exod 19:6, 11, 13).

Now all the people witnessed the thunderings, the lightning flashes, the sound of the trumpet, and the mountain smoking; and when the people saw it, they trembled and stood afar off. Then they said to Moses, "You speak with us, and we will hear; but let not God speak with us, lest we die"
(Exod 20:18-19).

And the Lord your God will circumcise your heart and the heart of your descendants, to love the Lord your God with all your heart and with all your soul, that you may live
(Deut 30:6).

God's original intent was not to impose upon Israel a set of laws, but to live in relationship with them, just as it had been with God and humans in the Garden of Eden (cf. Gen 2:7-25; 3:8; 15:6; Exod 14:31; 19:8). When God called Abraham to be the father of God's chosen people, it was so that God could develop a friendship with Abraham and with his descendants. God wanted to be their God and wanted them to be His people. It is for exactly this reason that God brought the Israelites out of bondage in Egypt (Exod 6:7).

So when Moses and the Israelites arrived at Mount Sinai, God did not initially give any laws to the people of Israel. Instead, God invited all the Israelites to the base of the mountain to speak with Him (Exod 19:11, 13). They were all welcome. He invited them to be a kingdom of priests (Exod 19:6), just as God had originally planned for humanity when He created Adam in the Garden of Eden (Gen 2:7). But when God drew near the people at Mount Sinai, the people became afraid (Exod 19:16; 20:18-19; cf. Gen 3:10). Due to their fear of God, the people asked Moses to be a mediator between them and God. They did not want to speak directly with God. They wanted Moses to speak to God for them and then pass on to them whatever God said. So although God desired a personal, one-on-one relationship with each Israelite person, the people rejected this close relationship with God, and instead asked Moses to serve as a mediator between them and God.

In life, there are only two ways of making sure that people get along with one another and live in a way that is mutually beneficial. They can either live according to love or according to law. When people live according to love, a list of laws about what should and should not be done only gets in the way. But where there is no love—or very little love—a list of laws becomes necessary in the attempt to create the harmony of love. Because love seeks the good of the other person, love naturally maintains boundaries, promotes peace, and builds up the other person. Where such goals fail, love takes responsibility for personal failure and offers forgiveness to others. But when love is absent and people are only looking out for themselves, laws are necessary to achieve similar results. The problem with laws, however, is that they tend to rapidly reproduce themselves, for no amount of laws can truly replace a relationship built on love. We looked at this in the previous chapter where I provided a fictional account of my marriage relationship.

All of this is exactly what happens to the Israelites when they reject a relationship with God built on love. In the absence of a relationship, they are given the Ten Commandments (Exod 20) and the Covenant Code (Exod 21–31). But these laws fail to keep them in harmony with God, and when God does not act as quickly as they would like, they create the golden calf and worship it instead of God (Exod 32). So, they are given more laws with greater degrees of intricacy and duty, which is the Priestly Code (Exod 34–Lev 16). Later, however, they are found guilty of making sacrifices to demonic idols (Lev 17:7ff), and so God adds further laws and regulations about the sacrificial system (Lev 17–26).

Each new addition of law is given in response to a failure on the part of the Israelite people to keep the law already given. The new law is added because of sin on the part of the Israelites, and as a way to close loopholes and provide further detailed instructions about the laws already given. In the Pentateuch, the ten laws eventually get amplified into the 613 commandments of the Mosaic Law.[18] None of this is because the law was better, but because law is needed where there is no relationship built on love. God desired love. But when love was rejected, and this rejection resulted in sin, laws were added to create the culture and actions of love, even when the attitude of love was absent.

As can be seen, this religion of laws was not God's ideal plan for the people of Israel, but He gave it to them because they did not want an intimate relationship with God where He spoke to them. Though God wanted and offered a relationship based on love, the people rejected this offer and asked for a religion based on laws. So God gave it to them, even though it was not best. God wanted a relationship with the people, but when they refused the relationship and turned instead to sin and religion, God was forced to incarnate Himself within the religion so that He could draw them out of it.

Just as God provided a human king in part to show the failure of human kings, so also, God provided a human religion in part to show the failure of human religion. This truth is one of the main truths we learn from the Pentateuch. God provided religion to show that religion does not lead people to God, but away from God. Religion separates and divides. It never restores and heals. So when the people of Israel reject a relationship of love in favor of a religion of law, it is not surprising that this religion of law exponentially increases in complexity. Laws only give birth to more laws. They never give birth to relationship.

What I find most interesting about all of this is that Moses knew every-

[18] See John H. Sailhamer, *The Meaning of the Pentateuch: Revelation, Composition, and Interpretation* (Downers Grove: IVP, 2009), 362-363.

thing we have said so far in this chapter about the Mosaic Law. Many Christians read the Pentateuch completely backwards. We believe that Moses wrote the Pentateuch as a way to record the history and laws of the Israelite people *so that* they would know who they were as a people and live according to the laws God provided. But this is just not true. A careful reading of the Pentateuch from start to finish reveals a completely different way of reading the five books of Moses. Moses is not seeking to uphold the law and call the people to obey it, but is instead seeking to subvert the law and show the people that they can never obey it, and so they should revert to God's original intent and purpose for them, which is to have a relationship with Him built on love.

Remember, Moses spoke to God as a man speaks to a friend, and so he knew what a relationship with God was like. Because of His relationship with God, Moses knew the dangers of law. He knew that where there is no love, law is necessary, but the dark side of law is that it only leads to sin and more law. This is the truth Moses sought to unveil when he wrote the Pentateuch. We see this not only in how the Pentateuch begins with God's creation of humans and God's stated desire for them, but also in how the Pentateuch ends.

At the end of the Pentateuch, Moses subversively shows the Israelites that just as they couldn't keep the Ten Commandments, they definitely won't be able to keep 613 either. In Deuteronomy 28, Moses describes the blessings that will come upon the Israelites for obeying the law and the curses that will come upon them for disobedience. One of the curses was that they would be driven out from the land by their enemies and scattered all over the earth (Deut 28:64-65). Yet in Deuteronomy 30:1, when Moses describes to the people what is actually going to happen to them, he says that they will remember God's law when they are "among all the nations where the Lord your God drives you." So after Moses lays out the blessings and curses, he tells the Israelites that he knows which way they will go. They will take the route of disobedience and will end up being scattered across the face of the earth. Moses knew the law would not "work." It would not lead them into a relationship. It would not lead them into love.

Moses does not leave the people without hope, however. He tells them that once they have learned that the law could do nothing to gain for them the relationship that God originally wanted, God would then circumcise their hearts and live with them in relationship as He had always desired (Deut 30:6-20). This also is what Jeremiah predicts when he sees God's people in his day having trouble obeying God's law (Jer 31:31-34). Paul understood Deuteronomy 30 in this way as well (cf. Rom 10:7-8). This relationship with God is what Jesus revealed and modeled for us, so that we also might have fellowship with Him and with one another (cf. 1 John 1:3).

When read from this perspective, the purpose of the Pentateuch is not for God to provide a set of laws which all people everywhere should follow. No, the point of the Pentateuch is to show that law and religion will never lead into the relationship of love that God wants with His people. From the beginning of the Pentateuch to the end, Moses consistently and repeatedly undermines the law, showing that it will not lead to love, that it will not help the people grow in their relationship with God or with each other, but that instead, it will only lead deeper into sin and the devastating consequences of sin. This is the tragic truth of the Pentateuch. The focus on the law throughout these five books is not for the purpose of calling people back to the law, but for calling people back to love.

Though it's somewhat lighthearted and humorous, here is a brief summary of how to read the Pentateuch as if it were a conversation between God and humans:

> **God:** I want a relationship with all of you, based on love, forgiveness, and reconciliation.
>
> **Israelites:** Yeah … We'll take religion based on law and sacrifice please, with Moses as our mediator.
>
> **God:** … Really? That's not going to work, but … okay. Here are the Ten Commandments (Exod 20).

Israelites: Yay! … Uh, wait (Exod 32). We can't keep these very well. The problem is that they're sort of vague. And the rivalry and violence keeps increasing. I know what our problem is … We need more laws, more sacrifices, and more religion!

God: … Really? I don't think that's going to work, guys, but okay. Here are some more laws, if that's what you want instead of a relationship with me (Exod 34–Lev 16)

Israelites: Yay! Now we know what to do! Uh, wait (Lev 17:7ff). We can't keep these very well. They don't answer all of the questions or speak to every situation we encounter. And the rivalry and violence keeps increasing. I know what our problem is … we need more laws, sacrifices, and religion!

God: … Seriously? That's your conclusion from this? Well, okay. Here's some more laws, if that's really what you want instead of a relationship with me (Lev 17–26).

Moses: Hey! How's this whole religion thing working for you? If you keep it, it will be great! But when you don't do it (as we should know by now, we won't), then it will only result in more chaos, rivalry, and violence (Deut 30–31).

And of course, it turns out Moses was right. The history of Israel as recorded in Scripture shows that where there is law without love, all it leads to is greater sin, and especially the sin of judging and accusing others based on the law, and then seeking to condemn and even kill those whom we believe to be the enemies of God based on their disobedience to the law. All religious history, including Christian history, reveals this same sinful pattern. The law, then, does nothing to help us get rid of sin, but only makes the problem worse when it leads to greater rivalry and violence.

This same truth is seen elsewhere in the Bible, including with other Old Testament Hebrew prophets.

THE PROPHETS

"To what purpose is the multitude of your sacrifices to Me?" says the Lord. "I have had enough of burnt offerings of rams, and the fat of fed cattle. I do not delight in the blood of bulls, or of lambs or goats. When you come to appear before Me, who has required this from your hand, to trample My courts? Bring no more futile sacrifices; incense is an abomination to Me. The New Moons, the Sabbaths, and the calling of assemblies— I cannot endure iniquity and the sacred meeting" (Isa 1:11-13).

"I hate, I despise your feast days, and I do not savor your sacred assemblies. Though you offer Me burnt offerings and your grain offerings, I will not accept them, Nor will I regard your fattened peace offerings. Take away from Me the noise of your songs, for I will not hear the melody of your stringed instruments. But let justice run down like water, and righteousness like a mighty stream" (Amos 5:21-24).

The Hebrew Prophets clearly state in numerous places that God never wanted the law and the sacrifices as the means for living in relationship with Him and others. It's a shocking idea, but when the entirety of Scripture is considered, and especially considered in light of Jesus Christ, we see that God didn't want the temple, the law, the sacrificial system, the priesthood, or any of the religious trappings that separate mankind from God and from each another. All such things are substitutes for the one thing God truly wanted, which is love.

Numerous prophets reveal this quite clearly. Though many people assume that the primary message of the prophets was to call the people back to obedience of the law, the real message of the prophets was to call people back to the *goal of the law*, which was love. We see this by the fact that many of the prophets are quite critical of how the people ignore justice and righteousness in the land. The prophets show that many of the people are quite observant when it comes to the law, but they neglect the greater goals of care for the poor, protection for the weak, and love for the outcast. A quick reading of some key prophetic texts reveals that their true concern was not adherence to the law, but living according to love (cf. Isa 1:10-20; 61:8; Jer 14:12; Hos 6:6; Amos 4:4-5; 5:21-25; Mic 6:6-8). Jesus, as the greatest prophet, reveals this same truth through His life, ministry, and teachings.

MATTHEW 5:17

Do not think that I came to destroy the Law or the Prophets. I did not come to destroy but to fulfill.

In Matthew 5:17, Jesus said that He did not come to destroy the law, but to fulfil it. The age-old question has been what Jesus meant by this, especially in light of later statements by Paul where he claims that Jesus did bring an end to the law (cf. Rom 10:4; Gal 3:23-25; Eph 2:15). Based on what we have seen already about the law, however, the solution to this dilemma is now clear. The law was only given as a substitute for love (and a poor substitute at that), but it could never actually lead anyone into love. The law could only create the appearance of love.

One interesting note about Jesus' fulfillment of the law is that there is no recorded instruction from Jesus to His own disciples for them to obey and follow the Law of Moses. Why not? Because He was modelling love, which is God's ultimate goal and purpose for our lives anyway. Where there is love, law becomes unnecessary. Loving God and loving others naturally leads to the fulfillment of the law (Matt 22:37; Mark 12:30-31; Luke 10:27). If loving God and loving others is the fulfillment of the law, then the law is "followed" simply by loving God and loving others. If we are guided by love, then we do not need the law to guide us, because love guides us to do the things commanded by the law.

Jesus, through His life and ministry, revealed what it looks like to live according to love. In so doing, He not only fulfilled the spirit and purpose of the law, but also did away with it in the sense that He showed that where there is love, law is not needed. Of course, where there is no love, the law is still better than nothing as a way to guide people into proper behavior. This is why Jesus said He did not come to destroy or abolish the law. He knew that love takes time to grow and spread, and that not everyone will live in love toward everyone else. Therefore, law, as defective as it is, still guides human behavior when there is no love. This was not only true of the Mosaic Law for the Israelite people, but is also true for the laws of any country or community today. The reason nations, businesses, and families have laws today is because love is not fully formed among us.

So what is clear from the rest of Scripture, as well as from Jesus' own words, is that love is the fulfillment of the law. Most Christians would agree that the law is accomplished and fulfilled when we love God and love others (Gal 5:14; Jas 2:8; Rom 13:8-10; 1 Tim 1:5; Deut 6:5; Matt 22:37; Luke 10:27; Mark 12:30-31). The way of love is the "more excellent way" (1 Cor 12:31). When Jesus said that He had come to fulfil the law, this was best seen in the fact that love was the defining characteristic of Jesus. Since love is the fulfillment of the law, and since Jesus loved God and loved everyone perfectly, He therefore fulfilled the law. This is what Jesus meant in Matthew 5:17. The rest of the Sermon on the Mount provides numerous examples of how love fulfills the law. To see this, let us briefly consider the Sermon on the Mount in Matthew 5–7.

MATTHEW 5–7

You have heard that it was said ... But I say to you ...
(Matt 5:21-22, 27-28, 31-32, 33-34, 43-44).

As with nearly everything Jesus said and did, there is a wide diversity of opinions about how to interpret and understand the Sermon on the Mount. We have neither the time nor space to delve into the various opinions, so let me simply summarize for you what I believe Jesus is doing in Matthew 5–7.

In His Sermon the Mount, Jesus is providing a description of what life looks like for the person who will follow Him. Since the average Jewish person listening to Jesus attempted to allow their life to be guided by the Mosaic Law and Jewish tradition, Jesus frequently compares and contrasts His way of life with the way of life that comes from following the Law. When we approach the Sermon on the Mount with this in mind, we see that Jesus calls people away from actions of legalistic obedience to a set of laws and toward attitudes of love for all people.

The Sermon on the Mount is a call to love. It focuses on attitude, rather than activity. Following Jesus is not about going through the motions but about living in love that comes from the heart. Jesus is not adding to the law, but is showing that love is the fulfillment of the law. He shows, for example, that while the law says "Do not murder" and "Do not commit adultery," such laws still allowed people to hate their brother or lust after women (Matt 5:21-30). In this way, it was possible to fulfill the letter of the law while completely ignoring its intent. But the person guided by love will neither hate nor lust, which fulfills both the letter *and* intent of the law. Jesus even goes so far as to call His followers to love their enemies (Matt 5:43-48), which is the ultimate representation of love and which no law could ever accomplish. The rest of the Sermon follows this same theme.

ROMANS 7:11-13

For sin, taking occasion by the commandment, deceived me, and by it killed me. Therefore the law is holy, and the commandment holy and just and good. Has then what is good become death to me? Certainly not! But sin, that it might appear sin, was producing death in me through what is good, so that sin through the commandment might become exceedingly sinful.

Paul's view on the law matches that of Jesus. Though there are numerous places he shows this, one of the clearest is Romans 7:11-13. Paul writes that the law is "holy and just and good." But this does not mean that the law is the ideal. Though the law is good, it is not God's "best." It is not what God originally intended or wanted. God wanted us to be guided by love, but when we failed to live in love, the only alternative was law. In the absence of a relationship built on love, law is a necessity for people to get along with each other.

Yet even though law serves a good purpose in this regard, it never serves as an adequate substitute for love. Law can never actually lead anyone into love. To the contrary, law often leads in the opposite direction, toward more rivalry, accusation, scapegoating, and violence, which is sin (see Part I on Sin). The law was given to help counteract sinful behavior, but one primary problem with the law is that it tends to create even more rivalry between humans.

Those who are able to keep the law look down on those who cannot, and often end up blaming, accusing, and scapegoating them for their failure. As Paul says, sin produces death through the law. It creates rivalry and causes us to judge and condemn others, and even think that God is on our side in such condemnation of others. This then leads to sacred violence where we kill others in God's name and feel righteous in doing so. Ultimately, then, while the law does bring order to a chaotic culture and introduce justice into society, it also sets up a system by which we are better able to blame, accuse, judge, condemn, and kill others, all while thinking we are doing God's will. This allows God's good commandments to be used for evil purposes. Though the purpose of the law was to prohibit imitative desire that led to accusation, violence, and scapegoating, it ended up inciting this rivalry instead.[19] All of this is exactly what Paul goes on to describe in Romans 7:13-23.

Of course, the fact that the law only increased imitative desire, rivalry, and violence has a silver lining. This increase made the power of sin that much more obvious. Paul says in Romans 7:13 that the commandments became exceedingly sinful. As a result of the law, the exponential increase of

[19] Robert G. Hamerton-Kelly, *Sacred Violence: Paul's Hermeneutic of the Cross* (Minneapolis: Fortress, 1992), 112.

sacred violence exposed this sin for what it really was: humans carrying out their own violent tendencies on others while blaming God for it (see my book *The Atonement of God*). Paul states at the end of Romans 7 (vv 24-25) and on into Romans 8 that Jesus is the one who delivers us from this problem of sin and death, but we have yet to see in this book how exactly Jesus did this. For now, let us look at another passage where Paul reveals his view of the law.

GALATIANS 3:19

What purpose then does the law serve? It was added because of transgressions ...

In multiple ways from multiple passages we have seen that while the law is a poor substitute for love, the law also only leads to further sin. When this happens, the human tendency is to create more laws. When current laws do not produce the righteous and loving life that we expected, the natural response is to add additional laws to rectify the problem. Our hope is that a few more laws will finally produce the behavior in others that we desire.

This is what Paul had in mind when he wrote in Galatians 3:19 that "the law was added because of transgression." People usually understand Paul to be saying that "the law was given to us so that it could reveal our sin to us," but that is not what Paul meant. Such an understanding does not fit the context of Galatians 3, nor does it fit with why laws are really added.

In the context of Galatians 3, Paul wrote that the law only brings a curse upon people because we can never truly keep the law. This also is what Moses stated at the end of Deuteronomy. Though the law can bring blessings to those who keep it, the fact that nobody can keep it means that it will only bring problems because it does not and cannot lead anyone to truly live in love. Keeping the law can never bring about the righteousness that God desires (Gal 3:10-14; 19-25).

The law, Paul wrote, was nothing more than a temporary tutor or mediator to lead us to Christ (Gal 3:24-25), and to living according to His way of love. The law served as a mediator in place of a personal relationship with God (which is what the Israelite people wanted at Mount Sinai). Of course, when there is no loving relationship, a mediator is required, but ultimately, the mediator, the guard, or the tutor must be set aside for the real relationship that God intended (Gal 3:20-25).

So when Paul wrote that the law was added because of transgressions, he was pointing the reader back to the truth of why all laws are created. Laws are created because someone messes up, and so a law is made to restrict that same behavior from happening again. Laws are always reactionary. This is not only true of laws and rules created by governments, companies, and families, but it is also true of the laws given in the Pentateuch.

As we learned previously in our discussion of the Mosaic Law, though God initially offered a relationship, the people rejected this in favor of religious law. And every time they broke, or transgressed the law, it showed that the law was empty of power and that they either needed to go back to a relationship built on love or get more law. In every case, more law was added as a result of transgressions. Eventually, the 613 commandments of the Mosaic Law became over 6000 laws in the days of Paul. When people reject a relationship of love in favor of a religion of law, this religion of law exponentially increases in complexity. Laws only give birth to more laws. They never give birth to relationship. So the truth in the Pentateuch is exactly what Paul states here: laws are added because of sin.

One final interesting note to point out from Galatians 3:19 is that the word sin, or transgression, is the Greek word *parabasis*, which we looked at briefly in the chapter on sin. This word is typically used in connection with the Mosaic Law (cf. Rom 2:23; 4:15; 5:14; 1 Tim 2:14; Heb 2:2; 9:15), but in the sense of breaking the law *by doing the exact opposite of the law while claiming to obey it.* But it is not to be confused with hypocrisy of self-deception. No, *parabasis* takes place specifically when religious people use the letter of the law to avoid following the spirit of the law. *Parabasis* occurs when people obey God's law as a means of disobeying the intent of the law.

It is a specifically religious form of sin which only comes from the law and which always and only produces more law.

LAW IS NOT THE SOLUTION TO SIN

Numerous texts in Scripture talk about the law, but the general theme in all of them is that while the law is good, it was given only as a substitute for a loving relationship. God's ideal is that we live in a loving relationship with Him and with one another. But where love is not possible, the law shows us what sorts of actions are found within a relationship of love. Yet while a strict observance of these laws will help us perform loving actions, the law itself can never produce actual love.

To the contrary, law tends to produce the opposite. Although the law is holy, righteous, and good, it only leads to more sin, and therefore to the proliferation of more laws. When there is no love, we must operate according to law. But since law can never truly lead us into love, it only produces a false imitation of love, which is sin. And in the attempt then to produce genuine love, more and more laws are created, which only take us further away from love.

Worse yet, the proliferation of laws leads us deeper into rivalry as we use the law to judge, condemn, and accuse one another. This rivalry often becomes sacrificial scapegoating and sacred violence as we seek to cast out or kill those we perceive to be the enemies of God based on their supposed "disobedience" to the laws of God. So law is not the solution to sin. Instead, law comes from sin and leads us deeper into sin. It is no surprise then, that the sacrificial system is not the solution to sin either, since it also is part of the Mosaic Law. It is to this topic we turn in Part III.

PART III: SACRIFICE

The sacrificial system of the Mosaic Law is seen by many as the evidence or proof that God requires death and payment with blood in order to forgive sins. But once we understand what sin is and why the law was given, it is then that we begin to understand the purpose and function of the sacrificial system. Sacrifices are not the antidote or cure for sin, but are actually part of the problem of sin!

The following two chapters provide an explanation for where sacrifices came from, why they were included within the Mosaic Law, and what Scripture reveals to us about the role and function of the sacrificial system. Through this study we will see that although God never wanted or needed sacrifices, we humans needed them. We engaged in the sacred violence of sacrificial rituals as a way of dealing with our own sin. Sacrifices, however, never really dealt with sin, but only added to the problem.

These two chapters on sacrifice also begin to reveal why Jesus had to die a sacrificial death on the cross. What we learn about sacrifices helps bring the cross into focus so that we can better understand and appreciate why Jesus died and how His death helps save us from our sins.

CHAPTER 6

DEFINING SACRIFICE

As hinted in previous chapters, just as the law was not God's idea, so also, the sacrificial system was never God's intended method for dealing with sin. Instead, the sacrificial system, much like the law, only increased the occurrence of sin in the world. Since sin is violence, and especially the violence committed in God's name, then any violence committed in God's name, including sacrificial violence, is a form of sin. Therefore, since God wants to rescue and deliver us from sin, sacrificial violence could not have been God's idea. All this, and more, will be seen in this chapter. As part of learning where sacrifice came from and why there are commands in the law about offering sacrifices to God, we will also begin to see why Jesus died as a sacrifice on the cross, and how this death worked to save us from our sin.

Let us begin by defining the word "sacrifice." The Greek word for sacrifice is *thusia*, and "sacrifice" is a good translation of the word, though "offering" is also acceptable. Most people are familiar with what a sacrifice is and the various forms a sacrifice can take. Just as in English today, the biblical concept of *sacrifice* can refer to a bloodless action through which we give something up or perform some task for God. Various New Testament authors, for example, write about offering ourselves and our service to God as a living sacrifice (Rom 12:1; Heb 13:15). The main way the word "sacrifice" is used, however, is in reference to the killing of humans or animals on a religious altar as a way of pleasing or appeasing God (cf. Lev 1:9-17; Judg 11:29-40). This second, more common understanding of sacrifice will be the focus of this chapter. In seeking to understand sacrifice, we must first consider where sacrifice came from and what sacrifice accomplished.

THREE PURPOSES FOR SACRIFICE

Almost every ancient religion and culture in the world practiced some form of sacrifice. Regardless of when, where, or how the sacrifice was performed, the logic behind the sacrifice was always the same. When these sacrifices in society, history, and culture are studied, we discover three basic purposes for sacrifices. In other words, all sacrifices can be categorized into three reasons they were performed, or three spheres in which they take place. The three reasons or purposes of sacrifices are sociological, psychological, and spiritual. To state these three more simply, sacrifice helps our interactions with others (sociological), with ourselves (psychological), and with God (spiritual). There is, of course, some overlap between all three sacrificial purposes, but let us consider each type of sacrifice separately.

Sociological Sacrifice

The first purpose for sacrifice is to maintain the social order. Sociologically, sacrifices help create peace in a given society or culture, and avoids the escalation of violence that threatens to overtake and destroy any given community. It does this in numerous ways. For example, sacrifices help in our interactions with other people, whether they are family, friends, or neighboring people. But it's not just with friends; sacrifice can also help with enemies, by creating peace with them or by allowing us to kill them in good conscience, depending on the situation.

In this way, sacrifice *saves* humanity in the sense that sacrificial violence serves as a substitute or escape hatch for the contagion of violence that can often sweep through society and culture as a result of interpersonal rivalry and tension. Sacrifice allows an outlet for that violence. A sacrifice is a way to expel violence and bloodlust within a society by directing and focusing all that violence upon one sacrificial victim. Whether it is with friends or enemies, ritualistic sacrifice provides a controlled outlet for violence so that the many forms of uncontrolled violence do not break out and obliterate a particular community, society, or culture.

This form of sacrifice did not develop in a vacuum. It rose logically from the systemic violence that often swept through communities. In any group (both ancient and modern), people often engage in activity that inevitably leads to bloodshed. Maybe it is adultery, theft, lying, or just anger. Usually, some sort of imitative rivalry is involved as well. But whatever the activity is, these sorts of behaviors tend to spiral out of control until blood is spilled (See Part V on Blood). But people also noticed that when the bloodshed occurred, a temporary peace came upon the town, community, or culture.

Ancient communities saw this pattern repeat itself over and over. Rivalry led to violence and death, which in turn led to peace. In this way, death restored peace to a society. Due to this restorative nature of death, societies began to ritualize death in the form of sacrifice as a way to prevent future outbreaks of rivalry and violence. As a way of trying to hold on to the peace in the community, ancient societies began to engage in ritualistic sacrifice. For them, sacrifice was a way to short-circuit rivalry and violence before it spun out of control. Sacrifice functioned as medicine for society, both restoring peace and preventing violence from breaking out.

There was, of course, a divine element to these sacrifices. People were not offering sacrifices to a nameless and faceless void so that the spread of violence might cease. In various ways and through various means, people believed that the violence which a community suffered was due to the judgment of the gods upon that community for their sin. They further believed that the peace which came to the community after the sacrifice was offered was likewise a gift from the gods in response to the sacrifice. When peace descended upon a community after engaging in such sacrificial violence, it was assumed that the peace was sent from God, and therefore, that God was now appeased through the sacrificial death. In this way, the practical effectiveness of sacrifice led to the belief in the divine requirement of sacrifice, which in turn made the offered sacrifices that much more effective.

So sacrificial practices from a societal perspective do not come from the command of God, but come instead from the human experience of peace that results from sacrificial violence. When we kill in God's name and experience peace as a result, we assume that our killing was in fact God's will. The peace that results from killing others in God's name leads us to believe that the killing of others was ordained and even commanded by God. But in reality, it was not. Killing others results in peace because the killing provides an outlet for the violent tendencies and bloodlust that resides in the hearts of all humanity.

This aspect of sociological sacrifices enters into the sphere of spiritual sacrifices, which will be considered shortly, but there is a psychological element to sacrifices as well, so let us consider this type of sacrifice next.

Psychological Sacrifice

Along with the social effects that sacrifice has on human interactions, sacrifice also helps individual humans deal with the psychological effects of sin and guilt. This is seen primarily in two areas: where people know about the wrong that has been done and seek to rectify it, and when people don't know the wrong that has been done, but try to correct it anyway. Let us briefly consider each.

Correcting a Known Fault

People often feel guilty for the bad things they do, and the natural human inclination is that we must do something to atone for these bad things. People feel like sin creates a debt which must be repaid. One of the best ways that humans have discovered to deal with feelings of shame and guilt is to make a payment of some sort to the offended person or deity. This payment comes in various forms, which may include money or service offered to the other party, but might also involve some form of sacrifice. Sacrifice is especially useful when a person is trying to repay a deity for sin. After all, how does one repay a divine being for a wrong done to them if you cannot see, hear, speak, or meet with this being? Sacrifice was the answer.

In this way, sacrificial systems and rituals alleviate human guilt. The person who has sinned feels that they have now done something to pay for their sin. Psychologically, sacrifice gives people a feeling of peace. It makes them think they have righted a wrong or rectified an injustice because they themselves paid for what they did by killing something that was of value to them. Of course, the payment given, service rendered, or sacrifice offered rarely actually corrects the wrong. If I kill someone you love, and then "pay" for it by letting you kill someone I love (or performing this sacrifice myself), this second murder does not bring the first murdered person back to life. But it does help both parties feel that something was done to correct a wrong. Sacrifice helps society, and maybe even the murderer, feel that something was done to pay for the murder. This same mentality is at work when the guilty party or community seeks to pay for an offense against some other person or deity. Sacrifice serves a psychological purpose in helping people deal with individual or communal guilt.

Correcting an Unknown Fault

People often try to pay for unknown sins. This happens as a result of trying to find explanations for the bad things that happen to us in life. When sickness, famine, disease, or disaster occur in life, the first human inclination is to believe that we are being punished by God for some unknown sin. If we have no obvious sin in our lives, we begin to search high and low for what this sin is, for why we have offended God so that He would treat us this way. Whether we are able to find this unknown sin or not, we typically engage in some sort of sacrificial ceremony as a way to appease God's wrath toward us and bring an end to the calamity that has come upon us.

Since ancient people knew nothing about weather patterns, viruses and bacteria, or the movement of tectonic plates, they assumed that the bad things which happened in this world were the result of God judging people for sin. Of course, even though people today know about such things, many still believe that God is the one who often sends disaster and destruction upon certain people because of their sins.

When people think that disease and disaster are sent from God, they often turn to sacrifice as a way to bring an end to these "divine acts of judgment." Very often, the people begin with a small sacrifice, such as a bird or lamb, but if the calamity continues, greater and greater sacrifices will be offered until "God is appeased." How do they know? Because the rains begin to fall again, the crops start to grow, or the disease ends. If the drought, disaster, or disease continues long enough, people might eventually end up sacrificing a son or daughter.

Of course, since most people today recognize that diseases, famines, and disasters are a result of various natural causes, we know that such things typically come to an end on their own. The blood of animals and humans does nothing to stop such events (and in fact, might only prolong them as in the case of disease). But in pre-scientific communities, as people offered more and greater sacrifices, and the disease, famine, or disaster eventually came to an end, the people believed that their sacrifice had appeased the wrath of the gods, thus allowing the judgment or punishment from the gods to cease.

In this way, sacrifice provided a way for people to "do something" about the problems they were facing in life. When disaster strikes, people like to feel that they can "fix it." One way that ancient people attempted to fix the bad things that happened to them was by offering sacrifices to the gods. Even if the people did not know exactly what the problem was or how they had offended God, they still turned to sacrifice as a way to atone for the unknown sins and faults of their community. Eventually, people began to offer regular, ritualistic sacrifices as a way to keep themselves on God's good side. People didn't wait until disasters occurred to offer sacrifices, but continually offered them as a way to keep God from sending disasters and diseases in the first place. Sacrifice was used as a preventative measure to ward off the wrath of God and keep the rain falling, the sun shining, and the diseases at bay.

So sacrifices help humans deal with guilt for some known sin and stop apparent divine punishment for unknown sin. These types of sacrifices are psychological in nature. They help us feel better about our sin, and help us feel that we are doing something about the perceived consequences of sin in our relationships, communities, and jobs. The sacrificial system alleviates our own guilt about our sin by psychologically cleansing our conscience from guilt (Heb 9:14). Such sacrifices are not for God at all, but are completely for us. Of course, just as with sociological sacrifices, psychological sacrifices also have many spiritual effects as well. This is the third and final reason for sacrifice.

Spiritual Sacrifice

In both the sociological and psychological spheres, sacrifice helps people deal with sin and guilt. For this reason, all sacrifices are performed for spiritual reasons. No matter what type of sacrifice is performed, we believe that we are ultimately offering the sacrifice "to God." This is especially true when sacrifices are performed in an attempt to appease God or bring an end to the events in this life that are perceived to be the punishment of God. The goal of satiating an offended deity is the primary purpose behind all types of sacrifice, and most people are familiar with this purpose for sacrifice. What most people don't know, however, is that these types of sacrifices were performed for three reasons.

For Unintentional Sin

The first type of spiritual sacrifice is the sacrifice for unintentional sin. An unintentional sin is when people sin without realizing they are sinning. This can happen in numerous ways, especially since there are so many laws and rituals to be remembered and obeyed. When there are over 600 laws (later amplified into over 6000), people become concerned about unknowingly breaking one of these laws. Who can remember and keep all of them? So the sin offerings and sacrifices were put in place as a way to atone for the sins of ignorance committed by the Hebrew people.

What is most interesting about these sin offerings and sacrifices in the Mosaic Law is that none of them were for willful sin. A willful, or intentional, sin is a sin that is committed with the full knowledge of a law or command being broken. Willful sins come in two types. They are committed either when a person knows the good they are supposed to do but doesn't do it (Jas 4:17), or when they know the bad they are not supposed to do but practice it anyway (Rom 7:19). In either case, there was no available sacrifice for intentional sin. Sin offerings and sacrifices were always and only for unintentional sins, for sins committed in ignorance (cf. Ezek 45:20; Heb 9:7). While Scripture does talk a lot about sacrifices, the Bible does not ever contain instructions for a sacrifice that covers intentional or willful sin.

What then was a person to do who sinned knowingly and willfully (which is true of most sin)? They were left with the only option that the whole of Scripture actually endorses: they were to depend and rely on the grace of God. Everywhere in Scripture, both in the Old Testament and the New, the only way to deal with willful sin is to thank God for His forgiveness and grace, which He freely extends to us.

So whatever it is we think about the sacrificial system of Scripture, it is not correct to think that God gave the sacrificial system as a way to deal with sin. He did not. While other cultures and people groups often used sacrifices as a way to earn forgiveness and grace from their gods, the Bible consistently reveals that sacrifices do nothing as far as God's grace and forgiveness are concerned. This is a key way that the sacrifices of Scripture are distinct from the sacrifices of other cultures and religions.

For Purification from Sin

The second type of sacrifice in the spiritual realm is the sacrifice of purification from sin. While this initially seems similar to the type of sacrifice most people are familiar with, this specific type of sacrifice has nothing to do with people, but is instead focused on the purification of temple precincts and temple furniture. As mentioned in the chapters on sin (see Part I on Sin), people believed that sin was contagious, that it somehow attached itself to the people, places, and animals that came into contact with it. Ancient people thought about sin the way we think about viruses and bacteria: it could be spread simply through proximity and close contact.

Since sacrifice had often proved to be effective in dealing with the social and psychological effects of sin, ancient people assumed that sacrificial blood was the "element" that purified places or items from the contamination of sin. So ancient people would take the blood of a sacrifice and sprinkle it on temple buildings, furniture, and utensils in an attempt to purify such items from the pollution of sin. The sacrifices were thought to sanctify, or repurify, the temple and its sacred items so that they could be used for holy purposes. Of course, since people continue to sin, the temple precincts continued to be contaminated by sin. Therefore, continual sacrificial purification was necessary (cf. Heb 10:4).

For Enacting a Will

The final type of sacrifice in the spiritual realm is also quite often overlooked and misunderstood. This third type of sacrifice was one in which the sacrifice symbolized, prophesied, or enacted the death of another person. This type of sacrifice is most often performed as part of a legal ceremony in which two or more parties sacrificed an animal to guarantee the terms of a covenant or to ratify and enact a legally binding Last Will and Testament.

When a sacrifice was carried out as part of a covenant agreement, both parties were effectively saying that if either of them broke the terms of the covenant, may that party be slaughtered and killed just like the animals before them. In this way, the sacrifice was a prophetic warning of what would happen if either member of the covenantal agreement broke the terms of the covenant. We see this type of sacrifice being carried out in Genesis 15 when God makes a covenant with Abram. In such a setting, both members of the covenant would typically walk through the sacrificed animals together. But in Genesis 15, after the sacrifices were made, God walked through the animals alone, thereby indicating that the covenant was completely one-sided. God promised to abide by the terms of the covenant, even if Abram did not.

A sacrifice might also be carried out at the enactment of a Last Will and Testament. As everyone knows, a Will is not put in effect until the person who made the Will dies (cf. Heb 9:16-17). I have a Last Will and Testament, but it has no power as long as I am alive. It will only become effective when I die. This has always been the case with such documents, even in ancient cultures.

There were, however, times when a person wanted to put their Last Will and Testament into effect before they died. A king, for example, might fear that there would be a war for succession after he died, and so in an attempt to avert such a war and to guarantee that his son became the heir to the kingdom, the king would perform a sacrificial death ceremony in which an animal was killed as a substitute for the king himself. When this happened, the death of the king was symbolized or enacted through the death of the animal. Through the sacrifice, it was *as though* the king himself had died. Afterwards, even though the king still lived, the son became king instead. This might be the type of sacrifice that is carried out in the story of the Prodigal Son. The father tells the older son, "All I have is yours" (Luke 15:31), which strongly indicates that the killing of the fatted calf was this type of sacrifice. It symbolized the father's death, so that now the older son was the sole heir. Just as the father had "died" in giving the younger son his inheritance, so also, the father now "died" again to give the older son his.

The most common practice of this type of sacrifice was when a king or priest was viewed as the heir of a god. Quite frequently in ancient times, kings and priests were thought of as divine sons of the gods. As sons, they were also viewed as heirs to the gods. Therefore, one religious ceremony that often took place was a ceremony in which the gods symbolically made a Last Will and Testament for themselves in which the king or priest was named as heir. The problem, however, was that when a god makes a Last Will and Testament, the human heir can never receive the blessings and benefits of this Last Will because the gods never die. After all, the enactment of a Will requires the death of the one who makes it. But if the gods do not die, then their heirs can never receive what was promised.

The solution to this problem was a symbolic sacrificial death. A sacrificial ceremony took place in which a person or animal went through a ritual that caused them to become inhabited by the god. Then this person or animal was sacrificially killed. In this way, the god symbolically died. No one believed that the god *actually* died in the sacrifice, but only symbolically so that the Last Will and Testament could be enacted and ratified.

QUESTIONING SACRIFICE

So we have seen the three main types of sacrifice. There are sociological sacrifices, which help maintain peace in a society, psychological sacrifices, which help individuals and communities deal with the guilt and shame they feel over sin, and spiritual sacrifices, which were used to atone for unintentional sin, to purify from the pollution of sin, and to help enact a covenant or Will. Sacrifice provides a release valve to the lust for blood that wells up in the heart of every human (sociological sacrifice), relieves our sense of guilt (psychological sacrifice), and helps people think that they have purified themselves from the pollution of sin (spiritual sacrifice).

One surprising truth about these sacrifices is that they are fairly universal in human history and human experience. The type of sacrificial thinking and sacrificial theology we discover in the Bible is also found in nearly every religion from every culture around the entire world throughout time. This is strange, is it not? Why do other cultures and religions also practice nearly identical forms of sacrifice? If sacrifices only worked when they truly pleased or appeased God, then they would only work when they were offered to the one, true God, the God of the Bible. But sacrifices "work" everywhere. Sacrifices do actually bring peace within a society, regardless of which deity is worshiped in that society. Sacrifices do help alleviate personal guilt in all people, regardless of which religion they practice.

Since this is so, people who worship and follow the God of the Bible are left with a serious dilemma. How is it possible that sacrifices "work" everywhere they are practiced?

There are only two answers. Either the one, true God of the Bible accepts sacrifices from all people regardless of which religion they practice, *or* sacrifices have nothing whatsoever to do with God. In other words, if sacrifices "work" everywhere for all people, then either God is accepting all these sacrifices everywhere and responding positively to them, or He is not. But if He is not accepting the sacrifices of other cultures and religions, and these sacrifices are just as effective at creating peace and alleviating guilt as the sacrifices offered directly to Him, then maybe God is not accepting "biblical" sacrifices either. Could it be that sacrifices have nothing whatsoever to do with God?

Let me state this idea more bluntly. It is the height of ignorance and arrogance to say that God accepts "biblical" sacrifices because they are properly performed to the one, true God, but He does not accept the sacrifices of other cultures because they are improperly offered to false gods, when the results of these sacrifices are identical in all cultures and religions around the world and throughout time. If the "fruit of sacrifice" is found everywhere, then who are we to say that only biblical sacrifices to the biblical God are correct? It is more logical to say that either all sacrifices are correct, or none of them are.

Indeed, when we once again consider the various forms of sacrifices surveyed above, we see that none of them are primarily *for* God. Instead, we simply use "God" as the explanation offered for *why* the sacrifices work. People see the peace that descends upon a community after a sacrifice is offered, and they explain this peace by saying "God was angry with us and so sent the strife, but when we offered a sacrifice to Him, His anger was abated, and so now He has sent peace." The same explanation is offered when sacrifice creates an alleviation of guilt, or when a string of sacrifices bring an end to famine or disease. But since sacrifices "work" regardless of the deity they are offered to, it seems that the deity has nothing to do with sacrifices at all. Since sacrificial practices "work" regardless of which god is being pleased or appeased, sacrifices having nothing whatsoever to do with God.

But if this is true, then why is there so much sacrificial language and imagery in the Bible? If God didn't need or want sacrifices, then why are there commands in the Bible about sacrifices? If sacrifices "work" regardless of which deity they are offered to, then why does God instruct the Israelites to bring offerings and sacrifices to Him and Him alone? In fact, if God doesn't care that much about sacrifices, why does the Bible include more sacrificial language, imagery, and terminology than any other ancient religious text?

And why is so much of this sacrificial terminology and imagery used in relation to the death of Jesus on the cross?

These are questions that must be answered if we are going to understand what the Bible says about sacrifice, as well as why Jesus went to the cross as a sacrifice. Let us begin by looking at the way Christians have traditionally understood sacrificial language in the Bible.

TRADITIONAL SACRIFICIAL THEOLOGY

Traditional Christian theology has typically argued that since sacrificial practices are so central to biblical revelation, this must mean that the sacrificial shedding of blood is required to please and appease God and to satisfy His wrath toward sinful human beings. Yet animal sacrifices were never enough. Though the blood of bulls and goats could temporarily appease God, they were not valuable enough to cover the infinite debt of sin that humanity owed to a perfectly righteous God. Sacrificing bulls and goats was like paying pennies on a trillion dollar debt; it was never going to even make a dent in what was owed. Therefore, God sent His one and only Son, Jesus Christ, to be the sacrifice to end all sacrifices. Because Jesus was God, His death was an infinite sacrifice to pay for an infinite debt. Now that the blood of Jesus fully satisfied God's righteousness, we no longer have to sacrifice humans or animals to God for our sin. Jesus has paid it all.

The vast majority of Christians believe something very similar to this. Many believe that God hates sin so much, He is filled with wrath toward sin and cannot even be in the presence of sin or sinners. The solution to this problem, they believe, is death through sacrifice. God requires that people pay for the eternal offense of sin against Him and His holiness, but since we are sinners, we can never repay this debt. Thankfully, the theory goes, since we could never repay our debt to God, Jesus became a human to repay it for us. He came to earth, died as a sacrifice for our sins, poured out His blood upon God's heavenly altar, and appeased the wrath of God. Now, when God looks at us, He doesn't see our sin; instead He sees Jesus. Therefore, because of the sacrifice of Jesus, God can now love us. This is the traditional view of sacrifice, which you have likely heard in sermons or read in books.

One additional point often made in connection with this view is that while God ultimately did not want or desire animal sacrifices, they were a redemptive move in the "right direction." People often point out that in the days of Abraham and Moses, the surrounding civilizations and cultures practiced human sacrifice. But God knew that it would be too much of a stretch to forbid all sacrifices, and so God helped His people move in the right direction by only asking for animal sacrifices, knowing that Jesus would eventually do away with all sacrifice.

The primary problem with this entire view, however, is that when God finally sets out to put a complete end to all sacrifice, He does so by reverting to the human sacrifice of His own Son. The sacrifice of Jesus to end all animal sacrifices turns out to not be a repudiation of the sacrificial system and human sacrifice, but rather an endorsement of it. In this view, the Bible talks so much about sacrifice because God wants and needs blood sacrifice, and the blood of bulls and goats only pointed people to the ultimate human sacrifice of the blood of Jesus being spilled for all. So when it comes to the traditional understanding of sacrifice and the death of Jesus, there are serious problems that confront the critical thinker. We now not only have to deal with why sacrifices "work" for other religions in other cultures, but also why God in the Bible seemed to move away from human sacrifice in Leviticus, only to end up committing the greatest human sacrifice of all at the crucifixion.

It seems better, therefore, to step back and reconsider what the Bible says about sacrifice. When we do this, we see that the Bible does not support or affirm sacrificial activity at all, but rather does away with it once and for all. To go back to the question about which sacrifices God accepts, the answer is that He accepts none of them. God never wanted or needed sacrifices. Sacrifices were never *for* God. Instead, the Bible undermines and weakens sacrificial thinking and theology.

THE BIBLE UNDERMINES SACRIFICE

To see how the Bible undermines sacrificial thinking and theology, we must return once again to the history and background of sacrificial practices. We have seen that there were a wide variety of reasons and circumstances in which a sacrifice might be made. Some sacrifices had sociological purposes, to protect families, cultures, and society from an escalation of violence, while other sacrifices had psychological purposes, to help individuals and communities alleviate the feelings of guilt and shame that often accompanies sin. Then there were several types of spiritual sacrifices that could be made, from the ones made by some religions to earn and gain forgiveness from God and those made for the purpose of cleansing the temple from the pollution of sin, to those made to symbolize the death of another person whether it was for a warning against breaking a covenant or for the enactment and ratification of a Last Will and Testament. These are the social, psychological, and spiritual reasons for sacrifice.

While these types of sacrifices can be found in numerous ways and places throughout the biblical text, the Bible also seeks to undermine and subvert all sacrificial thinking. Even within the sacrificial texts themselves, the Bible seeks to reveal that God has never wanted blood sacrifice of any kind, and that God does not need or desire sacrifice in order to love humans, extend forgiveness, or offer good gifts of health, peace, and prosperity to humanity. The next chapter will reveal this in more detail as we look at several key Scriptures about sacrifice.

For now, it is enough to note that the reason the Bible contains so much sacrificial language and imagery is so that it can reveal the true source of sacrificial violence to us. By including so much about sacrifice, the Bible reveals that sacrificial violence does not come from the heart of God, but from the human heart. All the teachings and commands on sacrifice in the Bible are there to subvert and undermine the entire sacrificial framework of human culture and society. The Bible shows us the true heart of God and the proper way out of the spread of sin and violence. The Bible talks a lot about sacrificial violence so that sacrifice can be exposed for the deception that it is and so that a substitution for sacrifice can be provided. The Bible contains so much about sacrifice because while sacrifice does have many positive social, psychological, and spiritual benefits, God always wanted something better for His people. The Bible repeatedly and creatively unveils what that "something better" is. While there are glimmers and glimpses of this "something better" all over the place in the Old Testament, it is most fully revealed in Jesus Christ through how He lived and how He died.

THE SACRIFICE OF JESUS

By taking a careful look at the sacrifice of Jesus, we begin to see how Jesus saves the world from sin. And once we begin to see what Jesus accomplished on the cross, it is then that we begin to understand why the Bible includes so much language about sacrifice. Through His death on the cross, Jesus perfectly and completely accomplished what biblical revelation had been doing all along. Looking at the sacrifice of Jesus helps us better understand the sacrificial imagery and instructions in the Hebrew Scriptures. In fact, *only* by beginning with the sacrificial death of Jesus will we properly understand the Old Testament sacrifices. If we begin with the Old Testament, it is much easier to misunderstand what is revealed within its pages, and therefore, much easier to misunderstand what Jesus revealed on the cross. So let us keep the cross of Christ front and center. Let us interpret everything else in Scripture through Jesus Christ and Him crucified (1 Cor 2:2).

To begin with, let us state the obvious: Jesus Christ was sacrificed. As many Old Testament Scriptures prophesy and many New Testament Scriptures explain, the death of Jesus was a sacrifice. But the key to understanding the sacrificial death of Jesus on the cross is to recognize that it was not God who demanded or required the death of Jesus; it was humans. Jesus did not die to please or appease God, but to please and appease men. In the Gospels, it is human beings who wanted Jesus to die; not God. Human beings called for His blood; not God. The sacrifice of Jesus was not a sacrifice from men to God for the purpose of pleasing and appeasing God, but was instead a sacrifice from God to men for the purpose of exposing sacrifice for what it truly is, thus bringing an end to it.

Yes, God sent His Son to die as a sacrifice, but this was not because God Himself wanted or needed the sacrifice, but because God wanted to reveal and expose to humanity once and for all the violent and sinful tendencies that reside in our own hearts. God did not want or need the death of His own Son in order to satiate His wrath toward sin and extend forgiveness to us. No, God has always loved and always forgiven all humans for all their sin, simply because that's the kind of God He is. He doesn't need or demand payment for sin. (In fact, if He *did* demand payment, then He wouldn't be forgiving; He would be getting "paid off.")

From the beginning of human history, we humans have engaged in rivalry, accusation, and violence, and we often do such things in God's name. Everything in Scripture is focused on revealing this one truth to us. But it did so imperfectly, because we humans could always justify our violent behavior toward others as "carrying out God's will against unrighteous people." In the name of justice we justify our violent behavior toward others.

But there was no way to justify our treatment of Jesus. He did no wrong. He never sinned. There was no unrighteousness in Him deserving of death. Yet we killed Him anyway, and we did so in God's name. We sent Jesus to the cross and we claimed that it was God's will. But it wasn't. It never was. Jesus allowed Himself to be sacrificed in order to reveal to us that all sacrificial violence comes from the heart of man rather than the heart of God. Jesus died to reveal to us once and for all that God does not want sacrifices. Jesus revealed that it is we who want to kill others and we who justify our violence against men and animals by blaming this violence upon God. Once we see this truth, we can see how Jesus is the sacrifice to end all sacrifices.

THE SACRIFICE TO END ALL SACRIFICES

God sent Jesus to die at our hands to show us that the murders we commit in His name were never His will or desire, so that, through such a revelation, we might no longer commit murder in His name. The death of Jesus redeems and reconciles, not because it buys forgiveness for us, but because it reveals to us that God has never been angry, and has always loved and always forgiven. When we thought God was angry at us, or that God wanted to kill our enemies, this was only our own anger and our own hatred reflected onto the face of God. But now in Jesus we have seen what God is really like, and we have been shown another way to deal with our own sin and the sin of others. In Jesus, we have been shown the way of love and forgiveness.

Only after we have seen this supreme revelation in Jesus about the heart of God and the condition of mankind, are we then able to go back into the Hebrew Scriptures to see what they say about sacrifice. And when we view the sacrificial system through the lens of the crucifixion (which I called the *crucivision lens* in my book *The Atonement of God*), we see that the sacrificial system contains the same revelation that came through Jesus Christ. Once our eyes are opened to see the human desire for blood and how this bloodlust is blamed on God, all the violent, warlike, and sacrificial language of the Bible comes into focus and makes much more sense.

The Old Testament sacrificial system (and all religious sacrificial systems), along with all the "holy" wars of human history (which is another type of sacrifice where we kill others in God's name), are exposed and revealed for what they are within the pages of Scripture. The biblical text emphasizes sacrificial violence in order to explain and unveil it rather than endorse and promote it. The Bible reveals that the common beliefs and practices about sacrifice are nothing more than religious myths. All sacrificial systems are built on the twin lies that the gods punish us for our sin through death and violence and demand payment for sin through further death and violence. Scripture shouts a big "NO!" to this entire myth.

When we read the instructions in Scripture to sacrifice in God's name, the proper response is not to nod our heads and go do the same, but rather to shake our head at how others justified their own violence, and then look deep into our own heart and mind to see how we do this too. Jesus revealed through His life and death what the prophets revealed as well (1 Sam 15:22; Ps 40:6; 50:9-13; 51:16-17; Isa 1:11-13; Jer 6:20; 7:22; Hos 6:6-8; Amos 5:21-25; Micah 6:1-4, 6-8), that God has never wanted or desired that we kill others (whether animals or humans) in His name.

This is why the Bible contains more violence than any other ancient religious text. The Bible places so much emphasis on war, violence, bloodshed, and sacrifice because God wants to reveal the true source of violence and sacrifice, and in so doing, put a stop to it. The Bible emphasizes sacred violence, not because God is violent, but because we are. The sacrificial system says more about humanity than it does about God, and the reason the Bible contains so much about sacrifice is because God wanted the truth about sacrifice revealed to us. This was done "as in a mirror dimly" through the Hebrew Scriptures, but has now been perfectly revealed in the person and work of Jesus Christ.

Due to the fact that there are so many passages on sacrifice in the Bible, it is impossible to take a careful look at even a small portion of them. Nevertheless, let us attempt to consider a few of the more critical texts on sacrifice in the Bible. As we look at these texts in the next chapter, we will see both the development of sacrifice in the Bible and how God both allowed sacrifice to be carried out while seeking to limit and subvert it at the same time. Through it all, we see God seeking to expose sacrifice for what it is, until He ultimately calls us to stop all sacrifice through Jesus Christ.

CHAPTER 7

SCRIPTURES ON SACRIFICE

The previous chapter summarized the various categories of sacrifices that people around the world participate in, and briefly showed why none of the sacrifices did anything to influence or change God's perspective toward humanity. God has always loved all people and forgiven everybody for all sin. He did not need sacrifice in order to do this. It is we humans who needed sacrifice in order to create peace in our communities, deal with personal and corporate guilt, and feel like we were doing something to correct wrongs that we had done. But in Jesus, God revealed to us a different way of accomplishing similar goals, and also revealed that He Himself has never wanted, needed, or commanded sacrifices in His name. This chapter seeks to provide the biblical evidence for all these claims. Let us begin at the beginning with several texts from the book of Genesis.

GENESIS 1

In the beginning God created the heavens and the earth (Gen 1:1).

Genesis is a book of beginnings, and among other things, it reveals to us the beginnings of sacrifice. But contrary to popular belief, the book of Genesis is consistently anti-sacrificial. This anti-sacrificial perspective begins on the first page, in Genesis 1. People are often surprised to hear that Genesis 1 contains teaching on sacrifice, because there is no sacrifice of any kind in the first chapter of the Bible. But that is actually the entire point of Genesis

1. Genesis 1 is not primarily about how God created the world. It does contain information about creation, but this is not the main point of this opening chapter of the Bible. The best reading of Genesis 1 is to see it not as a scientific treatise on how the world was made, but instead to read it as a poetic, polemical, theological narrative which contrasts the God of Israel from the gods of the surrounding nations.

All of the nations that surrounded Israel had religious stories they told about how their gods created the world. Egypt, Babylon, and Canaan all had creation myths that explained how the world came into existence, and what role humans and animals have within this world. One common theme in all of these creation myths is that they are extremely violent. In the Babylonian creation account, for example, the ocean goddess Tiamat rebels against the other gods, and so they send the storm god Marduk to defeat her. When Marduk is victorious, he cuts her body in half and forms the heavens and the earth from the two parts. So in the Babylonian account, the world is founded on violence, and specifically a form of sacrificial violence where a being is killed to appease the gods. Similar stories are found in the Egyptian and Canaanite creation myths as well.

For those who really dig into these other creation myths, one of the most surprising things about them is how many similarities they share with the creation account in Genesis 1 (I explain many of these in my One Verse Podcast). There are so many parallels and repeated images between Genesis 1 and the other creation texts of Egypt, Canaan, and Babylon, many scholars agree that the similarities cannot be pure coincidence. And since these other creation accounts existed long before Genesis was ever written, many believe that Moses (or whoever wrote Genesis) borrowed from these other creation accounts to write the account as it is found in Genesis 1. Liberal scholars have a heyday with this, claiming that such borrowing from other religious texts is proof that Genesis is nothing more than a plagiarized myth.

But that liberal position misses the point of Genesis 1 entirely. While it is true that Genesis 1 contains many signs of borrowing images and themes from the creation accounts of other religions at the time, there is one huge theme that is completely absent from the creation account in Genesis 1. It is the theme of violence, and especially sacrificial violence. Where all the other creation narratives of the surrounding countries contain violence, bloodshed, and sacrifice, Genesis 1 contains nothing of the sort. This is critical to understanding the message of Genesis 1.

When the Israelites were heading out of Egypt toward Canaan, and having heard of the creation stories of Babylon, one of the main questions this fledgling nation had was this: "What is our God like? Is the God of Abraham, Isaac, and Jacob like the gods of Babylon, Canaan, and Egypt?" These were legitimate questions. After all, Abraham came from Ur, which was in Babylon. Isaac had lived in Canaan. And Jacob had followed Joseph in moving in family to Egypt. So was Yahweh, the God of Israel, just a conglomeration of the deities from these other three religions? What was their God like? What did He expect? How did He behave? What did He want?

Genesis 1 (indeed, the entire book of Genesis) was written to answer these questions. And when the Israelites first heard the creation account of Genesis 1, they would have immediately recognized the similarities of this account to the creation myths of Babylon, Canaan, and Egypt, but they also would have seen the great difference. One of the main points that the original audience would have noticed about the Genesis 1 creation account is its complete lack of sacred violence. They would have come away with the certain sense that Yahweh, the God of Israel, is not violent in any way, and does not require or demand bloodshed or sacrifice to carry out His will.

A similar theme is found in the second creation account of Genesis 2 with its description of this world as the Temple of God in which no sacrifice is carried out. But let us move on instead to look at Genesis 3:21.

GENESIS 3:21

Also for Adam and his wife the Lord God made tunics of skin,
and clothed them.

Many people believe that God performed the first sacrifice in human history. According to the thinking of most Christians, while Genesis 1–2 are non-violent, and though these two chapters do not contain any references to sacrificial requirements, this is only because sin had not yet entered into the world. But once Adam and Eve ate from the Tree of the Knowledge of Good and Evil, God had to show them the seriousness of their sin, and so He performed the first sacrifice in the Bible. He took a lamb and killed it in front of them, and then made clothes for them from its skin, which would serve as a constant reminder that sin brings death. At least, this is how most people read Genesis 3:21.

Very often, pastors and Bible teachers also use the events in Genesis 3 to teach "substitutionary atonement." The typical teaching is that since Adam and Eve sinned, and since the wages of sin is death, God showed Adam and Eve the truth of substitutionary sacrifice. Rather than kill Adam and Eve for their sin, God killed a lamb instead. Then from the skin of this lamb, God made clothes for them. Again, this is how many people read Genesis 3:21.

Yet although this understanding of Genesis 3:21 is quite popular, a careful reading of the text reveals that it has no basis whatsoever in the biblical text. There is no mention of a lamb. There is no mention of death. There is no mention of blood. There is no mention of a sacrifice. Frankly, there is no mention of sin either. The only thing the text says is that God gave them clothing to wear. But was this clothing made from the skin of a dead animal?

Though Genesis 3:21 does say that God gave tunics of skin to Adam and Eve for clothes, it does not say that God sacrificed an animal—or even killed one!—in order to get those clothes. The Hebrew word for "tunic" normally refers to a linen tunic; not leather. The Hebrew word for "skin," however, can refer to the skin of an animal, but it also refers to the clothes that humans wear for covering (cf. Gen 37:3, Exod 22:26). The word used here also frequently refers to the linen tunics worn by kings and priests. So Genesis 3:21 simply means that God gave linen tunics to Adam and Eve to wear for their clothes. The pictures we all saw in Sunday school of Adam and Eve standing naked in the Garden of Eden while God slaughtered a young lamb on a sacrificial altar is not accurate to what Genesis 3 actually says.

The real picture of Genesis 3 is that Adam and Eve, with all their new-found "wisdom" from the Tree of Knowledge, made clothing for themselves out of scratchy fig leaves. God, out of His unending love for humans, decided to make something better for them. So he made linen tunics for Adam and Eve to wear as a covering. God did not want to send them naked out into the world, so He gave them royal, priestly, linen tunics to wear. This verse is not about God substituting an animal sacrifice for the death of humans due to human sin. No, it is about God's ongoing provision, protection, and care for the humans He has created, even though they have decided to go their own way without Him. So there is no sacrifice in Genesis 3:21. But what about Genesis 4:4?

GENESIS 4:4

Abel also brought of the firstborn of his flock and of their fat.
And the Lord respected Abel and his offering.

If Genesis 3:21 does not contain a description of the first sacrifice in Scripture, many people believe that Genesis 4:4 does. In this account, after Cain brought an offering of fruit to God, Abel brought an offering of the firstborn of his flock and of its fat, and gave it to the Lord (Gen 4:4). The typical way of reading this passage has Abel offering a sacrificial lamb to God. In this view, Abel learned to offer blood sacrifices to God from his parents, who learned it from the (supposed) sacrifice of Genesis 3:21. But since we now see that there was no sacrifice in Genesis 3:21, it might be wise to consider whether or not there was a sacrifice in Genesis 4:4.

Since God did not kill an animal when Adam and Eve were removed from the Garden of Eden, it also makes no sense to understand Abel as making a sacrificial offering to God in Genesis 4:4. A careful reading of the text reveals that blood sacrifice is not anywhere in view. While Genesis 4:4 does say that Abel offered a firstborn animal from his flock to God, the text does not say that Abel killed or burned the animal. This was not a blood sacrifice or a burnt offering. Abel simply gave a young, live animal from his flock to God. It was a gift of love and appreciation. Since Abel and his entire family at this point in biblical history were vegetarians, it would not have entered Abel's mind to think that God wanted a dead animal. A dead animal is a useless animal, and therefore, a bad offering.

But what about the offering of animal fat? The text says that Abel offered "their fat" to the Lord. Does not this mean that Abel killed and sacrificed the young animal? How else could he offer the fat? While the Hebrew word for "fat" can refer to the layers of fat that get burned in a sacrificial offering, the word also refers to rich, creamy milk or to the butter and cheese that can be made from milk (cf. Gen 18:18; 49:12; Exod 3:8; Judg 5:25; 1 Sam 17:18).

How do we know which of these Abel offered? Well, when the layers of fat of a sacrificial animal are mentioned later in Scripture, it is mentioned in a list of other body parts that have been cut out of an animal and laid out on a sacrificial altar, with an emphasis on blood and burning (cf. Lev 3:3-17). Genesis 4:4 contains no mention of death, blood, burning, or animal parts, and so it is most reasonable to conclude that Abel's offering to God consisted of a live animal from his flock and some milk or butter. There is no blood sacrifice made to God in Genesis 4.

And once again, at this time, what were the benefits of animals? They gave wool and milk. When Abel saw Cain giving the fruit of his labor, Abel decided to imitate his older brother, and also give to God the fruit of his own labor. But what was the fruit of Abel's labor? It was not a dead animal, but a live animal (for wool) and the milk, butter, and cheese that came from the flock.

So there is no sacrificial bloodshed in Genesis 4:4. Nevertheless, the very first mention of sin and bloodshed does occur a few verses later, showing that human rivalry leads to the sin of human violence. We looked at this in

Part I on Sin and will consider these events again in later chapters. For now, let us look at the very first sacrifice in Scripture. It occurs in Genesis 8:20-21 after the events of the flood.

GENESIS 8:20-21

Then Noah built an altar to the Lord, and took of every clean animal and of every clean bird, and offered burnt offerings on the altar. And the Lord smelled a soothing aroma. Then the Lord said in His heart, "I will never again curse the ground for man's sake, although the imagination of man's heart is evil from his youth; nor will I again destroy every living thing as I have done."

The first sacrifice in Scripture takes place after the flood, when Noah offers burnt offerings on an altar to God (Gen 8:20). Note carefully that this sacrifice was not commanded or instructed by God, but was initiated by Noah himself. The text also says that the smell of the burnt offering was soothing to God, and as a result, God says *in His heart* that He will never again destroy the earth. Since God said this "in his heart," one has to wonder how Noah knew what God said. How did Noah know that the smell of the burnt offering was soothing to God? And why does God need to be soothed in the first place? In light of such questions, it seems that what we read in Genesis 8:20-21 were not God's actual words to Noah, but are instead Noah's *impressions* of what God thought. God never commanded or instructed Noah to offer these burnt sacrifice, but when Noah killed and burned these animals, he himself felt more at peace, and he attributed this peace to God. This fits perfectly with the concept of "psychological sacrifice" that we looked at in the previous chapter.

This need for a psychological release from guilt fits with the thoughts that Noah ascribes to God in Genesis 8:21. When Noah gets off the ark, he recognizes that his heart is just as wicked as it was before, and that the thoughts and intentions of his heart are only evil continually. Since he senses this, he knows that God sees it as well. What is interesting about this description of humanity is that it is nearly identical to the description of humanity which was given as the reason for the flood in the first place (cf. Gen 6:5). Even though the flood nearly wiped out humanity, nothing has changed within the heart of humanity. Noah recognizes that the sin and evil and violence which brought about the flood in the first place continued to reside in his own heart. Though Noah survived the flood in the ark, the sin and violence that caused the flood survived in the heart of Noah.

Prior to the flood, sin led to violence against other human beings. But now, Noah takes a step to defuse the violence that is welling up in his heart. Rather than starting the cycle all over again by killing a family member (one wonders how many arguments and disagreements the family had in confined quarters during that year on the ark), Noah takes some of the animals and kills them instead. When he does so, he notices the delicious aroma of meat sizzling on a fire, and he also notices that he feels more at peace with himself and with his family than before. Although animals roasting over a fire do issue a wonderful smell (at least to us meat eaters!), I doubt very much that God can be "bought off" with BBQ. Yet Noah believes that the peace he feels is a gift from God, and attributes this feeling of peace in his own heart to what God must be thinking in His. Nowhere, of course, does God actually command Noah to offer these sacrifices, or say anything to Noah about being pleased by them. The sacrifice came from Noah, and was for Noah, and everything that Noah felt came from within himself as well. Yet he attributed it all to God.

This idea is critical for properly understanding the rest of the sacrifices in the Bible. When we kill animals "in God's name" or "for God," it is not actually because God commanded or wanted us to do so. Sacrifices make us feel better, which then leads us to wrongly believe that since we feel better about our sin, God must also feel better about us. This sense of relief we feel when we kill in God's name is the psychological response to sacrifice that we project from our own heart onto the heart of God. We think God wants sacrifices because these sacrifices help solve problems in our own life. But

God never wanted or needed sacrifice. It was a purely human invention which we projected onto the will of God.

Yet this first sacrifice was not only a "psychological sacrifice" to help Noah feel better about the evil in his own heart. Upon closer inspection, it turns out to also serve as a sociological sacrifice. God allowed this sacrifice to occur (and others like it) because they provide "a way out" from the escalation of violence that was characteristic of the pre-flood earth (Gen 6:5, 11, 13). The flood, of course, did not change the heart condition of humanity (Gen 8:21), and so rather than allow the escalation of violence to threaten the existence of humanity once again, God allowed humans to engage in sacrifice as a "release valve" for our violent inclinations. In other words, with the first sacrifice in the Bible, we see that sacrifice is not at all for God, but is instead entirely for humanity. Sacrifice is a way of escape from the contagion of violence that is always threatening the ongoing existence of mankind. The solution that Noah discovered, and which he then "blames" on God, is that the bloodlust of the human heart can be diminished through violence against animals before it escalates out of control and once again threatens the existence of all humanity.

This experience of obtaining social peace through sacrifice is a common human occurrence. When a violent contagion threatens the peaceful existence of a family, community, or culture, and they avert the threat of overwhelming violence through sacrifice, the peace that results seems to come from the gods. The violent bloodlust subsides and peace settles down upon all, and it seems so miraculous that they can only attribute it to the gods. Genesis 8:20-21 could not have stated the sociological significance of sacrifice any more clearly. Sacrifice is the preventative and curative solution to violence that threatens human existence. It does not come from God, but comes from man, and when we experience the peace that results from sacrifice, we attribute this peace to God Himself being appeased. As long as we do this, the text says, escalations of violence can be averted.

And since Genesis 8:21 is both a psychological sacrifice and a sociological sacrifice, it is not surprising to learn that it also serves as a spiritual sacrifice. Noah's sacrifice occurs in the context of creating a new covenant between God and mankind (Gen 8:22–9:17). This sacrifice enacts the terms of a covenant. So in this one sacrifice, we see all three purposes for sacrifice revealed. It is fitting, therefore, that this is the first sacrifice in the Bible.

Yet there is one truth about this sacrifice we have not yet seen. Although Genesis 8:20-21 does not contain a sacrifice that was commanded, instructed, or sanctioned by God, there is in fact a divinely-sanctioned sacrifice in Genesis 6–8. It is not the sacrifice at the end where Noah kills an animal; nor is it the sacrifice at the beginning where all human beings on earth (except eight) are killed in the flood. God did not want nor sanction any of these sacrifices. Instead, the divinely-sanctioned sacrifice in Genesis 6–8 is the one that takes place all the way through the text. It is the sacrifice which began as early as Genesis 3. No, not Genesis 3:21, but even earlier than that. The true divinely-sanctioned sacrifice in these opening chapters of Genesis is the sacrifice of God's own self. Since God allowed—even inspired—this text to be written as we have it today, and since God allows people then (and now) to blame Him for all the evil that goes on in the world (even though He is blameless), what we see is that God allows His name, His reputation, and His character to be sacrificed for the well-being of the humans He loves. There is a sacrifice in Genesis 3, Genesis 4, Genesis 6, and Genesis 8, but is a sacrifice of God's own self. This truth about sacrifice will be explored more deeply in Part IV on Scapegoating. For now, let us continue our study of sacrifice by turning to Genesis 9–11.

GENESIS 9–11

"And the fear of you and the dread of you shall be on every beast of the earth, on every bird of the air, on all that move on the earth, and on all the fish of the sea. They are given into your hand. Every moving thing that lives shall be food for you" (Gen 9:2-3).

Now this is the genealogy … (Gen 10:1; 11:10, 27)

> *Now the whole earth had one language and one speech ... But the Lord came down to see the city and the tower which the sons of men had built. And the Lord said, "Indeed the people are one and they all have one language, and this is what they will begin to do; now nothing that they propose to do will be withheld from them" (Gen 11:1, 5-6)*

Now that sacrifice has been introduced in Scripture, the book of Genesis shows how it creates peace in human culture so that humanity can develop and grow into a society rather than continually fall back into the contagion of violence that threatens to destroy all.

We begin to see this first in Genesis 9:1-7 where humans begin to eat meat. Prior to Genesis 9, it appears that humans were vegetarians. This is why Abel would not have offered meat to God in Genesis 4:4. Since no one ate meat, Abel would not have thought that God wanted meat either. The Bible reveals that the killing, cooking, and eating of meat is a form of sacrifice in itself. At the end of Genesis 8, Noah takes one of every clean animal and bird and sacrifices them on an altar as a burnt offering. As the meat cooked and sizzled over the open flame, Noah thought to himself, "Wow! That smells amazing!" So it is no surprise that only three verses later, we read that the very same animals which Noah burned as sacrifices on an altar are then given by God to humans as food (Gen 9:2-3).

Did God actually give them meat to eat, or is this also another projection by Noah upon God? We cannot say for sure (for most of the violence in the Old Testament is nothing more than humans projecting their own violence upon God), but it seems that in this instance (and also with the sacrifices in the Mosaic Law), God knew that humans needed a way of escape for the sin and violence that constantly welled up in our own hearts, and so rather than have us kill one another, God allowed us to kill animals as sacrifices and for food (which is a form of sacrifice). Our violent bloodlust for killing others is somewhat tempered by killing and eating animals. After God says that the earth will never again be destroyed the way it was in the flood, He provides the means to create peace with one another through the killing of animals. This is a clear picture of the sociological sacrifice.

Note, however, that God lays down restrictions and boundaries on sacrificial violence. First, the blood of these animals must be properly drained and the animal must be properly cooked (Gen 9:4-5). Second, only animals can be killed and eaten; not humans (Gen 9:6). The goal of this eating of sacrificial meat was that Noah and his family be fruitful and multiply upon the face of the earth (Gen 9:1) rather than suffering the consequences of escalating violence that destroys all (Gen 9:11). God allowed humans to kill and eat animals as a way to literally quench the human thirst for blood. Sacrificial killing for food helps restrict and control the violence of human hearts. Yet even through such an allowance, God sought to restrain such killing even further by reducing the emphasis on blood so that we are not drawn back once again into the lust for blood that threatens human existence.

The next several chapters of Genesis reveal how well this new sacrificial outlet worked. Rather than spiraling down into greater and greater violence, Genesis 9–10 records the first Table of Nations, and then Genesis 11 explains how humans were able to come together with a unified goal and purpose to accomplish the most amazing feats of architectural, scientific, and spiritual progress. The tower of Babel which the humans built in Genesis 11 was likely some sort of sacrificial structure. Humans recognized the importance of sacrifice as a way to maintain peace and build society. The clear point in Genesis 9–11 is that animal sacrifice was a great discovery which allowed humans to build society and culture. We could say that sacrifice is the foundation of continued human existence. To put it more bluntly, human civilization is built on blood. And though the initial sacrifice itself was never commanded or instructed by God, God did allow sacrifice for the purpose of food, but only under certain conditions and restrictions. Even then, when sacrifice took too prominent a role in human society with the construction of a giant sacrificial altar which reached to the heavens, God stepped in to limit sacrifices from having too much prominence in human culture. It is possible as well, though not explicitly stated, that this tower had also begun to be used for human sacrifice, which would also explain why God stepped in to stop it.

The basic theme we have seen throughout Genesis 3–11 is cyclically repeated over and over through the rest of Genesis. The first cycle is the one we have seen already. After God is introduced in the book as supremely non-violent (Gen 1–2), we then see that humanity enters into a cycle of blame, rivalry, and scapegoating (Gen 3) which ends in fratricide, the murder of one brother by another (Gen 4). This cycle is called "sin" (Gen 4:7), which is repeated twice in Genesis 4, first by Cain and then by Lamech. In both cases, the violence threatens to escalate out of control, from sevenfold retaliation to seventy-sevenfold. Yet it does escalate out of control in Genesis 6 when the cycle of inter-family violence covers the entire world and threatens the existence of humanity. Even in this flood of violence, however, we humans do not own up to our role in the violence, but blame God for it (Gen 6–8). He takes the blame and sacrifices Himself so that there can be a new beginning and a fresh start (Gen 9). But the cycle only begins again, with more rivalry, violence, blame, scapegoating, and death (Gen 10–11). Sacrifice is shown to be the key that holds humanity together, even while God seeks to limit and restrict the spread of human and animal sacrifice by sacrificing Himself.

The rest of the book of Genesis repeats the cycle that is found in Genesis 3–11. The patriarchal narratives often contain rivalry which leads to blame and accusations, which in turn leads to treachery and violence. There are three additional cycles in Genesis, the cycle of Abraham (Gen 12–25), the cycle of Jacob and Esau (Gen 26–36), and the cycle of Joseph and his brothers (Gen 37–50). The most interesting thing about these final three cycles, however, is that a new element to the cycle is introduced and emphasized. We see that the cycle of rivalry and accusation does not need to end in death. There is another way it can end as well, which is the non-violent way of God as introduced in Genesis 1–2. This is the way of self-sacrifice through forgiveness and reconciliation. To see this, let us briefly consider the three cycles of Genesis 12–50.

GENESIS 12–50

The primary reason that God calls Abraham is to begin showing the world another way to deal with the human problem of sin. As Genesis 3–11 has so clearly revealed, the sin cycle of rivalry, accusation, and violence leads only to the destruction of humanity. God's only activity in this cycle has been to reduce the damage and rescue humans. But now, beginning with Abraham, God shows how we humans can also work with God to save humans from the cycle of sin. God does this by calling us to follow His example in sacrificing ourselves for the sake of others through forgiveness and reconciliation. Forgiving others when they sin against us is a form of sacrifice, for it sacrifices our desire, our pride, and our position in society for the sake of reconciling a broken relationship with others. This was not seen in any human in Genesis 3–11, but was only seen in God. Now, beginning with Abraham, we begin to see that God calls humans to follow His example in offering forgiveness and seeking reconciliation.

The Abrahamic cycle of rivalry, retaliation, and reconciliation is less pronounced than the other cycles in Genesis, but it is there. This is because Genesis 12–25 only introduces us to how we can be a blessing to the world by turning away from interfamily rivalry and violence and instead offer forgiveness and seek reconciliation. As with Genesis 1–11, this cycle begins with God "creating" or "calling" forth a new man to be His ambassador to the world. Abram, in a sense, is a fresh start, a new Adam. In Genesis 12, just as God called Adam to spread God's work upon the world, God calls Abram to be a blessing to the world. Nevertheless, just as with Adam and Eve, there is a little bit of rivalry between Abram and Sarai in Genesis 12 and 16. The rivalry between Abram and Lot in Genesis 13–14 is parallel to the rivalry between Cain and Abel. Then in Genesis 15, Abram renews his commitment by entering into a covenant with God, just as Noah did with God in Genesis 9.

Most people have heard sermons about the Abrahamic covenant in Genesis 15:9-12. Abram cut several animals in half and then separated the animal halves so that a walkway was created between them. The idea was for the two parties of the covenant to walk through the animal halves together, and then make the agreement on the other side that if either of them broke the agreement, they would be cut in half like these animals. In Genesis 15, God walks through by Himself indicating that He would keep the covenant even if Abram and his descendants do not.

For our purposes in this chapter, however, note that the ancient practice of "cutting a covenant" reveals that violence was the standard operating procedure for all societies and cultures at the time. Even legally binding agreements were "written in blood" and enforced with blood. This is the form of "spiritual sacrifice" which helped enact a covenant. When God walks through alone, He is not indicating His blessing on such a practice, but is simply allowing Himself to be bound by the methods used in that day for making contracts. By walking through alone, God not only indicated that He will carry out the terms of the contract by Himself, but also that He had no desire for the sacrificial blood of others. What is more, by walking through alone, God is indicating that He alone is taking on any and all failure in this covenant. If Abram or his descendants fail in their part of the covenant, God will take this failure upon Himself, sacrificing Himself according to the terms of the covenant. So in numerous ways, God wants Abram to know that even if Abram fails in his part of the covenant, God wants all bloodshed to cease. This truth is further reinforced in Genesis 22, which we will look at in the next section.

The second cycle of violence is found in Genesis 26–36. Jacob and Esau are classic brother rivals. They are in conflict in the womb (Gen 25:22) and Jacob seems to compete with his brother Esau even during birth (Gen 25:25-26). The rivalry continues when Jacob persuades Esau to sell his birthright for a bowl of stew (Gen 25:29-34) and when Jacob tricks their father, Isaac, into blessing him instead of Esau (Gen 27). In the end, however, this sibling rivalry does not conclude with one brother murdering another, but with forgiveness and restoration of the relationship (Gen 32–33). Nevertheless, it appears that while progress is being made, Jacob does not fully trust Esau, and so lies to his brother once again in order to protect himself and his family (Gen 33:14-20).

The third and final cycle is the best of all. Genesis 37–50 provides an account of rivalry of all-against-one. All of Joseph's brothers condemn, accuse, and cast Joseph out of the family, and then lie to their father about how an animal killed Joseph. Joseph, however, ends up as the second in command over all of Egypt, and when given the chance to retaliate against his brothers, chooses instead to forgive and bless. The end result is that an entire family experiences reconciliation and restoration.

The overall theme and message of Genesis, then, is that although rivalry, blame, scapegoating, sacrifice, and violence is the foundation of civilization and culture, and although all people live according to these activities, God does not endorse or approve of them. Instead, God provides a different way to create peace, build community, restore families, and generate civilization and culture. God's ways are not ways of rivalry, sacrifice, and violence, but ways of love, forgiveness, and reconciliation. God modeled this alternative method in Genesis 1-11, and then calls people to follow His example in Genesis 12–50. Joseph is the best example of how this can work in a family and in a culture. Having seen this, let us turn back to look at one final sacrificial text from the book of Genesis before moving on to other sacrificial passages in the Bible.

GENESIS 22:1-14

Abraham's attempted sacrifice of Isaac in Genesis 22:1-14 is a central biblical passage that must be understood if we are going to grasp what God wants humans to see about sacrifice. It is here that God reveals something crucial to Abraham about sacrifice, and by studying this text, we are allowed to see it as well.

Most humans believe that God wants and needs sacrifice in order to forgive sins and bless people with life, health, and prosperity. In Genesis, God sets out to show that He is not violent and does not want death and killing of any kind. In Genesis 12, when God called Abram out of all the peoples of the earth to bring His new revelation of Himself to humanity, one of the primary truths God wanted to impress upon Abram was that God did not want or need sacrifice. We saw previously how God did this in Genesis 15. God impresses this truth upon Abraham even further in Genesis 22.

In Abraham's day, it was very common for other religions to practice human sacrifice. So when God instructs Abraham to take Isaac up onto a holy mountain and offer him as a sacrifice, it appears that Abraham is not surprised. This is a normal and typical request for a god of that time. So early the next morning, he gets up, takes Isaac, and heads toward Mount Moriah as God instructed. Though much is often made of Abraham's swift obedience, no other response was possible. When a deity demands a human sacrifice, a swift response was required, lest the wrath of the deity increase and many more people die. This was well-known and widely accepted.

Yet in Genesis 22, something very strange occurs. Just as Abraham is about to kill Isaac on the altar, God stops him. God calls out to Abraham and tells him to not kill his son (Gen 22:12). By stopping the killing stroke, God shows that He is opposed to all such sacrificial killing. The lesson for Abraham is that God is a God of life, not death. God does not want sacrifice, either human or animal.

But did not God provide a ram for Abraham to offer up as a substitute for Isaac? This is, after all, how many read and teach Genesis 22. It is not uncommon for pastors and preachers to point to this text as a clear reference to the substitutionary death of Jesus. The way this chapter is often taught, we humans are like Isaac on the altar, but rather than kill us, God provides a substitute in Jesus, just as He provided a ram as a substitute for Isaac.

The main problem with this way of teaching Genesis 22 is that it is not taught anywhere in the Bible. Furthermore, a careful reading of Genesis 22 itself reveals that there is no mention of God Himself providing the ram for Abraham. It simply says that Abraham saw a ram caught in a thicket. It does not say that God caused the ram to get tangled in the thicket, nor does it say that God provided the ram as a substitute for Isaac. Further still, the text does not say that God asked Abraham to offer the sacrifice of the ram as a substitute for Isaac, or even offer the ram at all. Much like Noah, Abraham offered the sacrificial animal on his own, and believed that this was what God wanted. But nothing in the text affirms that the death of the ram was expected, demanded, commanded, or even blessed by God. God does not desire sacrificial victims, whether they are human or animal substitutes. Modern Bible scholars and pastors read these sorts of ideas into the text as a way of justifying sacrificial, substitutionary theology, even though the Bible nowhere affirms or supports this way of reading the text.

Briefly consider the theological *ram*ifications of this sacrificial, substitutionary teaching of Genesis 22. Such a theology implies that in the days of Abraham, God wanted to teach Abraham that He did not want human sacrifice, for animal sacrifice was preferable. However, when it comes to Jesus, we see that God truly *does* want human sacrifice after all. The problem with Isaac, apparently, was that he just wasn't perfect enough. Ultimately, according to sacrificial, substitutionary theology, God has always wanted human sacrifice, and animal sacrifice only kept God partially satisfied until we could offer to Him the best and most perfect human sacrifice of all, the sacrifice of His own perfect Son.

But this approach is not only logically poor; it is theologically bankrupt. The substitute in Genesis 22 is from a human life that is "more" valuable to an animal life that is "less" valuable. If Jesus were truly "our" substitute, His death would be the opposite. His death would be a substitute from human life to the infinitely more valuable divine life of Jesus. Therefore, this connection between Genesis 22 and the Gospels leaves us with a God who not only wants and demands human sacrifice, but wants and demands the best, the brightest, and the most pure sacrifice of all. This way of reading Genesis 22 does not shut the door on human sacrifice, but jams it wide open. Thinking of Jesus as our substitute in the way that the ram was a substitute for Isaac invites us to believe that God only wants the best humans as sacrifices. Such a God might conceivably want virgin sacrifices or the sacrifices of young children. But this is not the God of the Bible, and is not the God revealed in Jesus.

As you can see, this substitutionary, sacrificial reading of Genesis 22 is reprehensible at best. God has never wanted any sacrifice, whether human or animal. God's intent from the very beginning has been to do away with all murder, death, and violence. This is the truth from Genesis 22 which must be taught, and which is right in line with the rest of the revelation of Scripture. Though violence against animals was allowed from time to time (as we saw in Genesis 9), this was not what God wanted or desired. Animal sacrifice was allowed purely as a temporary fix for the sinful human condition, as a way of release for the violent bloodlust of the human heart. Though God abhors all violence, if the choice is between humans killing humans and humans killing animals, God allows the lesser of two evils.

Genesis 22 is the first step in this major revelation of Scripture. Abraham learns that God does not want human sacrifice. Yet even though God does not provide a ram for Abraham, Abraham is not quite ready to accept that God does not require *any* sacrifice at all, and so rather than kill Isaac, he kills the ram that happened to be caught in the thicket nearby, and then he says that God provided the ram (Gen 22:14). Yet God would have been just as pleased, if not more pleased, with Abraham if Abraham had simply untied Isaac, walked back down the hill, and gone home.

While it is true, according to the New Testament, that Jesus is our substitute, the important point of the New Testament is that Jesus did not die "in our place to appease God," but rather died "in the place of all the sacrificial victims we have killed in the name of God." Jesus did not die because God needed or demanded a human sacrifice. God did not substitute Jesus in our place. No, Jesus died because we humans demanded a human sacrifice, and God allowed us to kill His own Son so that we might finally see what we were doing when we killed others in God's name. Jesus did die as a substitute, but He was a substitute for all sacrificial victims of the world. He died to reveal the truth about sacrifice. What truth? The truth that God does not desire sacrifice; we humans do. Jesus died to reveal how we kill others in God's name and to reveal that the sacrificial inclination comes from within our own hearts, not from the heart of God. Jesus died to reveal these truths to us so that we will put an end to the making and killing of all sacrificial victims. This truth will become clearer in Parts IV and V on Scapegoating and Blood. But we have several more sacrificial texts to consider first.

EXODUS–DEUTERONOMY

The Mosaic Law contains numerous instructions about sacrifices. The law provides the reasons and methods for sacrifice, what should and should not be sacrificed, who should make the sacrifices, and numerous other such topics. In light of these numerous and detailed instructions regarding sacrifice, many believe that it was God's plan, purpose, and will to provide a sacrificial system to the Israelite people. This idea, however, comes from a basic misunderstanding about the purpose and origin of the law itself, as well as a failure to understand what Genesis really teaches about sacrifice. So to understand what the Mosaic Law teaches about sacrifice, we must first understand what Genesis teaches about sacrifices and secondly, the role, function, and purpose of the Mosaic Law itself. Thankfully, both of these topics have been previously covered in this book. But for the sake of clarity, let me summarize what we have seen so far.

A proper understanding of Exodus–Deuteronomy begins with the recognition that the book of Genesis is not just the historical account of the beginning of the world and the founding of Israel. Instead, it is a story with a theological message and purpose. The book of Genesis provides the people of Israel—who were coming out of Egypt and anticipating an entrance into the land of Canaan—with an introduction to the person and character of Yahweh, and how Yahweh differed from the gods of Egypt, Babylon, and Canaan. The basic message of Genesis is that while all the gods were unpredictable, unreliable, vindictive, and violent, Yahweh was faithful, dependable, loving, forgiving, gracious, caring, and kind. The various cycles of stories in the book of Genesis take the reader from actions of blame, scapegoating, rivalry, retaliation, and revenge to outcomes of forgiveness, reconciliation, and restoration. God seeks to show the people of Israel that just as He is different than the gods of the surrounding nations and religions, so also, He calls His people to live differently as well.

Based on this foundational understanding of Genesis, God calls His people in the early chapters of Exodus to live with Him in an intimate relationship built on love. But this way of living was so foreign to the people of Israel, they refuse the offer of a relationship with God and ask instead for lists of laws mediated by Moses. God agrees to give this to them, but only as a way of teaching them that there can be no substitute for an actual loving relationship with Him. The only alternative to living outside of a relationship with God is living inside the system of rivalry, blame, scapegoating, and violence which the rest of the world operates by (cf. Gen 4). This pattern is repeated over and over in the Pentateuch, not only in Genesis, but also in Exodus–Deuteronomy. The specific additional insight of Exodus–Deuteronomy is that where there is no love, laws are required to create peace. But laws only lead to more rivalry, blame, and violence (sin), which in turn leads to the addition of more laws. And so the cycle continues (see Part II on Law).

So even though God does provide the sacrificial system in the Mosaic Law, it was not because such things were His plan or desire. God desired a relationship built on love, grace, and forgiveness. But in the absence of such a relationship with God and with others, people degenerate into the default behavior of rivalry, blame, scapegoating, and violence. Such sinful actions lead only to escalating violence. The sacrificial system provides the sociological, psychological, and spiritual release valve for such escalations of violence. And if the only choice is between a contagion of violence that threatens to destroy all of humanity and sacrificial violence that helps keep violence from escalating out of control, the second option is better by far. In this way, we can say that sacrificial violence is a good/bad thing. It is good in that it works, but it is bad in that it is not what God wanted, planned, or desired. Yet in the absence of what God wants, plans, and desires, the only remaining choice was between allowing humanity to destroy itself and allowing humanity to use sacred violence as an outlet. God chose the latter and gave Israel the sacrificial system. Just as God allowed Noah and Abraham to offer sacrifices as a release valve for the violence and guilt in their own hearts, so also, God allowed Israel to do the same, especially since the nation refused God's offer to live in a loving relationship with Him. Thus, we have the reason for God's sacrificial instructions in the Mosaic Law.

Of course, just as we saw in Genesis 9 and Genesis 22, the sacrificial laws in the Pentateuch are a redemptive move in the right direction. Though much of the surrounding culture practiced human sacrifice, God forbade such practices, and limited the Hebrew people to animal sacrifice only. It was not perfect, but it was a move in the right direction. We must be careful to not reverse this redemptive move by saying that through the cross of Jesus, God wanted human sacrifice after all. Such a teaching is a move backward, not forward, in the biblical revelation about sacrifice. This truth is further emphasized in various passages from the Prophets about sacrifice.

THE PROPHETS

For you do not desire sacrifice, or else I would give it; You do not delight in burnt offering (Ps 51:16).

"For I did not speak to your fathers, or command them in the day I brought them out of the land of Egypt, concerning burnt offerings and sacrifices" (Jer 7:22).

"Though you offer Me burnt offerings and your grain offerings, I will not accept them, nor will I regard your fattened peace offerings" (Amos 5:22).

The truth that God never wanted sacrifices is reinforced over and over in the writings of the Prophets. Jeremiah 7:22 may be one of the more significant prophetic texts on this topic, for it says that when God brought Israel out of Egypt, He did not give them commands or instructions about burnt offerings and sacrifices. Yet everybody knows that the instructions about offerings and sacrifices in Exodus and Leviticus are clearly attributed to God. So is this a contradiction in the Bible? Exodus and Leviticus say that the instructions about offerings and sacrifices are direct commands from God, but Jeremiah says they are not.

The solution is to recall the purpose and function of the law. The law, along with its numerous sacrifices and offerings, could never produce the relationship that God wanted or desired with His people (see Part II on Law). God knew this from the very beginning, and initially tried to have a relationship with them without any law. But they rejected a relationship with God, and asked for a priestly mediator and religious laws instead. In the absence of a relationship built on love, grace, and forgiveness, there is nothing left but law, and so God gave law to them. The sacrifices and law were a poor substitute for relationship, but were necessary to help preserve and protect God's people from the destructive power of sin (see Part I on Sin).

One of the great problems with law, however, is that people find ways to obey the law which have no impact whatsoever on their heart or motives, and therefore, do not really obey the intent of the law at all. A strict observance of law tends to result in a legalistic keeping of lists of rules and regulations while completely ignoring the actual purpose for which the law was given. God knew this, as did all the Prophets of Israel. So it is not surprising to read various statements throughout the Prophets that God never wanted or desired sacrifices.

Jeremiah says that God never commanded his people to offer sacrifices and burnt offerings (Jer 7:22-23). Amos says that God hated their religious festivals and burnt offerings (Amos 5:21-24). Micah points out that God doesn't need thousands of rams and rivers of oil, and definitely not a family's firstborn son. Instead, God wants justice, kindness, and humility (Micah 6:6-8). God is not delighted with sacrifices and offerings, says the

Psalmist, but with a broken and contrite spirit (Ps 51:16-17). There are numerous other similar passages as well (cf. 1 Sam 15:22; Ps 40:6; 50:9-14; 51:16-17; 69:31; Isa 1:11-13; Jer 6:20; 7:22; Hos 6:6-8; Amos 5:21-25; Micah 6:1-4, 6-8).

The basic message of the prophets regarding sacrifice is that God owns the cattle on a thousand hills. He doesn't need us to give Him more. Besides, He prefers them alive. God is not a God of blood and death, but a God of love and life. So do you want to worship God? Do so with love and justice, grace and mercy, generosity and peace. This is what the prophets proclaim. Jesus followed this prophetic tradition by teaching similar things during His life and ministry.

THE GOSPELS

"But go and learn what this means: 'I desire mercy and not sacrifice'" (Matt 9:13; Mark 12:7).

In many ways, the four Gospel accounts are anti-sacrificial in theme and focus. Over and over in the Gospel accounts, Jesus undermines the sacrificial system along with its temple structure and priestly administration (Luke 19:45-48). The one time He does instruct someone to make a temple offering, it is not because He wants or requires the offering (or thinks that God does), but because it serves as a testimony to the temple priests (Luke 5:14). Through His words and actions, Jesus shows that God freely loves and forgives without any need for the blood of bulls and goats. Jesus refocuses the temple, the priesthood, and the sacrificial system on Himself, showing that what He does and how He lives is the true way to worship and follow God (cf. Luke 5:17-26).

By His life and example, Jesus shows that there is no human mediator between God and man, and that God has not separated Himself from mankind because of our sin, but has instead become one of us, sharing in our pain and releasing us from our shame. This teaching got Jesus in a lot of trouble with the religious leaders of His day, because they (rightly) understood that what He was saying was undermining the entire sacrificial system that supported the temple and the priestly class. Strangely, many religious leaders today side with the religious leaders of Jesus' day in saying that the religious buildings, clergy, and sacrifices are all required by God. Of course, the religious leaders who argue this today believe that they are following the teachings of Jesus, but they twist the words and actions of Jesus to make it sound like they are in agreement with Him.

This hermeneutical twist is primarily seen through a re-interpretation of the death of Jesus on the cross. While the Gospels clearly and consistently reveal that the death of Jesus was at the hands of men to please and appease religious and political rulers and satisfy an angry mob, many religious leaders today see the death of Jesus on the cross as a sacrifice which pleased and satisfied God. But this interpretation sides with the religious and political leaders who called for the death of Jesus. Many religious leaders then and now believed that God wanted Jesus to die, and that peace would come only through His death. The more modern Christian theologians who argue for this view teach that while the blood of bulls and goats could only temporarily cover our sin, the death of Jesus was the ultimate and perfect sacrifice which God needed and demanded as the complete payment for sin. This way of thinking about the sacrifice of Jesus does not undermine the sacrificial system, but supports and buttresses it as never before.

The best way (and the most ancient way) of understanding the death of Jesus on the cross, however, is to see it not as something demanded or required by God in order to extend forgiveness of sins to humanity, but instead as something demanded and required by humans as a way to reinforce the great lie which we have lived beneath since the beginning of the world. The great lie is that God is angry at us because of sin, and when bad things happen in life, it is because God is angry at us, and so the best way to deal with sin and an angry God is to find the "sinner" in our community and kill him or her in the name of God. Then God will be pleased that we have taken care of sin and will bless us once again.

Jesus was viewed by the people of His day as a sinner and blasphemer who needed to be condemned, accused, and executed in accordance with the will of God. But it was not God's will. No execution or sacred violence is ever God's will. How do we know? The death of Jesus revealed this truth to us. The death of Jesus did not reveal that *God* wants death, but that *we* want it. His death reveals *our* vile hearts and violent ways, while at the same time revealing the heart of God as always forgiving and only loving. The death of Jesus called us to the one thing God has always wanted for us, which is to live as He lives, with nothing but love, grace, mercy, and forgiveness extended toward others. This truth will be looked at in more detail in Parts IV and V on Scapegoating and Blood.

So while there is sacrificial language used in the New Testament about the death of Jesus, the sacrificial language is used to reveal to us the origins and nature of sacrifice, that it is not something wanted or desired by God, but is instead wanted and desired by humans as a way to deal with sin and violence in our own lives and cultures. In giving Himself up to us in this way, Jesus both exposed our own hearts to us and revealed how God wants us to truly live. Jesus is the sacrifice to end all sacrifices, *not* because God is finally appeased, but because the heart of man and the heart of God are both finally revealed for what they are. We condemn and kill while God loves and forgives.

ROMANS 12:1

I beseech you therefore, brethren, by the mercies of God, that you present your bodies a living sacrifice, holy, acceptable to God, which is your reasonable service.

People occasionally refer to Romans 12:1 as a passage which teaches that God wants sacrifices. Yet while Romans 12:1 does invite us to present ourselves to God as a sacrifice, it is as a *living* sacrifice that He wants us; not as a dead one. God does not desire death, but life. If we offer ourselves to God and to His service, it is as a living, breathing human being. This may mean, of course, that we die to ourselves and some of our past dreams and desires, but doing so will not lead to a failure to be who God made us to be, but instead to a resurrection of our true self and all that God planned for us.

HEBREWS 9:23–10:18

But now, once at the end of the ages, He has appeared to put away sin by the sacrifice of Himself (Heb 9:26).

Therefore, when He came into the world, He said: "Sacrifice and offering You did not desire, but a body You have prepared for Me. In burnt offerings and sacrifices for sin You had no pleasure. Then I said, 'Behold, I have come—in the volume of the book it is written of Me—to do Your will, O God'" (Heb 10:5-7).

Sacrifice is one of the overarching themes in the book of Hebrews. Even where sacrifice is not specifically mentioned, other themes such as the priesthood and the tabernacle are referenced, which, of course, were centered around and founded upon sacrificial rituals. Nevertheless, Hebrews 9–10 focus on the rite of sacrifice itself. The author of Hebrews does this in various ways.

First, in Hebrews 9:11-15, 21-22 we learn about the purification that was accomplished through blood. This is the form of spiritual sacrifice in which blood was used to cleanse or purify the temple precincts from the pollution of sin. A second sacrifice is mentioned in Hebrews 9:16-20. This sacrifice was for the enactment of a Last Will and Testament. This also was a form of spiritual sacrifice in which a sacrificial death symbolized the death of God so that His covenant with the people could go into effect. Both of these themes are then brought into Hebrews 9:23–10:18 to show how the sacrificial death of Jesus accomplished both of these things, but in a way that was perfect and permanent.

In many traditions, this passage is understood to be saying that God wanted and needed blood sacrifice all along, but the blood of bulls and goats was not enough to satisfy God. Instead, God needed the perfect sacrifice, which was the death of His only Son Jesus. Once Jesus was sacrificed, God's wrath against sin was satisfied once and for all, so that no more sacrifice was needed.

There are numerous problems with this way of reading the text. It not only makes God look like a bloodthirsty pagan deity who cannot love or forgive unless He receives payment in blood, it also portrays God as a petty and ignorant ruler who makes His subjects needlessly kill their animals for Him, even though He knows these sacrifices do nothing to actually appease His wrath. This way of reading the text also makes God appear foolish. After all, didn't He know that the blood of bulls and goats would accomplish nothing? Didn't He know that what He was really looking and waiting for was the sacrificial death of His own Son? Couldn't He look forward in time and see that the one truly effective sacrifice was coming? Since the answer to all these questions is "Yes," the instructions in the Mosaic Law about sacrificing bulls and goats makes God appear foolish. Or at least impatient. Was He so impatient that He simply could not wait for the blood of Jesus, and needed to get an appetizer of the blood of bulls and goats to hold Him over until He could feast on human blood, the blood of His own Son, Jesus? This depiction of God starts to make Him sound like a Vampire. Do we worship a Vampire God?

May it never be! Instead, these sorts of questions reveal that this way of understanding sacrificial language in Scripture must be wrong. God is not like any of these caricatures. He is wiser and more loving than we can ask or imagine. He is patient and kind beyond comparison. Therefore, since God could not have been asking for the blood of bulls and goats to simply hold Him over until He received the blood of Jesus, what then does the text mean?

The true point of the text is summarized in Hebrews 10:5-10. The truth is stated twice that God never wanted or desired sacrifices, nor did He take any pleasure in them. Instead, what God wanted was someone who would do His will. Jesus perfectly obeyed God's will, which made Jesus the perfect *living sacrifice.* Yet Jesus did die. He died a sacrificial death. Through His death, He shed His blood for the sins of all mankind. The Bible clearly reveals this truth, as does the book of Hebrews. But the question is *Why?* Why did Jesus die? Why did Jesus shed His blood? Why did the shed blood of Jesus accomplish what bulls and goats never could?

The author of Hebrews has the answer. Jesus did not die because God required or needed sacrifice. He died to take away and bring an end to sacrifice. Jesus did this by revealing through His own sacrifice at the hands of men that God does not want sacrifice; we do. People sacrifice to God, even though God didn't want such sacrifices. We sacrificed to God because we wanted sacrifice, and because sacrifice seemed to bring peace into our lives and communities. But when Jesus died and rose from the dead, He revealed that God does not want sacrifices, but instead wants people to live their lives in faithful obedience to Him, as He told Saul so long ago, "To obey is better than sacrifice" (1 Sam 15:22). Living in a relationship with God is what God has always wanted (cf. Heb 10:16). The sacrifices of the Mosaic Law were given as a substitute for relationship, but now that we have seen from Scripture and through Jesus that God never wanted or desired sacrifices, but only wanted us to live in a loving relationship with Him and each other, we can put away all sacrifices and live as God desires. Best of all, this is the only true way to find the peace we all seek. When we generously love and freely forgive as God has done for us, we then find peace with God and with one another.

SACRIFICES ARE NOT THE SOLUTION TO SIN

This book is searching for the solution to sin. We saw in Part II that the law is not the solution to sin, but actually only adds to the problem because we use the law to accuse and condemn others. This study on sacrifice has showed the same thing. Sacrifice is not the solution to sin, and never has been. Instead, sacrifices are part of the problem of sin, and are sometimes even sinful themselves. Since sin is the dehumanization of others so that we can accuse, condemn, and maybe even kill them in God's name, the law and the sacrificial system do not stop sin, but only aid us further in the practice of sin. Therefore, neither the law nor sacrifices are the solution to sin.

What then is the solution? What is the fix? What is the cure? It's Jesus, of course. But how does the sacrificial death of Jesus save us from our sin? Well, we have already begun to glimpse the truth of what Jesus accomplished on the cross and how His death delivers us from our sin, but Part IV of this book will present the truth even more clearly. Part IV looks at a special type of sacrifice, the scapegoat sacrifice, which lies at the foundation of all human society and civilization, and which is one of the primary truths revealed in the Bible. Once we see the truth of the scapegoat, we will better understand what Jesus revealed on the cross.

PART IV: SCAPEGOAT

The human problem of sin is a human problem of violence. And whereas many consider the law and the sacrificial system to be the cure for sin, Scripture reveals that law and sacrifice only add to the problem of sin and human violence. While law and sacrifice do provide some positive benefits for humanity in the absence of genuine relationships built on love, they are not what God wants or desires. So what does God want and desire? How is it that God reveals to us where we have gone wrong and how He wants us to live? The answer to both questions is "Jesus."

Almost all Christians know that Jesus provides a positive example for how to live. His life, ministry, and teachings are the source of endless encouragement and instruction for the type of life God wants for us. Yet at the same time, most Christians fail to understand that Jesus also provides a clear picture to humanity of where we have gone wrong. Jesus provides the clearest explanation ever provided in human history for the nature of sin, the problem of the law, and the truth about sacrifice. Jesus does this all by becoming a scapegoat sacrifice.

The following two chapters look at the scapegoat sacrifice, not only in how it is revealed and explained in Scripture, but also how this type of sacrifice forms the foundation for all human civilization and culture. Chapter 8 will define the scapegoat sacrifice and show how all humans are involved in this foundational and sinful human activity. Chapter 9 will then look at various passages from Scripture which clearly reveal the scapegoat sacrifice to us. Through these two chapters, we will discover what the scapegoat sacrifice is, how it forms the foundation to human civilization, and how Jesus revealed to us the shocking truth about the scapegoat sacrifice.

CHAPTER 8

DEFINING THE SCAPEGOAT

The New Testament never specifically refers to Jesus as a scapegoat sacrifice. As a result, some might think it is strange to study the concept of the scapegoat as a way to understand what Jesus accomplished on the cross for the sins of the whole world. However, once we understand what a scapegoat sacrifice is and what it accomplishes, we see that the death of Jesus upon the cross was clearly a scapegoat sacrifice.

Furthermore, when we understand that all scapegoat sacrifices are invisible to the ones who perform the sacrifice (this will be explained later), it becomes obvious why Jesus is never specifically referred to as a scapegoat. Jesus is not referred to as a scapegoat by the New Testament writers for the same reason that the author of Esther never mentions God. But just as God is everywhere in the story of Esther for people who have eyes to see and ears to hear, so also, the theme of Jesus as a scapegoat is everywhere in the New Testament for those who have eyes to see and ears to hear. And once the Spirit has opened our minds to see this truth in the New Testament, it is then that all of Scripture opens before us with a whole new light, and we also begin to see ourselves, culture, economics, politics, history, religion, relationships, and pretty much everything else in a whole new way as well. Yes, the truth of the scapegoat is *that* pervasive and *that* important. Let us begin to see this by defining the word *scapegoat.*

DEFINING SCAPEGOAT

The English word *scapegoat* is derived from the phrase "escape goat" which is a reference to the practice in Leviticus 16 of selecting two goats, one to be sacrificed and the other to "escape" into the wilderness as it carries the sins of the people into oblivion. In Leviticus 16, the term *scapegoat* is a translation of the Hebrew word *azazel.* There is some debate, however, about whether or not *scapegoat* is a good translation of this Hebrew word. Some believe that that the word *azazel* actually refers to a goat demon. Others claim the word simply refers to the wilderness or a deserted place, while a few argue that the word should simply be translated as "entire removal."

Of greater interest, however, is the fact that other cultures had similar rituals in which the sins of a community were symbolically placed upon some person or animal before being driven away and cast out from the rest of society. The Babylonian New Year festival, for example, included the activity of laying all the sins of the people upon a sheep and then casting this sheep into a river to carry the sins away.

So whether we are thinking of the scapegoat ritual of Israel or the "scapesheep" ritual of Babylon, the central function of this type of sacrifice is the same. In all cases, the sins of the people are symbolically laid upon the animal, which then carries the sins of the people away. This idea has great ramifications in connection with Jesus and how He took away the sins of the world. Yet to properly understand how Jesus did this, we must start at the beginning. We must understand where the scapegoat ritual came from and why it was practiced.

THE WAY OF THE SCAPEGOAT

You have likely heard someone in modern times speak or write about a "scapegoat." When you hear on the nightly news that the CEO of a company became a scapegoat, or when you read in the newspaper that a certain group of people are being scapegoated, what is it that is being said? The answer is that this person, or group of people, is being blamed for numerous problems in the company or culture, most of which they had nothing whatsoever to do with. This is what the image of the scapegoat represents. When you "scapegoat" someone, you are blaming them for all the problems in the company or culture, even though they are mostly innocent of the things for which they are blamed. A similar term or concept is when someone is "framed." To frame someone is to blame and accuse them for things which they are mostly innocent. Typically, when someone is framed, or scapegoated, both the scapegoat and the accusers are equally guilty for the same crime or problem, but one person or group is selected to bear the blame for all. When this happens, they become the scapegoat.

After a scapegoat is selected, they are "sent away" in some fashion. In ancient societies, the scapegoats were often sacrificed, or at the bare minimum, exiled into the wilderness or some far off country. In today's society, however, scapegoats usually get "cast out" from society so that they can no longer properly participate in the culture. They might get shunned, boycotted, imprisoned, or confined to the slums of inner cities. Of course, even today we find ways to kill our scapegoats. One popular method is to declare war upon them.

This practice of scapegoating has roots in the earliest ages of human history. In Scripture it begins as early as Genesis 3, but the practice can be found in all cultures and societies from all parts of the world throughout all of history. Due to the pervasiveness and universality of scapegoating, many scholars believe that it is this practice which is at the core of every culture and exists at the foundation of every civilization. The practice is so pervasive, some anthropologists, sociologists, and psychologists have given it a name, referring to this practice as the "the scapegoat mechanism." Some sociologists and psychologists have noted that there are five basic stages in the scapegoating process. They are Imitation, Desire, Rivalry, Violence, and finally, Scapegoating. Let us consider each.

Imitation

You have heard it said, "Monkey see; monkey do." This is because monkeys are imitative creatures. But monkeys are not the most imitative creatures on the planet; human beings are. Humans are imitative by nature. When we are born, the first thing we begin doing is watching, listening, and imitating. We learn how to speak languages, walk on two legs, and show emotions by imitating other people around us. As we age, we do not leave imitation behind, but only become more adept at observing and imitating others. It can be argued that nearly all of our tastes, desires, interests, goals, and values are gained through imitation. Cultural fads, popular foods, hit music, and common clothing styles all center upon the human tendency to imitate what we see.

So whether we recognize it consciously or not, nearly every interaction with every person throughout every day is full of imitation. In fact, recent scientific studies of the brain have shown humans have something called "mirror neurons" which fire when we observe someone else doing something. When we see a person mowing their lawn, mirror neurons fire in our brain *as if* we ourselves were doing the mowing. In other words, brain scans of a person mowing the lawn look identical to brain scans of a person who is watching someone else mow the lawn.

For the most part, imitation is good and healthy. After all, imitation teaches us to speak, walk, and behave. Yet imitation has a dark side too. If we imitate a bad example, then we learn bad behaviors and bad habits. But we can also imitate people in their selfishness, greed, anger, and violence. Very often, when two or more people are arguing or fighting with each other, it is due in part to each group imitating the other. But whether the object of our imitation is good or bad, imitation creates a second step toward scapegoating, which is desire.

Desire

Imitation leads to desire. Due to the power of imitation, we desire to own or do that which we see others owning or doing. Because of imitation, we desire what others desire. We see the things they have, or the things they want, and we want to have these things as well. Of course, when *they* see that we desire what they have, or even that we desire what they desire, *their* imitation kicks in, and they desire the object even more. We desire what they desire; so they desire what we desire, and our mutual desires feed off each other, increasing in power and potency as we each seek to gain for ourselves the object of our desire.

As with imitation, desire is mostly good, but can also become quite bad. Desire is good because it gives us common values, interests, goals, and cultural norms. Desire also helps sell products so that stores stay open and people have jobs. But desire becomes bad when we desire things that are off limits, that should not be desired, or which cannot be obtained. The Bible often refers to this as "coveting." Bad desire is when we desire our neighbor's wife, or we desire to become like God in a way that He has reserved for Himself (cf. Gen 3:6). The problems really begin when this bad form of desire takes root in two or more people who desire the same object. It is then that desire leads to rivalry.

Rivalry

When someone desires what they should not, or when two or more people desire the same object, rivalry is the result. The two people or groups who both desire the same object, and whose desire feeds off of and is amplified by seeing that others desire the same thing, enter into a competitive rivalry with each other. They simultaneously try to gain the object of desire for themselves while hindering their rival from obtaining it.

This rivalry is intensified when there is a limited supply of whatever object is desired, such as the last television on the shelf, the most beautiful woman in town, or the land which has a seaport. But even when there is unlimited supply of the object of desire, rivalry still occurs, for we decide in our minds that the *one* object which our rival desires is the best, even when there are others to choose from.

Consider an example. Imagine that I examine a pair of shoes at the shoe store and then put them down and walk away because I am not certain about whether or not I like them. Soon after, I see another customer examine that exact same pair of shoes. In my mind, having seen that this other person is looking at the shoes I previously examined, my desire for that particular pair of shoes is amplified, and I now enter into rivalry with that other customer. When he puts them down, I scurry over to grab them back and buy them. Even if there are other identical shoes in the store, I desired *that particular* pair, because I perceived in my mind that they were somehow better than the others. Maybe the stitches seemed straighter or one of the other pairs had a small nick or smudge on the side. So regardless of how many other identical shoes were in the store, I wanted *that* particular pair because I saw the other man looking at it.

But imagine if the other customer did not put down the shoes, and I had gone over and said, "Excuse me, I was just looking at those shoes and had only put them down for a second, but I did want to buy them." What would happen then? The rivalry would only increase, for now, the man would see my desire for these shoes, and this would cause desire to rise up in himself as well. If this rivalry continues to increase in intensity, it is possible that the rivalry over the shoes can lead to violence.

Violence

Not all rivalries lead to violence, but many do. This is especially true when we recognize that not all violence is physical violence. In the case of the shoes, the first forms of violence would likely come in the forms of verbal violence. Maybe the other customer would tell me I was a fool for putting the shoes down and walking away. If I wanted them, I should have held on to them. Now, having been called a fool, I might imitate him and return the insult, which will likely only escalate the violence further. Most arguments, family feuds, political and economic struggles, and even wars between countries begin as innocent rivalries that rapidly escalate as each person or group imitates the desire and violence of the other.

The great problem with violence is that it nearly always escalates. If I insult you, you slap me in return. So I shove you, but you punch me. I feel like I didn't deserve this, so I tackle you. You feel like you must defend yourself, so you stab me. Now I feel endangered, so I shoot you. But it doesn't end there. Your brother gets upset that I shot you, so he comes and shoots me and my wife. My family feels like you took your revenger too far, so they go and burn your brother's house to the ground with everyone in it. Eventually, the entire community is caught up in the contagion of violence until everybody is at war with everybody else. This cycle of retaliation and vengeance continues until the entire village is caught up in the violent contagion, and most of the town is destroyed and the people killed. This is how the cycle of violence nearly always happens, in both ancient and modern cultures.

Thankfully, modern societies often have police forces to help maintain the peace and stop these cycles of violence before they escalate out of control. But even today, if the cycle is allowed to continue long enough, or if the "peacekeepers" join one of the groups, the result will be a war which can destroy entire communities and countries. A perfect modern worldwide example of this is the events that led up to World War I, which in turn led to World War II. A political insult became an assassination which led to Word War I. Adolph Hitler was a soldier in World War I, and he felt that he and his country were so mistreated after World War I that the rest of the world must suffer. And suffer they did. The entire world suffered during these two World Wars, and is still suffering.

The tricky thing about the escalation of violence is that it sometimes occurs between family members. We humans typically don't mind violence too much, as long as it is directed at enemies or foes. But very often, the initial steps of imitation, desire, rivalry, and violence occur between family members or among people who love and need each other. When this happens, those who are in a rivalry with others look for a way out. They know where rivalry and escalating violence leads, and they do not want to destroy their marriage, their family, their neighborhood, or their business. So what are they to do? They cannot afford to allow the rivalry and escalating violence to continue, but at the same time, they cannot afford to surrender to their rival and abandon the object of their desire. The solution to this problem is the scapegoat.

The Scapegoat

When there are two or more groups of people who find themselves in a situation where violence is threatening to escalate out of the control, and neither group can afford to let the violence go any further, but nor is any group willing (or able) to back down, a scapegoat provides the way of escape. A scapegoat is a third party individual or group which gets blamed for the initial rivalry and the violence that resulted from it. The scapegoat is typically an outsider, someone who is different from the two initial rivals. They might be of a different race, religion, political persuasion, or economic class. They might be deformed in some way, or be a newcomer to the town or neighborhood.

Regardless of who becomes the scapegoat, the two groups of people who are in rivalry with each other subconsciously (or nonconciously) agree together to turn all their anger, malice, hatred, and violence upon this outside third party. It is almost magical or spiritual the way both groups simultaneously "realize" that their rivalry and violence only began when the outsider showed up. Through a series of conversations and what seems to be "inspired revelation from God," they recognize that their problem is not with one another. Instead, their problem comes from that other person. So the two groups who were formerly at odds with one another, now come together in unity to redirect their violence toward the outsider.

And even though this outsider usually has almost nothing whatsoever to do with the cause of the original rivalry and violence, they get blamed for all of it. This outsider is accused and condemned for creating the problem and causing the rift. As this "scapegoating mechanism" continues, the hatred and violence against this person continues to escalate. The two groups who were at odds but have now united together against the scapegoat realize that "something must be done" with this person who caused all the problems. So they begin to dehumanize this other person, and describe them in monstrous terms. They are called names. They are ridiculed, insulted, and mocked. Eventually, they become outcasts and rejects. Frequently, they are beaten, tortured, and killed.

The beauty of selecting and then casting out or killing the scapegoat is that it really works. Where there used to be only rivalry and violence, peace comes upon those who engage in this scapegoating process. This peace is seen as clear evidence that the scapegoat victim truly was the cause of the problem. But really, the problem was never actually solved, and given time, it will resurface and a scapegoat victim will be needed once again.

The tragedy of this scapegoat mechanism however, is that it requires the death or destruction of an innocent victim. Though they are never completely innocent of all wrong doing, they are mostly innocent of the wrongdoing for which they are accused. But regardless of their guilt or innocence, they are selected and cast out by society in the name of peace. They are despised, rejected, hated, beaten, and maybe even killed. Yet peace is restored, and the cycle of imitation, desire, rivalry, and violence is temporarily put to rest. Brothers and lovers and partners and allies can now live in peace once again because they have destroyed a scapegoat victim.

As you can see, it is the scapegoat that allows people to live in peace with each other. Without the scapegoat mechanism, peace could not exist and society could not function. When violence threatens to destroy a community or culture, the scapegoat sacrifice allows a way of escape from the escalating cycle of violence. Their death, even when people see it for what it is, almost seems like a "necessary sacrifice."

But is it necessary?

It turns out that while the scapegoat mechanism does create a temporary peace in human relationships and society, there is a better way to create peace. There is another way of escape from the cycle of violence that threatens humanity. While the scapegoat mechanism is the most common approach humans use to create peace, it is not the only way. Jesus reveals this other way to create peace, and in so doing, reveals that this "other way" has been God's way of peace all along. But to see what Jesus reveals about this way to peace, and how He reveals it, we must first understand a bit more about scapegoats. We must see how scapegoats are chosen, and how to recognize the scapegoat mechanism at work in our own lives and culture. Let us begin with the three types of people who make good scapegoats.

THREE TYPES OF SCAPEGOATS

The selection of the scapegoat is usually nonconscious (one step beneath our unconscious decisions). That is, people typically do not consciously think to themselves, "We need someone to blame, so let us look about for a scapegoat." There are usually no "scapegoat selection meetings" or votes cast for whom to blame. Instead, in times of crisis, people naturally and nonconsciously look about for someone to blame, and will quickly point the finger at almost anyone nearby as a target for scapegoating. Since humans do this so naturally, the scapegoat selection often seems to come from various sources and voices all at the same time, which only serves to affirm and support the selection of the scapegoat. Eventually, there is almost unanimous agreement by the crowd that the one person, or one group, is guilty of the sins for which they are charged. Yet even though almost anyone can become a scapegoat, they are most easily and most often selected from three types of people: the ones who are different, the ones at the top, and the ones at the bottom.

The most popular type of scapegoat is the outsider, the one who is different from everybody else. They might be of another race, gender, religion, political persuasion, or socio-economic class. They might be a foreigner. Maybe they do not speak the language of the populace. They might be sick or deformed in some way, or simply look and act different than everyone else. Humans are inherently suspicious of people who are "different," and so they often get selected as a scapegoat for society's ills. The next two types of scapegoats are really just subsets of the first type, but they are popular enough that they deserve their own discussion.

The second type of scapegoat comes from among those at the top. They are different from everyone else because they are in charge. They are the kings, rulers, and presidents. They make good scapegoats because they are easy to blame. When things go wrong in a community, country, or company, people look for heads to roll, and usually the one in charge is the easiest one to blame. When a company fails or a country collapses, sometimes the leaders are blamed. Though there are a myriad of reasons for why a company might fail or a country might collapse, and often the failure was decades in the making and was brought about by numerous decisions and events from previous leaders, the leader who is in charge when the fail occurs often gets the blame. They become the scapegoat.

The third type of scapegoat is found among those at the bottom. They are different from everyone else because they are viewed as being the dredges of society. The poor, the sick, and the weak make good scapegoats because they are voiceless and powerless to defend themselves. It is easy for the rich and powerful to blame the weak and poor because they cannot usually rise up in self-defense and rarely have the resources or education to explain why they should not be blamed for what has gone wrong.

So these are the three main types of scapegoats, but really, they are all just "different" from everyone else. Of course, a scapegoat victim can come from almost anywhere. And if they are not different from everyone else, the scapegoating process makes sure that they become different, that they become less than human. But this is one of the three signs of scapegoating, which are also important to understand.

THREE SIGNS OF SCAPEGOATING

Since scapegoating is so prominent throughout culture and history, it is important to understand when scapegoats are being made. There are three major signs of scapegoating. First, scapegoats are always dehumanized. Humans typically do not want to kill other human beings, or drive others out of society, yet such things must be done to the scapegoat. So to justify the unfair and unjust treatment of the scapegoat, people always try to turn the scapegoat into a monster. They do this through a variety of means, which include name-calling, slander, and fabricated or embellished stories about the evils of the scapegoat.

This practice of turning a human into a monster provides the very best indication of scapegoating. Whenever a person or group is demonized and dehumanized, this is a clear indication that scapegoating is occurring. The end result of scapegoating is that we kill or exile another human being, but before we can do such things, we must turn them into a monster. We do this by blaming them of horrible sins, of accusing them of monstrous deeds, and by telling stories or passing lies about what this person does in secret. Today, we might dehumanize a scapegoat by calling them animalistic names such as "monster, dog, pig, bitch, or predator," or by labelling them with derogatory titles such as "racist, bigot, sexist, thug, xenophobe, or homophobe." All such labeling and name-calling is a popular form of accusatory scapegoating.

When we successfully dehumanize our scapegoat, we become so convinced that they truly are guilty of everything for which they are accused, we do not even realize we *are* scapegoating. This is the second tell-tale sign of scapegoating. Most scapegoats are "invisible." That is, when we scapegoat someone, we rarely realize that we are scapegoating them. What this means is that the more convinced you become that a person truly is a monster, the more likely it is that you are scapegoating them. As long as you can see good in somebody and redemptive qualities in their character and behavior, the scapegoating tendency is held at bay. But once you view someone as completely depraved, beyond redemption, having no ability to do or say anything good, you can then be sure that you have turned them into a scapegoat.

This does not mean that scapegoats are innocent. While the scapegoat may not be guilty of *everything* for which they are charged, the scapegoats are also usually guilty of *some* of the things. But this just adds to our certainty about the scapegoat. The best scapegoats are guilty scapegoats. There are almost always a few sins for which the scapegoat truly is guilty. People point to these obvious faults as clear evidence that the scapegoat must also be guilty of all the other faults which are not so clear. The glaring character flaws convince and persuade us that "the stories must be true." Once these obvious sins and failures are pointed out to the mob, it becomes easy to then blame the scapegoat for the numerous sins and failures for which they are innocent. The few clear failures are extrapolated out into numerous faults until the scapegoat becomes a sinner of monstrous proportions and people do not realize they are turning a person into a scapegoat. The scapegoat itself becomes invisible, and we think we are just speaking the truth, calling out evil where it is found, and crying for the expulsion of the monster from our midst.

This leads to the third sign of scapegoating. After we dehumanize or demonize a person until they become so monstrous we do not even realize we created a scapegoat out of them, we make one final move which allows us to kill or expel the scapegoat. This final move is that we get God involved. Almost always, as the mob pronounces its judgment upon the scapegoat and condemns them as a monster and consigns them to exile or death, the name of God is called upon to justify and reinforce the decision and actions of the victimizing crowd. They say that it is "God's will" for them to kill this wicked, evil enemy. They say things like, "God has revealed to us the truth about this evil monster! God has shown us that this person is the cause of all our problems! God has brought judgment down upon us because of this vile sinner! God wants us to expel and kill them so that there can be obedience in our midst and peace in our nation once again!" And so they slay or destroy the scapegoat victim with God's name on their lips.

The fact that scapegoating "works" to create peace only reinforces in the people's mind that the death or expulsion of the scapegoat victim truly was the will of God. The fact that former enemies are now able to walk arm in arm off into the sunset singing "God Bless America" is viewed as clear evidence that God helped them successfully select and kill the true "enemy of God" who caused all the problems in the first place. This nearly miraculous peace between former enemies is seen as clear proof that God truly did reveal the source of the problem. This peace proves that the scapegoat was truly guilty of the sins for which they were accused. When peace comes upon a people after they successfully kill or expel a scapegoat victim, the peace is viewed as a blessing from God for obeying His will.

But note something quite shocking about this final sign of scapegoating. Although humans believe that God revealed the truth about the scapegoat victim to them, and that it was God's will for humans to kill or expel the scapegoat, we have also seen that God is not actually behind such killings. The people only use God's name to justify their own treatment of the scapegoat victim. "It was God's will" is a convenient excuse that people use to blame God for their own terrible treatment of others. In this way, God gets accused of the most terrible crimes against humanity.

Do you see what this means? It means that God Himself has become our scapegoat. Scapegoating others in the name of God leads us to make a scapegoat out of God Himself!

SCAPEGOATING GOD

When we set out to kill others "for the sake of peace," we do it in God's name. We kill because "it is God's will." But it is not. We blame God for our own violence because this makes violence against others easier to commit. So God is blamed for the violence that is in the heart of mankind. Religion needs a violent God, because we can then blame our own violence on the God we serve. But what we are seeing is that the violence of God is nothing more than the violence of humans projected upon God. The violence of God is the result of blaming God for our own violence.

Whenever humans blame an outside third party for things which that other party is innocent, this is the scapegoat mechanism at work. And since God is often blamed for that which He did not command or do, God has been the most scapegoated person in all of human history. When two warring parties say that their cause is just, righteous, and divinely ordained, they are scapegoating God. When these two warring parties create peace by selecting, accusing, and killing a scapegoat victim and then say that it is God who revealed the guilt of this person to them, and that it is God who wants this person killed, the two warring parties have actually created two scapegoat victims: the human and the divine. This then allows the two warring parties to unite together in peace with each other while they violently kill and murder another human being, all the while believing that they do so in obedience to God.

As we can now see, all the signs point to the fact that God has become the ultimate human scapegoat. God fits all three types of scapegoat victims. God is, of course, far "different" from human beings. And since He is God, He is at the very top. Then, in Jesus, God also took on a role at the bottom, revealing that He has always been a servant to humanity.

The three signs of scapegoating are also evident. Throughout history and even in the teachings of many religions (Christianity included) God gets blamed for a wide number of horrendous activities. Who has been blamed for more crimes than God? Who else but God gets blamed for all death and disease, sickness and storms, or famine and warfare? If people are to be believed, God is the greatest mass murderer in existence. If it is God's will, as some say, for women to be raped, children to be molested, and wars to be fought, then God is the greatest monster in the universe. But since people typically do not want to worship a monster, they make the monstrous side of God "invisible" by saying that we humans just don't understand the "greater good" of God's will. With our limited human perspective, we must trust that God is good even when He allows children to be raped dozens of times a day. In this way, God is demonized, then made invisible, and the name of God is invoked as justification for the acts of God. After all, God is God and He can do what He wants, right?

This practice of scapegoating God also occurs when the violence is perceived to have come from God Himself. Though human violence is often blamed on God, there are many types of violence in the world that do not seem to have any direct connection with human action, and therefore, these types of violence are also blamed on God. These non-human types of violence include things like storms, famines, diseases, floods, earthquakes, and hurricanes. People (both ancient and modern) tend to believe that such things are sent by God. Even modern secular insurance companies refer to these sorts of events as "acts of God."

Typically, when these "acts of God" occur, people assume that God does not randomly send such tragedies upon people, and therefore, such events must be some sort of divine punishment. So when the storms come, the floodwaters rise, the food gets scarce, or the children get sick, people assume that God is angry and they start looking around for someone to blame. And once again, the scapegoat mechanism comes into play. This time, however, the scapegoat mechanism is not used to create peace between two warring groups of people, but instead between humans and God. The violence of nature is viewed as violence from God, and if God is angry at humans then it must be because someone sinned, and so the way to appease God is to find the sinful person or people group and destroy them. These guilty people have angered God, and so the way to stop God's anger is to kill the people who angered Him.

Of course, after the people are killed, one of two things happens. Either the natural disaster continues, or it ends. If the disease or disaster continues, then the people assume that while they killed some of the guilty people, there are still more who need to be cleansed from society, and so the search for sinners goes on. This "cleansing" process continues until the disease or disaster finally ends, as they always do. The people see the conclusion of the disease or disaster as a sign that God is now appeased and that the sin has been properly cleansed from the community.

Many people today (though not all!) realize, however, that diseases and disasters have nothing whatsoever to do with God punishing people for sin, but are instead simply the natural events that occur in a chaotic world. Therefore, the conclusion of these disasters also has nothing whatsoever to do with appeasing an angry deity through sacrifice. When bad things happen in this world, God is not punishing people for sin, and to blame Him for doing so is simply to make a scapegoat out of God.

Certainly, there are Scriptures which can be used to support the idea that God is behind floods and disasters and famines, and these texts are used by people today who still want to teach that God punished people for their sin, but more and more people are waking up to the fact that Jesus perfectly reveals God to us, and Jesus never punishes people for their sin, but instead only loves, forgives, heals, and rescues. Therefore, those passages from Scripture which portray God as a vindictive divine being who sends storms and sickness is not actually revealing God Himself, but instead reveal the mentality of mankind who likes to blame God for the bad things that happen in this life. The Scriptures which reveal a violent God are still revelatory and inspired, but they do not reveal the true actions and heart of a God who punishes sinful and rebellious humanity. Instead, they reveal the actions and heart of a humanity who scapegoats and blames a loving and gracious God. We have made a scapegoat of God, and we use texts from Scripture which also scapegoat God to support our view that God is guilty of the crimes for which we accuse Him, when in reality, it is we who commit these crimes and do them in His name.

The reason we know that we have made a scapegoat out of God, and that He has not ever been involved in the crimes we attribute to His name is because of what we see revealed in Jesus Christ. There are three ways that Jesus reveals the truth about scapegoating, and in all three ways we also learn the truth about God's involvement with scapegoating and how we scapegoated God to justify our scapegoating of others.

THREE WAYS JESUS REVEALS SCAPEGOATING

The entire life of Jesus (including the entire Bible) is a revelation about scapegoating, and how God wants this practice to cease. We see this in three main ways.

First, Jesus revealed the truth about scapegoating by never scapegoating anyone. Although scapegoating is a universal practice, Jesus stood out starkly from the mass of humanity by refusing to participate in the scapegoating of others. Jesus never dehumanized anyone, never demonized, and never called on God to justify violence against others. Instead, Jesus always did the opposite of scapegoating. This leads to the second way Jesus revealed scapegoating.

Beyond just refusing to participate in scapegoating, Jesus actually went out of His way to befriend and identify Himself with the scapegoats in that day. Jews often scapegoated Gentiles, especially the Roman military, yet there are numerous instances in the Gospel accounts where Jesus healed, blessed, and spoke positively of Roman military officials or their families. The rich tax-collectors were also popular scapegoats, and Jesus repeatedly befriended and offered forgiveness to them. Similarly, Jesus frequently hung out with those on the bottom of society, the "sinners" and prostitutes. Then there were the lepers. These were the ones scorned, despised, and judged by everyone. It was even believed that lepers were under the judgment of God. Lepers were exiled from society and sent off into wilderness areas to die. But Jesus often went out of His way to welcome, touch, and heal those stricken with leprosy. Beyond this, Jesus healed the blind, the deformed, and a woman with issues of blood, all of whom would have been viewed as potential scapegoats for society. In every case, Jesus partnered with them, identified Himself as one of them, and revealed that God had accepted them into His family.

This practice of Jesus partnering with the outcasts and scapegoats of society could only lead to one thing: the scapegoating of Jesus Himself. Society nearly always scapegoats and kills those who stand up for other scapegoats. Why? Because society needs scapegoats to maintain the peace of society. Without scapegoats, society is left defenseless against the ravages of escalating violence (forgiveness is not viewed as a realistic option). So when Jesus went against the grain of society by refusing to scapegoat and by identifying with the scapegoats, Jesus Himself became a prime target for scapegoating. Becoming a scapegoat is the main way in which Jesus reveals the truth about scapegoating.

When Jesus was killed, He was accused of crimes He did not commit. He was accused of blasphemy and threatening to tear down the temple. They turned Jesus into a monster. They beat and tortured Jesus until He was unrecognizable. Then they crucified Him as a common criminal. And they did all this in obedience to the laws and commands of God. Jesus was crucified in the name of God. But was God the cause of the crucifixion of Jesus? No. Quite to the contrary, God raised Jesus from the dead, thereby vindicating Jesus and proving that the death of Jesus was not His will. God wanted Jesus alive, just as God also wants humans alive. God does not want death, but life. He is not a God of the dead, but of the living.

JESUS, THE LAMB OF GOD

The most surprising thing about Jesus being presented as a scapegoat victim in the Gospels is that He is never referred to as such. Jesus is never actually referred to as a scapegoat anywhere in Scripture. There are numerous reasons for this. One reason, for example, is that scapegoats are invisible to the ones doing the scapegoating. Jesus does not get called a scapegoat because scapegoats are never recognized for what they are. As mentioned earlier in this chapter, the revelation in Jesus about scapegoating is only for those who have eyes to see and ears to hear.

The main reason, however, that Jesus is never referred to as a scapegoat in the New Testament is that scapegoats are usually guilty of *some* of the things for which they are accused. Remember, the best scapegoat is a guilty scapegoat. But unlike every other scapegoat in history, Jesus was innocent of all wrongdoing. There was no sin found in Him, nor was He guilty of any crime. But does this then mean that Jesus wasn't a *true* scapegoat? No. It means the opposite. Because He was innocent of all wrongdoing, He alone is the perfect revelation about the truth of scapegoating. Let me explain how this is so.

While scapegoating themes are found on nearly every page of the Gospel accounts, it is in the events surrounding the arrest, trial, crucifixion, and death of Jesus that we find the most concentrated revelation of scapegoating in all of literature. Yet the Gospels do something which almost no other literature in history does: they portray the scapegoat as completely innocent of any wrongdoing. Most scapegoating literature sides with the scapegoating mob, keeping the scapegoat invisible, and cloaking the innocence of the scapegoat in robes of blame, accusation, and monstrous descriptions. But Jesus in the Gospels is shown to have done nothing wrong. He is fully innocent of everything for which He was accused.

So rather than refer to Jesus as a scapegoat, the New Testament refers to Him as the Lamb of God. Jesus still performs the function of the scapegoat, carrying away the sins of the world (John 1:29), but He does this without any personal guilt of His own. "The Lamb of God" is another name for the scapegoat, but with an emphasis on innocence. The term "scapegoat" has a negative connotation which implies that even if the scapegoat victim might not have been guilty of all the crimes for which they were condemned, they were still nonetheless guilty of some sort of the crime, which means their condemnation and killing are justified. But to speak of Jesus as the Lamb of God, is to speak of Him as being completely innocent of all wrongdoing. We killed Him as a scapegoat, but there is no way we can pin any wrongdoing upon Him, which means that our murder of Jesus was completely unjustified and wrong.

In this way, Jesus reveals the truth about scapegoating. Jesus reveals what no other scapegoat in history can reveal. While no other scapegoat in history was innocent like Jesus, the absolute innocence of the scapegoat Jesus proves that all other scapegoats throughout history are also innocent of most of the crimes for which they are accused. The perfect innocence of Jesus reveals the relative innocence of all other scapegoats. Although the best scapegoat is a guilty scapegoat, Jesus was not guilty of anything, and yet He was still scapegoated. In this way, by scapegoating a completely innocent victim, the lie of scapegoating is revealed for all to see.

In the process of allowing Himself to be scapegoated so that He could reveal the scapegoat mechanism, Jesus also revealed something else. When we killed Jesus, we killed Him in God's name, as we usually do with scapegoats. We justified our killing of Jesus by saying that it was God's will that He be killed. Surprisingly, many Christians today continue to say the very same thing. Most atonement theories argue that it was God's will for Jesus to suffer and die (See my book *The Atonement of God* for more on this topic). But through the death and resurrection of Jesus, we learn that it was not God's will, but man's will, for Jesus to die. Jesus died, not because God needed a sacrifice, but because mankind did.

Once again, since Jesus perfectly reveals God to us, and since Jesus was perfectly innocent of all the crimes for which He was accused, we can know, therefore, that God also is perfectly innocent of all the crimes against humanity for which He is accused. Just as Jesus was innocent of all wrongdoing, so also is God. Jesus always loved and only forgave, and the same is true of God. Jesus never killed anyone, nor did He command anyone to do so. The same is true of God. One of the greatest revelations we received from Jesus is the revelation of scapegoating, and not just how we scapegoat others, but also how we have scapegoated God. This idea alone will allow you to read your Bible with brand new eyes. When the Bible is read with the revelation about scapegoating that we have in Jesus Christ, we see that all the violence and bloodshed attributed to God in the Old Testament is nothing more than people making a scapegoat out of God. So ultimately, Jesus reveals three truths about the scapegoat, all of which relate to the three previous truths we have seen so far in this book.

THREE REVELATIONS ABOUT THE SCAPEGOAT

This book began by looking at sin. Sin was defined as the process by which we dehumanize others so that we can kill them in God's name. This is exactly what happened to Jesus when He became a scapegoat victim. But although Jesus was dehumanized, accused, condemned, and crucified, He was innocent of all wrongdoing. Even though most scapegoats are guilty of *some of the things* for which they are accused, Jesus was completely innocent. In this way, Jesus revealed that other scapegoats are mostly innocent as well. If we can accuse a completely innocent man of horrible sin, then we can also accuse relatively innocent people. Though the best scapegoat is a guilty scapegoat, the perfect innocence of Jesus reveals that scapegoats are typically not guilty of *everything* for which they are accused. This is why the Bible never ends up speaking about Jesus as our scapegoat. Though Jesus did serve in the function of a scapegoat, He is not called a scapegoat because He could not justifiably be accused of any wrongdoing. Jesus was a scapegoat, but He was an innocent scapegoat. So through our great sin of dehumanizing, condemning, and killing Jesus, it was revealed to us that this is the sin we all commit when we dehumanize and condemn others, or call for their deaths in God's name. The sins for which we kill the scapegoat are the sins for which we ourselves are guilty.

By becoming a scapegoat victim, Jesus revealed that all the accusations thrown at the scapegoat do not actually indicate crimes of the scapegoat themselves, but instead reveal the crimes of those doing the scapegoating. Scapegoats are a mirror into our own lives, culture, and society. We do not like what we see in our hearts, or in our society and culture, and since we find it so difficult to own up to such things, we lay the blame for them on someone else. We lay the guilt for our own actions on the scapegoat, saying that the only reason we did these horrible deeds is because that evil, monstrous villain tricked and deceived us. We say that it is the scapegoat's fault for why we behave like animals. Therefore, because the scapegoat led us into such sin, they must die. When we kill them, we feel like we have destroyed the evil that was in our midst, even though the sad reality is that we have done nothing whatsoever about it. We kill the scapegoat to drive out the sin that is in our own hearts, but the sin that is in our hearts is only strengthened and amplified through the blaming and killing of the scapegoat. This is the first truth Jesus reveals about scapegoating.

The second truth is that we use the law of God to do the exact opposite of the reasons for which the law was provided. Due to a lack of love, the law was given as a tutor, to show us what love looked like and how love acted, until the time when we could love God and love others without the law. But instead, we used the law to further our own sin. We used the law to justify our sinful behaviors of dehumanizing, condemning, and killing others. We used the law to make scapegoats. This truth was perfectly revealed through the life, ministry, and crucifixion of Jesus when the law was quoted and cited as evidence against Him.

People often say today that the proper use of the law is to reveal our own sin to us. In some circles, this is referred to as "using the law lawfully." But the truth revealed in Jesus is that the law does not reveal our sin to us; instead, it allows us to sin in ways we cannot see. If we really want to see our sin, we should not look to the law, but to how we use the law to condemn and accuse others. It is there, in the scapegoating victimization process, that our sin is held before our eyes if we have the courage to see it. This second deep truth that Jesus reveals about scapegoating is that when we use the law to condemn and kill others, our very use of the law proves that the problem is not in others, but in ourselves. Jesus reveals that the scapegoat is nothing more than a reflection of our own hearts and the sins in our own society, and how we are misusing and abusing the law to accomplish the exact opposite of what was intended by the law.

This leads to the third and final truth Jesus reveals about scapegoating, which is a truth about sacrifice. Just as killing an animal sacrifice brings a temporary peace to humans, so also, condemning and then casting out or killing a scapegoat victim bring a sense of peace. Yet this peace is a lie. This peace tricks us into thinking that the problem was dealt with and that God is pleased by our actions. But the opposite is actually true. The sacrificial slaying of our foes causes us to feel that we have done something about the sin in our midst, but really, it only serves to hide our sin from us. Sacrificial killing and scapegoating are nothing more than a form of sin that hides the true nature of our sin. Scapegoating is a sin that casts out sin, thereby only strengthening sin. By becoming a sacrificial scapegoat victim, Jesus revealed this truth to us. He literally *became sin*, that is, became a scapegoat victim, so that we could see in Him the shocking and horrifying truth about all scapegoat victims. What is this truth? It is the truth that such sacrificial victims are not pleasing to God. They are pleasing to us, and we are the violent ones who kill others in God's name. We have made scapegoat victims out of innocent people, and we have made a scapegoat victim out of God. And God wants all of it to cease. This is what we see when we turn to look at some Scriptures about scapegoating in the next chapter.

CHAPTER 9

SCRIPTURES ON THE SCAPEGOAT

Almost every passage in the Bible teaches the truth about scapegoating in one fashion or another. The biblical revelation about scapegoating may be one of the central revelations in Scripture. But this is not surprising, for scapegoating is a foundational human activity upon which all society is founded and all culture functions. Since God wants to call us away from killing innocent victims in the name of God, it is completely normal for the Word of God to primarily serve as a revelation about scapegoating.

In fact, this revelation about scapegoating is one of the things that sets the Bible apart from all other religious texts. The biblical revelation about scapegoating makes it unique among the "Holy Texts" of world religions, and is also one of the reasons we can trust that the Bible is divine revelation. As we saw in the previous chapter, the truth about scapegoating is a truth that most humans are blind to. A true scapegoat is typically invisible to the ones doing the scapegoating. Therefore, only divine inspiration can reveal the truth of scapegoating to us. Only God, in light of Scripture, through the crucivision lens of Jesus, and by the illuminating and convicting work of the Holy Spirit, can reveal where and how we scapegoat others. And since the Bible reveals the truth about scapegoating like no other religious text, this shows that the Bible is uniquely inspired. Yes, all other religious texts contain the truths and ideas of scapegoating, but no other religious book exposes scapegoating for what it truly is. Outside of the Bible, no other religious text so clearly reveals and explains the scapegoating mechanism as the sacrificial killing of an innocent victim for the sake of temporary peace.

But this chapter is not about proofs for the inspiration and authority of

Scripture. Instead, this chapter will look at several of the key passages from Scripture which reveal the truth about scapegoating. Due to the pervasiveness of scapegoating themes in the Bible, it was difficult to select only a few texts to examine, but the following passages are representative of what the Bible teaches on almost every page. We begin with Genesis 3.

GENESIS 3:12

Then the man said, "The woman whom You gave to be with me, she gave me of the tree, and I ate."

The first step toward scapegoating involves dehumanizing and demonizing the potential scapegoat victim. The best way to do this is to accuse and condemn them. And typically, the crimes we condemn and accuse scapegoats of committing are actually the things for which we ourselves are guilty. Rather than own up to our own faults, we tend to point the finger at others. One of the first places this is seen in the Bible is in Genesis 3, immediately after Adam and Eve eat from the Tree of the Knowledge of Good and Evil. After God finds the first couple hiding in the Garden, He asks Adam why he ate from the forbidden tree, and Adam blames Eve for giving the fruit to him (Gen 3:12). In this way, Eve becomes the first scapegoat, revealing the historical truth that women often become the scapegoats for the faults of men. Those who are physically stronger often select those who are physically weaker to be the scapegoat. Women, children, the poor, the sick, and the deformed are often scapegoated by the strong, the rich, and the powerful.

There are some today, of course, who say that Adam was justified in blaming Eve, for she is the one, after all, who gave the fruit to Adam. But such a mindset only shows the power of the scapegoating mentality in the human psyche. A careful reading of the text shows that Adam is completely to blame for this event. He did not properly pass on God's instructions to his wife. He introduced his wife to the temptation of the tree by bringing her to it. He stood idly by without saying a word while the serpent deceived her. He did nothing to stop her when she ate the fruit from the tree. Yet despite all the failures on the part of Adam, he puts the blame on Eve, and many Bible teachers have been doing the same thing ever since (I cover this in more detail in my One Verse Podcast). The first scapegoat in the Bible is Eve, and the first scapegoat in the Bible is still invisible to most people today.

Yet there is another invisible scapegoat in Genesis 3. Eve is not the only scapegoat in the text. After Adam points the finger at Eve, he then points the finger at God. Adam says, "the woman, *whom you gave to be with me* …" (Gen 3:12). Though Adam first blames Eve, Adam implies that the real guilt lies with God, for God is the one who gave the woman to him. Adam's attempt to blame God mirrors the truth we saw in the previous chapter. Although women, children, the poor, the sick, and the deformed are often selected as scapegoats, God is the most scapegoated person in history. Throughout Scripture and human history, God gets blamed for most wars, sicknesses, diseases, and death. When famine and storms fall upon us, we say that God sent them. When we march off to slay our enemies, we do so with God's name on our lips. One of the clearest signs that scapegoating is occurring is when we bring God into it and say that our blame, accusation, condemnation, and killing of others is all according to the will of God. To blame God for the evil we ourselves commit against others is the most prominent form of scapegoating in the Bible (and in human history) and we see it occur right here in Genesis 3.

GENESIS 4

Then the Lord said to Cain, "Where is Abel your brother?" He said, "I do not know. Am I my brother's keeper?" (Gen 4:9).

This human attempt to blame others for our own mistakes is seen again in Genesis 4 when Cain attempts to rescue his family by giving God an offering of fruit (see Part III on Sacrifice). When his offering of fruit is not accepted by God, Cain blames and murders his brother, Abel (Gen 4:3-15). Cain is upset that God did not accept his offering of fruit, and believes that this entire situation could have been avoided if God had just acted the way Cain expected him to (cf. Gen 4:5). So just as Adam blamed Eve, Cain blamed Abel for the sibling rivalry that ensued.

But also, just like his father, Cain does not stop with blaming Abel. He also blames God. Cain implies that it is God's fault for not doing a better job protecting Abel. When he asks, "Am I my brother's keeper?" (Gen 4:9), Cain is essentially pointing the finger at God, saying, "Don't ask me where my brother is. Don't you know? I am not my brother's keeper; You are!" So once again, Cain blames his brother, but also implies that the blame ultimately rests with God.

Immediately after the murder of Abel, the scapegoating continues with Lamech, who murders a young man and then blames him by essentially saying, "He had it coming; it was his fault" (Gen 4:23-24). And once again, Lamech brings God into it. He tells his wives that if God put a sevenfold protection around Cain against vengeance, then God would put a seventy-sevenfold protection around Lamech, for Lamech was more justified in killing the young man than Cain was in killing Abel. So again, everyone justifies their own violence by blaming others for it, as well as blaming God in the process.

GENESIS 6–8

So the Lord said, "I will destroy man whom I have created from the face of the earth, both man and beast, creeping thing and birds of the air, for I am sorry that I have made them" (Gen 6:7).

And God said to Noah, "The end of all flesh has come before Me, for the earth is filled with violence through them; and behold, I will destroy them with the earth" (Gen 6:13).

The opening verses of Genesis 6 must be read in light of what was seen in Genesis 4. The murders by Cain and Lamech reveal that violence always and only lead to more and greater violence. One act of violence leads to an ever-increasing cycle of revenge and retaliation. God warned about the sevenfold retaliation which would come upon anyone who murdered Cain (This was not a threat by God, by the way, but a warning statement about the consequences of revenge). But when Lamech killed a man, he said that anyone who tried to kill him should get seventy-sevenfold retaliation. You can see that the cycle of violence and vengeance rapidly spins out of control.

So it is no surprise when Genesis 6 describes the earth as being filled with violence (Gen 6:5, 11, 13). The opening scene for the flood account is that sin and violence have become an all-consuming contagion upon the earth which threatened to destroy all who lived upon it. Sin and violence have had their way, and they have covered the whole earth.

What is most curious about the flood account is that it is here, for the first time in Scripture, that God appears violent. Throughout the opening chapters of Genesis, God is portrayed as consistently non-violent. Violence was starkly absent from the creation stories of Genesis 1–2, even though both stories drew numerous themes and elements from other common—and violent!—creation stories of that day. In Genesis 3, when humans disobey and rebel against God, God does not lash out in anger, but instead shows up for His daily walk with Adam and Eve, and then kindly creates comfortable clothes for them before sending them away from the Garden. In Genesis 4, after Cain kills Abel, God's only response is to try to protect Cain from getting murdered himself. And while death comes upon almost everyone in Genesis 5, God is never said to be the agent of this death. The only time God took anyone in Genesis 5 was when He took Enoch to save him from death (Gen 5:24).

So in Genesis 6, when the text records God's declaration that He will send a flood to destroy every living thing upon the earth, our first response should be shock and confusion. This is quite out of character for everything we have learned about God up to this point. And even if God decided it was necessary to destroy all humans, why does He also decide to destroy all the birds and animals? Doesn't this seem like overkill? Stranger still, after declaring that He is disappointed with humanity because of the sin and violence that covers the whole earth, God sets out to engage in even greater violence by drowning every living person and animal upon the earth. So in response to the all the violence, Genesis 6–8 portrays God as the most violent one. Yet if violence was such a problem for God, why did God then turn around and engage in the greatest act of violence possible? How are we to read this? Is worldwide genocide okay if it is performed by God? Such an idea seems contrary to everything Genesis has revealed about God up to this point.

The solution is multi-faceted, and depends in large part on what has already been revealed about God in Genesis 1–4. There are four basic truths about God that Genesis has revealed so far. First, God does not send storms, but calms them and rescues people from them (Gen 1:2, 6). One strange thing about the flood account is that when the flood waters do in fact come upon the earth, God is never specifically stated as the one who sends them (Gen 7:10-12, 17-20). The only specifically stated activities of God was when He shut the doors of the ark (Gen 7:16), and sent the wind to blow back the waters (Gen 8:1).

The second truth about God which has been revealed in Genesis 1–4 is actually about humans. We humans tend to blame God for the bad things that happen in life, and for the bad things that we ourselves do (Gen 3:12, 4:9). This is also true for natural disasters like floods, famines, storms, and disease. When we blame God for causing natural disasters, we almost always use terminology and language that is identical to what we read in Genesis 6.

The third truth is that just as God worked to deliver Adam, Eve, and Cain from the pain they had brought upon themselves (Gen 3:24; 4:15), God spent decades warning the people through Noah about what was coming and trying to save as many as He could (Gen 5:32; 6:3, 14; 7:6).

The fourth truth revealed about God in Genesis 1–4 is also critical for helping us understand the flood account. This fourth truth is that humans are the evil and violent ones, while God is not. And strangely enough, one of the final verses of the flood account states that humanity was just as evil and violent as they were before (Gen 6:5; 8:21). Isn't that shocking? Genesis 8:21 is a surprise ending to the flood story. It subverts and turns upside down the traditional reading of the flood account. The fact that the condition of humanity did not change one bit as a result of the flood means that if God sent the flood to stop the violence and evil of mankind, then His own violence against humanity was a complete and utter failure.

But was God so foolish as to not know that His violence against humanity would fail to reform and rectify our violent behavior? Of course not! We cannot accept that an omniscient God would be that foolish and shortsighted. So instead, we must admit that Genesis 8:21 was written to help the reader see a truth about violence that few people ever recognize. The truth about violence which Genesis 6–8 reveals is that violence solves nothing. The truth about violence is that violence always and only leads to more violence.

But did God really kill everyone just to make this point? No! We see this by noting an even greater truth revealed in the flood account of Genesis 6–8. Unless we are ready to say that God is a violent mass murderer who drowns all men, women, children, and animals (except for those on the ark) just to prove that violence never solves anything, we must step back and reconsider the flood account from another perspective. What perspective is that? It is the perspective revealed through Noah's sacrifice in Genesis 8:20-21.

We looked at these two verses previously in Part III on Sacrifice, but they are critical for not only understanding sacrifice, but also for understanding what happened in the flood. The fact that Genesis 8:21 describes the sinful and violent condition of humanity as being identical to the way it was before the flood raises a big, red flag over the entire text. This big, red flag screams at us, saying, "Look at me! Look at me! Do you want to know what you just read? Let me show you!" Then Genesis 8:21 goes on to describe the sacrifice that Noah offered to God, even though God never commanded or instructed Noah to do such a thing. Yet Noah is convinced that God did in fact command him to kill animals. Noah kills animals to create peace in his own heart, and part of what creates that peace is the belief that killing these animals was God's will. Noah believes that killing these animals is what God wanted, even though it was not. He ascribes his violence toward these animals as being the will of God, even though it was not.

When we see this truth about sacrificial killing in Genesis 8:20-21, we are then invited to go back and re-read Genesis 6–8 in the same light. All the violence in the flood did not solve or cure human violence, any more than the sacrificial violence of Noah would cure the violence that resided in his own heart. And just as Noah blamed God for the sacrificial killing of animals, so also, we humans blame God for the killing of other humans, whether it be by our own hands, or through natural disasters like storms and floods.

What this means is that it is not proper to read the Genesis flood account as an account of what God *actually did* in response to the violence that covered the earth. Instead, we must read it as an account of how humans blame God for the bad things that happen in this world. The alternative (and traditional) explanation is monstrous. If we say (as many do) that God responded to world-wide violence with a world-wide genocide, then we must not only say that God is the most violent being in the universe, but we must also say that He is the most foolish, for this supreme act of violence did nothing to solve the violence. It is much better, therefore, to approach the flood account as Genesis 8:20-21 indicates. Just as Noah killed animals to create peace in his own heart and then blamed this violence upon God, so also, we humans, due to the sin and violence that is in our own hearts, blame God for all the violence that goes on in this world.

This way of reading the text allows us to see that God is not the greatest mass-murderer in history. The verses in these chapters which indicate that God is the source and cause of the flood waters (6:7, 13, 17; 7:4, 23; 8:21) do not reveal what God *actually did*, but instead reveal *what humans believe*

God did. The verses which talk about God destroying all humanity are verses which reveal the religious heart of humans when we believe that the bad things which happen to us are sent upon us by God.

When floods destroy cities, when houses burn to the ground, or when babies die in their sleep, there are always some who say that God sent such things. The human tendency is to blame all violence and storms and pain upon God. This tendency began at the very beginning when Adam blamed God for giving Eve to him as his partner (Gen 3:12), it continues through the stories of Cain and Lamech, and comes to full fruition in Genesis 6–8 when God gets blamed for the flood that covers the whole earth and horrifically destroys every living thing upon it. God inspired the biblical flood account to be written as it was to reveal this tendency to us. Genesis 6–8 does not reveal what God is like, but what humans are like. God inspired this text to be written, not to reveal to us how He really behaves, but instead to reveal how we humans often blame Him for the horrific things that happen in our life.

Most significantly of all, we see here that once again, God becomes the scapegoat. In Genesis 6–8 (as in Gen 3:12), God allows His character and reputation to be destroyed and maligned for the sake of those He loves. He takes the blame. He willingly becomes the scapegoat for the flood that destroyed the earth.

The crucifixion of Jesus supports this way of reading the text. To the average person watching Jesus die on the cross, Jesus appeared to be just as guilty as the two criminals on either side of Him. Jesus was crucified among thieves and rebels, and as such, it would be logical for the average person to assume He also was guilty. But was Jesus guilty when He died on the cross? No. Though He appeared guilty, He was innocent of all wrong doing. So also with God in the flood (and everywhere else in Scripture and history as well). God very often appears guilty of great crimes against humanity. And many people do indeed accuse God of great sin and violence. But God allows such things to be said of Him for the very same reason that Jesus allowed Himself to appear guilty on the cross. God, like Jesus, has always been a scapegoat for humanity.

As we see in Genesis 6–8, God very often takes the blame for the horrible things that happen to (or are done by) humans. The reason God does this is because of what God knows about sin and violence. We humans engage in rivalry, which leads to accusation, scapegoating, and violence. This cycle of sin will endlessly repeat, destroying more and more human victims in its wake. Since we often seek human scapegoats to blame even for natural violence (we blame "sinners" in New Orleans for Hurricane Katrina or "Muslims" in Indonesia for the Tsunami), God frequently inserts Himself into the cycle of violence as the scapegoat so that there can be no more retaliation and revenge. For who can retaliate against God?

When storms, famines, earthquakes, sickness, disease, and flood occur, we blame God for them. We say that God sent them. When read this way, Genesis 6–8 is not so much an inspired revelation about how God acts, but is more of an inspired revelation about how humans behave. Genesis 6–8 provides a mirror into the heart of humanity. We are supremely violent, and we engage in so much violence that it covers the face of the earth. We usually blame this violence upon God, making Him the scapegoat for our violence. Therefore, when natural violence occurs, it is only natural that we blame this violence upon God as well. We humans require explanations for human and natural violence, and "God did it" is the most common explanation and easiest way out.

God inspired the human author of Genesis to write the text in a way that makes God appear guilty, because God is most concerned with revealing something to us that we humans rarely see. God is not as concerned with revealing Himself to us as He is with revealing ourselves to us. Most humans around the world understand the basics about a good and powerful God, but few humans ever really get a glimpse into the sin of scapegoating violence that lurks in all our hearts and crouches at our door (cf. Gen 4:7). God inspired the biblical text to be written in such a way that both exposes our scapegoating tendencies, and at the same time, calls us to live in a different way.

But beyond this, God inspired the biblical text to be written as it was because God would rather that He become the scapegoat for our sins than have us make other humans into our scapegoats. Ultimately, God wants all scapegoating to cease, but if it is a matter of scapegoating humans or scapegoating God, God prefers to offer Himself as the scapegoat sacrifice so that human lives can be spared. Remember, scapegoating brings peace to human society and culture. God knows this, but He also knows that the price of peace through scapegoating is that someone gets blamed. God would rather take the blame Himself than allow humans to get blamed, scapegoated, and killed. This is what God is doing throughout Scripture, and is ultimately what is revealed through the crucifixion of Jesus. But this jumps too far ahead of the story. Let us continue the study of scapegoating by turning to the scapegoat sacrifice itself in Leviticus 16.

LEVITICUS 16–17

Then Aaron shall cast lots for the two goats: one lot for the Lord and the other lot for the scapegoat. … But the goat on which the lot fell to be the scapegoat shall be presented alive before the Lord, to make atonement upon it, and to let it go as the scapegoat into the wilderness (Lev 16:8, 10).

Leviticus 16 contains instructions to the Hebrew people about the scapegoat ritual (cf. Lev 16:8, 10, 26). In this ritual, two goats were selected as an offering, one for the Lord and one for the scapegoat. The one for the Lord was killed on the altar, and the one for the scapegoat was sent out into the wilderness. This second goat is referred to as the "scapegoat." Yet as indicated in the previous chapter, not all Bible scholars agree that the Hebrew word used here should be translated as "scapegoat." The Hebrew word is *azazel*, and some believe it should be translated as "wilderness," "entire removal," or even as "evil spirit" or "demon."

What is most curious about the scapegoat ritual, however, is that it was instituted in the historical context of the people worshiping demons (Lev

17:7). We do not know exactly what this worship of demons entailed, or why it is referenced in the context of sending out the scapegoat, but the two events do seem connected somehow.

Regardless of how to understand the historical, cultural, and religious meaning of the word a*zazel,* the point of the scapegoat offering is quite clear. The goat is intended to carry away the sins of the nation into oblivion. When the priest laid hands on the scapegoat, this symbolized passing the sins of the nation onto the goat before exiling it into the wilderness. The scapegoat ritual was a way for the sins of one group of people to get passed to an innocent animal, which then carries the sins away into forgetfulness. Similar practices are seen when lepers "pass their disease" to a bird and then release it so that it carries the leprosy away (Lev 14:1-9), or in the Babylonian practice of putting the sins of the people on a sheep and then casting it into a river to be carried away by the current.

Yet while Leviticus 16 is a key biblical passage about the Hebrew scapegoat ritual, what many fail to recognize is that this practice did not originate with the Hebrew people or the instructions from Moses in Leviticus 16. The practice of scapegoating is much more ancient and much more significant than most realize. Furthermore, these animal scapegoat rituals were preceded historically by human scapegoat rituals. Cultural anthropologists note that nearly all ancient civilizations practiced human scapegoat sacrifices as a way to create peace and unity in a society. When violence threatened to escalate out of control and annihilate a tribe or town, peace was created between the warring factions by selecting one outsider to bear the blame for everything that had gone wrong. This outsider was then violently murdered or sacrificed by the two warring factions, who were then able to live in peace with each other once again. Some sociologists and anthropologists call this the "scapegoat mechanism." It was the means by which society dealt with violence and created peace by forcing the sacrificial victim to carry their sin away. All of this was considered at length in the previous chapter.

Somewhere along the way, early human societies realized that the peace created by these human sacrifices could be refreshed and renewed on a regular basis through a repeated ritual which commemorated the first sacrifice. While some cultures repeated the sacrificial ritual by using another human sacrifice, most cultures eventually discovered that an animal made a sufficient substitute. The effects of this sacrifice, though, were only temporary. The blood of the sacrificial ritual never created a lasting peace, and so it had to be repeated every so often to maintain peace and keep human bloodlust at bay. Human sacrifice kept it at bay the longest, but animal sacrifice was easier and less costly. This history of sacrifice helps explain *all* of the sacrifices in Scripture, but especially the scapegoat sacrificial ritual of Leviticus 16 (see Part III on Sacrifice).

So while much of what is going on in Leviticus 16–17 is shrouded in mystery by history, the roots of sacrificial thinking and the scapegoat ritual are clearly evident. One is blamed for the sins of all, and this one carries the burden of the sins of all away from society and culture into oblivion. The scapegoat disappears and the sins are remembered no more. The most important point to note, of course, is that the scapegoat ritual is not so that God can forgive and forget, but so that humans will. The scapegoat is a necessary sacrifice to create peace between humans; it is not necessary to create peace between God and humans. This point is critical to understand as we move forward in the biblical text.

Outside of Leviticus 16, the word "scapegoat" is not mentioned anywhere else in the rest of Scripture. Nevertheless, now that we understand what a scapegoat is and what purpose it serves in society and culture, we can begin to see scapegoats all over the biblical text. We humans not only make humans into scapegoats, we also justify our scapegoating by laying blame on God. One clear sign of scapegoating is when we dehumanize or demonize someone else. We call them names, turn them into monsters, and blame them for all sorts of terrible crimes. Then, once we have successfully turned the human scapegoat into a monster, we call on the name of God to help us kill our scapegoat enemies in His name. The Bible repeatedly reveals how this historical process occurs, not so that we can imitate it, but so that we can be wary of it. The Bible is a mirror which reveals the scapegoating tendencies of the human heart. If we ignore what we see, we will never be able to change.

JOSHUA 7:10-26

Then Joshua, and all Israel with him, took Achan the son of Zeruh, the silver, the garment, the wedge of gold, his sons, his daughters, his oxen, his donkeys, his sheep, his tent, and all that he had, and they brought them to the Valley of Achor. And Joshua said, "Why have you troubled us? The Lord will trouble you this day." So all Israel stoned him with stones, and they burned them with fire after they had stoned them with stones (Josh 7:24-25).

The historical events in the book of Joshua are classic scapegoating accounts. There is rivalry among the people of Israel regarding the leadership of Joshua and the divisions of the land in Canaan, and there is rivalry between Israel and the Canaanites over the land. There is also quite a bit of trepidation on the part of Joshua that the people will not follow his lead into Canaan but will instead rebel as they did with Moses (cf. Num 13–14). Joshua was one of the two original spies who thought that the Israelites would be victorious in Canaan (Num 14:6-9), and now, forty years later, he wants to make sure that Israel does not make the same mistake. In the opening chapters of Joshua, he protects himself against this lack of confidence in a variety of ways. Among them include only sending two hand-picked spies instead of twelve (Josh 2:1), performing special ceremonies (Josh 3–5), and even visiting with the Angel of the Lord (Josh 5:13-15). Note carefully that when the Angel of the Lord is asked whose side he is on, the answer is "Neither" (Josh 5:14). Though we humans always claim that God is on our side against our enemies, God Himself does not take sides; He is on the side of all humans.

In the events that follow, Jericho is destroyed and then the people of Israel set their eyes on their next target, the city of Ai. But the Israelites are not successful in their attack on Ai, and Joshua knows that his position of leadership is in jeopardy. So in Joshua 7:10-26, the people of Israel undertake a classic scapegoating ritual as a way of blaming one for the sins of all and uniting everyone else together under the leadership of Joshua. Joshua states that one person among them is guilty for the failure in the attack against Ai. They cast lots to determine who the guilty party is, thereby making it appear that God is helping them expose the guilty party.

Now, if you know anything at all about humanity, and if you know anything at all about ancient warfare, then you know that of all the thousands of soldiers who entered into Jericho on the day it fell, it is almost certain that despite Joshua's command to give everything in Jericho to "the treasury of the Lord" (Josh 6:19, 24), quite a large number of soldiers kept back some of the gold and silver for themselves. No, the text of Joshua 6 does not say that this happened, but can it be imagined that the people of Israel, who had repeatedly disobeyed God and complained about God's provision, would now, after this first victory at Jericho, almost universally obey God and take none of the spoils of war for themselves? Did they now all of a sudden start trusting God? Did they now all of a sudden start obeying God completely? Such a rapid and complete change of behavior is unlikely in the extreme. Instead, based on what we know about human behavior and Israelite history, it is more likely that while *most* of the gold and silver was turned over to the treasury, nearly every man took *some* gold and silver for himself.

So on that fateful day outside the walls of Ai, if you had been there observing the casting of the lots tribe by tribe and family by family, you would likely have seen numerous nervous glances, shuffling of feet, and sighs of relief as the lots passed them by. Joshua likely knew what we all know, that it did not really matter who was selected by the casting of lots. Whoever it was, they would likely be found guilty. So when Achan was chosen by lot and gold was found hidden in his tent, Achan became the scapegoat for the sins of all Israel. Though all were guilty, he bore the sin and shame of all. So they stoned him and then burned him, along with his sons, his daughters, his animals, and all his possessions. The reason that his family, animals, and possessions had to be destroyed as well is because scapegoat victims must always be sent away into forgetfulness and oblivion. Family members would carry on Achan's memory, as would any animals or possessions which were given to others. A scapegoat must be completely destroyed, and so they were all stoned and then burned.

If you have ever struggled with the stoning of Achan and thought to yourself about how barbaric it seemed to not only stone Achan, but also his innocent children and animals, then you have correctly understood the point of the text. It is only when we try to explain away this text and justify the scapegoating activity of Joshua and the Israelites that we miss the point of Joshua 7. This text out of Joshua is a classic scapegoating text, and it is written in a way that makes his relative innocence and the guilt of everyone else plain for all to see. Was Achan guilty? Yes. But he was no more guilty than anyone else. Yet Achan became a scapegoat to bear the sins of Israel into oblivion, and in so doing, unite the people of Israel together under the leadership of Joshua so that they could go forward with one mind and one purpose to defeat the city of Ai, which is exactly what they did.

Ironically, the victory over Ai in Joshua 8 is ascribed to God and how the people of Israel had rooted out the sin in their midst. Yet the text somewhat mocks this interpretation, for it says that they won because they took 30,000 soldiers into battle instead of 3,000 (cf. Josh 7:3; 8:3), and laid an ambush for Ai instead of engaging in a frontal assault (cf. Josh 7:4-5; 8:4-7). And this time, the soldiers were allowed to keep the spoils of the city for themselves (Josh 8:2, 27), which was quite a relief to many men, since they were now able to add the spoils of Ai to their spoils from Jericho, thereby hiding their own guilt.

Yes, this way of reading Joshua 7 looks behind the surface details of the text. But this way of reading the text also helps the text make better sense in light of what we know about God, human nature, the Israelite people, Joshua's concern for his leadership, and general warfare practices at that time. When all these factors are taken into consideration, the scapegoat reading of Joshua 7 becomes the most obvious reading.

Seeing the scapegoat mechanism at work in Joshua 7 also helps us understand the "ban" (Heb., *cherem*) in the book of Joshua. Repeatedly in this book, God is reported as saying that everything is "under a ban" or "devoted to destruction" (Heb., *cherem*) for God (cf. Josh 6:18-24; 7:11-13; 8:26; 10:1, 28, 35-40; 11:20-21; etc.). Some modern teachers and pastors try to explain this genocidal destruction by saying that the Canaanites were monsters, and so God needed to destroy them. We are told that the Canaanites raped women, tortured children, performed human sacrifices, owned slaves, and participated in all sorts of deviant behavior. God, we are told, viewed the Canaanite people as beyond redemption and worthy only of death. The Canaanite evil was a threat to the "purity" of the Hebrew people and so they must be exterminated. It was so bad, even the women and children needed to die. The scapegoat reading of Joshua 7 causes us to wonder about the truth and validity of this description of the Canaanite people.

Besides, if you have ever listened to the rhetoric of any genocidal leader as he calls on his people to exterminate some other group, you will recognize all such language about the Canaanites for what it is. The description of the Canaanites in Joshua (and by many Bible teachers and pastors today) is scapegoating rhetoric. Such language portrays one's enemies as subhuman monsters who deserve only death. As a result of how evil these people are, we are told, it is a righteous and godly act to kill them. It is even merciful to put them out of their misery. The book of Joshua, like much of the Bible, is written to expose such thinking for the lie that it is. Such thinking about other people is one of the foundational lies of scapegoating, and the Bible seeks to expose this lie so that we will no longer participate in such scapegoating practices. When you read Joshua, do not read it as an account of how God kills evil people. Instead, read it as an account of how we humans enter into a rivalry with others, and as a way to win this rivalry, we demonize and dehumanize our foes so that we can kill them in God's name.

JOB

And so it was, after the Lord had spoken these words to Job, that the Lord said to Eliphaz the Temanite, "My wrath is aroused against you and your two friends, for you have not spoken of Me what is right, as my servant Job has" (Job 42:7).

Another Old Testament book which exposes the practice of scapegoating is the book of Job. The book of Job provides an excellent example of how the scapegoat mechanism works. Due to all the bad things that happen in Job's life, Job's friends see this as evidence that Job is an unrepentant sinner under the judgment of God. This is *always* how people view their scapegoat victims. The book of Job, however, does not end the way most other classic scapegoating texts conclude. Typically, a scapegoat narrative ends with the victim being condemned and killed "in the name of God," and the reader goes away from the text believing that the scapegoat truly was guilty of everything they were accused of. A true scapegoating narrative persuades the one who hears it that the scapegoat victim was not a scapegoat at all, but was simply another guilty sinner who was condemned and killed for their many crimes.

This is what makes the book of Job so important. Though much of the story follows the typical scapegoating pattern, the story contains one critical difference which allows the reader to see Job in a completely different way. The difference is that at the end of book, God shows up and defends Job. Usually, the standard scapegoating texts introduce the voice of God to support the claims of the accusers and justify their expulsion or killing of the victim. But this account does not end with Job dying because when God weighs in, He speaks in Job's defense. This shocking turn of events reveals the even more shocking truth that God is on the side of the scapegoat victims, that God does not speak to accuse and condemn, but speaks instead to defend, reconcile, and redeem.

One surprising truth from the book of Job, then, is what it reveals about true "satanic" activity. The book begins with Satan gaining permission to test Job, and many people assume that this satanic testing concludes by the end of chapter 2 after Job loses his health, wealth, and children. But this is not true. The most "satanic" activity in the book of Job occurs when Job's friends accuse him of wrongdoing. The name Satan, after all, means "accuser." Many Bible teachers believe that the main point of the book is that humans don't know why bad things happen to good people. While that truth may be a minor point of the book, the main point is that we humans often engage in the satanic activity of accusing and blaming others and that we do so "in the name of God." But when God finally shows up, His only response is, "You who accuse others know nothing, so stop accusing!" The message of the book of Job is that all accusation, blame, finger-pointing, and scapegoating must stop, for God is not in agreement with our accusations. Instead, God is on the side of those we accuse. It is this truth that we see consistently in the life and ministry of Jesus, to which we now turn.

JOHN 1:29, 36

The next day John saw Jesus coming toward him, and said, "Behold! The Lamb of God who takes away the sin of the world!" (John 1:29).

Entire books could be written on how the four Gospel accounts reveal the truth about scapegoating. The Gospels contain scapegoating themes on almost every page. It is not an exaggeration, then, to say that the four Gospels are long exposés of scapegoating. This is only logical, for if the sin of scapegoating is the primary sin of humanity since the foundation of the world, then the primary task of Jesus would be to deliver us from our slavery to this sin by both exposing it to us and showing us how to live differently.

One of the primary ways that Jesus exposed and revealed the truth about scapegoating to humanity is by becoming a scapegoat Himself. Jesus submitted Himself to the scapegoat mechanism so that He might unveil and dismantle it from within. One of the first places we see this purpose explained is in John 1:29, 36 when John the Baptist declares that Jesus is the Lamb of God who takes away the sin of the world. Some people assume that the "Lamb" which John is referring to is the Passover lamb. But the law never describes the Passover lamb as taking away the sin of the world. In fact, there is no lamb of any kind in the Mosaic Law that takes away sin. So what lamb is John referring to?

The most likely answer is that John has Isaiah 53:7 in view, where the Messiah is viewed as a lamb who carries the sins and transgressions of all people upon His own body into death. Isaiah 53 is full of scapegoat imagery, but rather than speak of a scapegoat, Isaiah speaks of an innocent lamb who has done no violence and tells no lies (Isa 53:9). This lamb does not even speak in its own defense (Isa 53:7). By using scapegoat imagery in reference to a lamb, both Isaiah and John are making the point that unlike most human scapegoats, Jesus as the Messianic Lamb of God was completely innocent of all wrongdoing. Human scapegoats are usually guilty of some of the things for which they are accused, but Jesus exposes the scapegoat mechanism by being completely innocent of everything, yet still being accused and scapegoated. In this way, He exposes scapegoating for what it is: a wrongful accusation of an innocent victim. By being a *completely* innocent victim who still gets accused, condemned, and killed, Jesus reveals the truth that all scapegoats throughout history have also been *mostly* innocent of the crimes for which they too are accused, condemned, and killed.

This is why John (and Isaiah) speaks of Jesus as the Lamb of God who takes away the sin of the world. The "sin of the world" is not "all the individual shortcomings and moral failures of the world" but rather, "the foundational sin that all the world commits and which every culture, community, society, religion, and political party is built upon" (see Part I on Sin). The "sin of the world" is a founding sin which forms the basic building block of everything in the world. When Jesus as the Lamb of God (as the innocent scapegoat) takes away the sin of the world, He does not primarily do this by removing this sin *from* the world, but by exposing this sin *to* the world so that we can no longer commit it in good conscience. He takes away our ability to commit this sin blindly. He takes this sin away by revealing this sin for what it is.

The primary mission and message of Jesus is that we must give up practicing "the sin of the world," which is the way of scapegoating through accusation and blame, and must instead follow His way of peace through forgiveness and grace. Jesus is the Lamb of God who takes away the sin of the world and leaves us only with the grace of God. Now that the sin of the world has been exposed and removed as an option, the sin of the world no longer works as an outlet for our violence, and we must learn to live in the divine realm of forgiveness and grace lest we destroy ourselves. This is the consistent and insistent message of Jesus in the Gospels.

LUKE 11:49-51

"Therefore the wisdom of God also said, 'I will send them prophets and apostles, and some of them they will kill and persecute,' that the blood of all the prophets which was shed from the foundation of the world may be required of this generation, from the blood of Abel to the blood of Zechariah who perished between the altar and the temple. Yes, I say to you, it shall be required of this generation."

The truth that the sin of scapegoating is the foundational sin of the world is taught by Jesus in Luke 11:49-51. In this passage, Jesus speaks about all the blood spilled from the foundation of the world, from the blood of Abel to the blood of Zechariah. Jesus also mentions the altar and the temple, as a reference to the fact that the sin of scapegoating is primarily a *religious* sin. Since humans who scapegoat others often do so in God's name, and then usually kill their scapegoat victims as a sacrifice to God, the sin of scapegoating is often associated with religion.

One of the strange features of the scapegoat mechanism is that scapegoat victims often become venerated heroes in later generations. Jesus indicates this as well, by pointing out that while their Jewish ancestors killed the prophets, later Jewish generations built tombs of veneration for the prophets. Ironically though, people rarely learn from the scapegoating practices of the past, but continue to engage in scapegoating in their own day. Jesus says that this is what His generation will do with Him. Though every generation says that if they had lived in the days of the prophets, they would not have killed them, every generation also has "prophets" of their own day which they then scapegoat and kill (cf. Matt 23:30). Jesus came to bring an end to all such scapegoating, and He did so by becoming a scapegoat Himself.

JOHN 11:49-53

And one of them, Caiaphas, being high priest that year, said to them, "You know nothing at all, nor do you consider that it is expedient for us that one man should die for the people, and not that the whole nation should perish" (John 11:49-50).

John 11:49-53 is one of the numerous passages in the Gospels which clearly reveals the truth about how scapegoating creates peace. A scapegoat victim is chosen when two or more warring groups seek to end the escalation of violence by blaming an outside person or group for the sins of all. In the days of Jesus, the greatest rivalry that existed was between the Roman Empire and the Jewish religion. Yet Caiaphas realizes in John 11:50 that in order to create peace between politics and religion, a single victim can be chosen by both parties to bear the blame for all. Through the arrest, trial, and crucifixion of Jesus, the two warring sides of this conflict came together and created peace. Jesus submits Himself to this process to expose it for what it is and call us to live a different way.

ACTS 5:1-11

Then Ananias, hearing these words, fell down and breathed his last. So great fear came upon all those who heard these things (Acts 5:5).

> *Then Peter said to her, "How is it that you have agreed together to test the Spirit of the Lord? Look, the feet of those who have buried your husband are at the door, and they will carry you out." Then immediately she fell down at his feet and breathed her last. … So great fear came upon all the church and upon all who heard these things (Acts 5:9-11).*

I am not certain that the death of Ananias and Sapphira in Acts 5 is actually a scapegoating text. But it certainly has all the signs. For example, the cause of their death is hidden in the text. It just says they fell down and breathed their last. But this is strange, is it not? Especially since their crime involved not being honest about how much money they received for selling a piece of land. If God struck dead everybody who lied, our churches would be nearly empty. So it seems that what we have here is part of the scapegoat mechanism, in which two victims are killed, but their death is attributed to God. Of course, the text does not actually *say* that God killed them, but it is strongly implied.

In the same way, scapegoating accounts from other religions texts often say that scapegoat victims were "struck down by the gods." But if you had been present, watching events unfold in these other accounts, you would probably see an angry priest or a bloodthirsty mob striking down and killing a scapegoat victim. The "gods" had nothing to do with it. In such occurrences, since priests are viewed to be the "instruments and vessels of the gods," and since mob violence is often attributed to the gods, scapegoat victims are sometimes described as being divinely killed, even though they are killed by humans. Some scholars wonder if something similar occurred in Acts 5.

Maybe Peter was the one who was *truly* upset at not getting all the money from Ananias and Sapphira. It appears that maybe Peter was alone in the room with Ananias and then Sapphira, since he tells them that the feet of the men are at the door. Furthermore, at this point in the history of the church, Peter still did not fully understand the grace of God or how the Kingdom of God works (he starts to get a better understanding in Acts 8).

So maybe he is the one who killed Ananias and Sapphira because he was still operating under an old covenant mindset. Maybe, just as Peter had tried to kill Malchus in the Garden of Gethsemane (John 18:10), he tries to defend God's honor and the reputation of the church here in Acts 5. If this is the case, Ananias and Sapphira might have been strangled or poisoned since the text says they fell down and breathed their last. All of this is pure speculation, of course, but the events of this text have much in common with other religious scapegoating texts.

A few other details also raise red flags. The repeated statements that fear fell upon all who heard about the death of Ananias and Sapphira (Acts 5:5, 11) makes people doubt that God was really behind these deaths. After all, perfect love casts out fear (1 John 4:18). How could God, who is love (1 John 4:8), perform such actions that result in fear? On top of this, there are the numerous parallels between Acts 1–5 to the three primary "Creation and Fall" texts of Genesis 1–4, Genesis 6–9, and Joshua 3–7, all of which contain clear scapegoating themes. The "fall of the church" in Acts 5 is parallel to the fall of humanity in Genesis 3–4, the fall of the new humanity in Genesis 8–9, and the fall of Israel in Joshua 7.

I wish I knew what was going on in Acts 5, but I don't. It certainly seems like a clear scapegoating text, but there are just not enough details within the account to provide any certainty about how Ananias and Sapphira died. The one thing we can know for sure, however, is that God did not kill them. The text does not say He did. We assume that God killed them because we believe this is the way God acts, and so we read such an idea into the text even though it is not there. Furthermore, since we cannot ever imagine Jesus killing someone for lying to Him, this also proves that God was not behind the deaths of this couple. The fear that results from this sad event is further proof that their deaths were not the work of God. It seems possible that scapegoating was at work, but we cannot see behind the veil of history to discern how.

REVELATION 5:5-6

But one of the elders said to me, "Do not weep. Behold, the Lion of the Tribe of Judah, and Root of David, has prevailed to open the scroll and loose its seven seals." And I looked, and behold, in the midst of the throne and of the four living creatures, and in the midst of the elders, stood a Lamb as though it had been slain, having seven horns and seven eyes, which are the seven Spirits of God sent out into all the earth.

These two verses near the beginning of the visions of John reveal the differences between the way people thought about God throughout most of human history and what Jesus revealed about God during His life and ministry. Throughout most of human history, people have thought that God was a violent being who engaged in retribution and vengeance on His enemies. This portrayal of God can also be found in many passages from the Old Testament. Such a picture of God is represented by the Lion of the Tribe of Judah. A lion is a predator, using fangs and claws to kill its foes and feast on their blood.

But in Revelation 5:5-6, John is invited to look at the Lion of the Tribe of Judah, and when he looks, he does not see a lion at all, but a Lamb that has been slain. When God is revealed through Jesus Christ in the Gospels, and here in the opening chapters of the book of Revelation, God is not portrayed as a being who kills, slaughters, and makes scapegoats out of others, but instead as a being who allows Himself to get killed and slaughtered for the sake of others. God creates peace, not by killing others, but by allowing Himself to get killed for others. This vision of God in Revelation 5 is a critical key for understanding the rest of this prophetic book.

The fact that the lamb is slain since the foundation of the world reveals that this is the way God has always been. He has always been an innocent Lamb who allows Himself to get slain for the sake of others. He is the premier scapegoat of humanity, but as a perfectly innocent scapegoat, it is best to describe Him as a Lamb. As the scapegoated God, Jesus identifies with all scapegoated, sacrificial victims since the foundation of the world.

When we kill others in God's name, Jesus is right there, with the sacrificial victim, being killed alongside the one we condemn, accuse, cast out, expel, dehumanize, and kill, all in the name of God. Through this revelation, we once again see that we can no longer scapegoat others in God's name, for God is not a God who blames, accuses, and condemns, but is a God who loves, forgives, and accepts. And He calls us to do the same.

SCAPEGOATING IS NOT THE SOLUTION TO SIN

Sin is the human problem. But just as law and sacrifice only adds to the problem of sin, so also, scapegoating does nothing about sin. Instead, scapegoating is sin itself. The biblical revelation about scapegoating is that it is the foundational sin of humanity. Scapegoating is the sin which allows us to create peace with one another by blaming all our sins on an outsider, and then killing them in God's name.

Jesus, through His life, ministry, and teachings, exposed the truth about sin and scapegoating. But the ultimate revelation about scapegoating occurred on the cross, when Jesus became sin for us (2 Cor 5:21). On the cross, Jesus became a scapegoat. He let Himself be accused and condemned of the sins for which all people are guilty. He let Himself be dehumanized and demonized. He let Himself be whipped, beaten, and tortured until He was unrecognizable as a human being. He let Himself be killed on the cross as a common criminal. Then He was buried in the grave.

And if the grave was where Jesus had stayed, He simply would have been another scapegoat victim in the long line of human scapegoats. But He did not stay in the grave. Three days later, he rose from the dead, thereby defeating sin, death, and the accusations of the devil, proving His vindication before God. Through His resurrection, we were shown how we had unjustly and incorrectly scapegoated Jesus. And once we see this, we see that all scapegoats have been unjustly and incorrectly killed for the sins of the people.

In this way, Jesus calls for all scapegoating to cease. But it is not just scapegoating. Jesus calls us away from all sins of rivalry and violence and accusation. This is the truth revealed by His shed blood, which we look at in the final Part of this book. Once we see what Jesus reveals through His blood, we then finally understand how the sacrifice of Jesus saves the world from sin.

PART V: BLOOD

Now that we have seen the truth about sin, law, sacrifice, and scapegoating, the following two chapters on blood are almost unnecessary. Once we understand that sin is basically violence and everything that leads to violence, that the law and sacrifice don't rescue us from sin but only lead us deeper into it, and that scapegoating is the only human practice which creates a temporary reprieve from human violence even though scapegoating itself is the greatest and most foundational human sin of all, we then see how the blood of Jesus rescues us from sin as nothing else can.

The blood of Jesus rescues us because it reveals the truth to us. The death of Jesus on the cross reveals the truth about sin. It reveals the truth about the law and sacrifice. It reveals the foundational truth about scapegoating. It also reveals the truth about the heart of God and the heart of mankind. And through His violent, lawful, sacrificial, scapegoating death on the cross, Jesus shows a better way to peace. Chapter 10 will explain how Jesus reveals all this through His death on the cross, and then Chapter 11 will look at several key texts from the Bible which clearly unveil the truth about the blood of Jesus.

CHAPTER 10

DEFINING BLOOD

Everybody knows what blood is. It is the life-giving liquid substance that flows through the veins of every living creature. Yet this chapter is not so concerned with defining blood as the red liquid in our veins, but instead with understanding the symbolism and significance of the term *blood* in Scripture and history. As we will see, a lot of the Scriptural references to blood refer to concepts already discussed in this book, such as the sinful shedding of blood through religious violence that comes from the law through holy wars and sacred sacrifice, and the entire scapegoating process in which blood is shed in the pursuit of peace. Therefore, by way of defining *blood* in this chapter, all of these concepts will be considered again. In the process, we will see how the blood of Jesus rescues and delivers us from our sin.

BLOODY SIN

In biblical literature and theology, blood is frequently associated with violence. This is seen in phrases like "bloodshed" or "the spilling of blood." Such terms are close synonyms for murder and warfare. Therefore, while the word *blood* can refer simply to the liquid that runs through the veins of living creatures, it can also serve as a shorthand way of saying *bloodshed.* When used in reference to bloodshed, the word *blood* is referring to violent events like sacrifice, war, death, or murder (cf. Matt 23:30-35; 27:4, 24; Luke 11:50; Acts 5:28; Rev 16:6).

So whenever we read about blood in the Bible, it is helpful to pause and consider whether the reference is simply speaking of the red liquid that flows through our veins, or if some sort of violent imagery is in view instead. When we study the biblical references to blood in this way, we discover that most of the references to blood in the Bible are related to some sort of violence. Therefore, violence is the main concept which blood symbolizes. Yet as Part I of this book showed, violence is also the main concept behind sin. In Part I, we learned that sin is violence and the things that lead to violence. And since blood also points to violence, this means that sin, blood, and violence are all connected. Sin leads to bloodshed, and bloodshed is a sign of sin. Both come from violence and result in greater violence.

This close relationship between the concepts of blood and violence is especially true when the New Testament speaks of the blood of Jesus. Nearly every time the New Testament speaks about the blood of Jesus, it has in view the way His life was violently taken from Him on the cross. To speak of the blood of Jesus is not simply to say that Jesus died and that the red liquid in His veins was poured out. No, to speak of the blood of Jesus is to speak of His violent death. References to the blood of Jesus point to His sacrificial, bloody death on a Roman cross.

This is a critical point to grasp, for it shows that the crucifixion of Jesus on the cross was the greatest sin humanity has ever committed. The crucifixion of Jesus on the cross was not for the purpose of appeasing the wrath of God, for how can another violent death bring pleasure to a God who is opposed to all violent deaths? No, the bloody, violent death of Jesus on the cross was the greatest human sin in a long line of human sins that stretches back to the very beginning of human history. And the death of Jesus on the cross did not appease the wrath of an angry God (for He was never angry to begin with), but rather revealed the sin and violence that is in the heart of all mankind. The violent and bloody death of Jesus on the cross reveals where violence comes from and calls us to forsake such violent ways and follow Jesus instead into love and forgiveness.

But notice what this means. It means that the violent death of Jesus was necessary. There was no other way to reveal the truth about sin and bloodshed. The truth about sin and violence which Jesus unveiled on the cross could not have been revealed in a non-violent way. We humans are blind to our own sin and our complicity in violence, and we never would have believed that it was possible for us to violently shed the blood of an innocent victim unless such sin was clearly revealed to us. But this is what Jesus did reveal through His violent and bloody death on the cross.

In other words, what Jesus accomplished through His death could not have been accomplished if it had been non-violent. Jesus didn't just have to die; He had to die violently at the hands of men. The death of Jesus would not have accomplished the same thing if He had stumbled off a cliff or if a pot had fallen from a building and landed on His head. The book of Hebrews talks a lot about the blood of Jesus being sprinkled in a heavenly sanctuary. This doesn't mean that Jesus literally took a bowl of His blood to heaven and sprinkled it here and there. No, it is not the death or the blood of Jesus *itself* that does anything. The blood of Jesus is not magic blood. Instead, the fact that the blood of Jesus was *shed through human violence* is the key ingredient to what He accomplished on the cross. The blood of Jesus, then, reveals that violence is the central component to sin.

BLOODY LAW

Blood also reveals that religious law only leads to more sin and violence. We saw this in Part II when we looked at the law. The law was initially given because a true relationship built on love was rejected by the Israelites. Nevertheless, in the absence of a genuine relationship, the law served a good purpose in curbing violence and limiting retaliation. Prior to the law, violent sin and bloodshed quickly escalated out of control and became a contagion of violence that threatened to destroy entire civilizations and cultures. But the law created limits to revenge and retaliation.

However, the law also leads to more human violence and bloodshed. Because the law allows violence to be "sacred," that is, commanded and commended by God, the law actually "sanctifies sin." It makes the sin of violent bloodshed something to be sought after, rejoiced, and celebrated. As a result of the law, violence against others can be rationalized and justified as "God's divine punishment upon others." Rather than marching out to kill others for the sake of honor, for the cause of justice, or simply because one group wants more land, the law allows killing and war to occur in the name of God. The law of God allows any war to become a holy war. We still see this today when people cry "Death to the infidels!" or when we march off to war with the prayers of our pastors supporting death in God's name.

The blood of Jesus on the cross revealed this side of the law as well, for Jesus was crucified in obedience to the law. The crucifixion was not primarily a political execution on the part of Rome, but was instead a religious killing in the name of God. Jesus was accused of teaching against the Sabbath, for threatening to destroy the temple, and for speaking blasphemy against God. Jesus was innocent of all such things, of course, yet nevertheless, the law was used to justify the murderous intent in the hearts of those who sought His death. So the shed blood of Jesus on the cross allows us to see that a reliance upon the law leads to using the law as a way to kill and murder others in God's name. One other clear way the law leads to bloodshed is through sacrifices.

BLOODY SACRIFICES

The law also provided the means by which an animal could be killed instead of a human being. Human revenge and retaliation often led to more and greater human death. But the law allowed the death of animal victims to serve as the substitute for human victims. But this doesn't mean that the death of animal victims was good. Violence against animals might be preferable to violence against humans, but it is still violence. Shedding the blood of animals allowed humans to more easily refrain from shedding the blood of humans, but it was still bloodshed.

When thinking about sacrificial bloodshed, it is important to remember that there were three types of sacrifices: sociological, psychological, and spiritual (See Part III on Sacrifice). Blood was shed in all three, but the function and purpose of the blood was different in each. The sociological sacrifices served as a substitute for violence between warring factions in which animals were killed instead of humans, thus creating peace. Psychological sacrifices took place when someone felt guilt over a personal sin, and the shedding of blood from a sacrificial victim helped them feel like they had paid the price to rectify what they had done wrong. Finally, there was a spiritual purpose for sacrifice as well, in that since sin was viewed as a contaminating substance which covered and defiled everything it came into contact with (sort of how we view bacteria), blood was used to cleanse an item and wash away sin (the way we might use Lysol spray or an anti-bacterial sanitizer). We must keep these three types of sacrifice in mind when we think about bloodshed in the Bible, for they help us understand the *reasons* for blood being spilled in sacrificial rituals.

Notice as well that whether we are talking about sociological, psychological, or spiritual sacrifice, the blood of the sacrificial victim is shed in an attempt to stop the escalation of violence and bloodshed in a family, town, or community. Blood is shed in an attempt to stop *even more* blood from being shed. But the fact of the matter is that blood is still being shed. Life is still being taken. Sacrifice is nothing more than bloody violence carried out in the name of God, so that hopefully, less overall violence will occur.

Yet while sacrifice does achieve a temporary peace, this does not mean that God wants or needs the sacrifice. As we learned in our study of sacrifices, God never wants or needs them. It is we who want and need sacrifice. It is we who kill in the name of God as a way to create peace and feel like we are doing something about our sin. God, in the process of allowing sacrifice, put restrictions upon it. He prohibited human sacrifice, and gave requirements that the animals would be killed quickly and efficiently, and not tortured or allowed to suffer. Again, none of this was God's will, but just as God takes us "just as we are" so that He can then transform us into the image and likeness of Jesus Christ, so also, God took the sacrificial system so that He could make it more humane and less violent with the goal of ultimately revealing the truth about sacrificial violence in Jesus Christ.

And the truth is exactly what Jesus revealed. Jesus died as a sacrificial victim. He suffered a bloody sacrificial death. Yet Jesus did not die because God wanted or needed sacrifices. God does not want animal sacrifices, and He definitely does not want human sacrifices—especially not the sacrifice of His own Son. The blood of Jesus was shed through human, sacrificial, *religious* violence. Though Jesus wasn't killed on an altar the way most sacrifices are, He was killed in the name of God. Through His death on the cross, Jesus willingly submitted Himself to the violent death of ritualistic sacrifice as a way of revealing to us the sin to which we are enslaved.

Jesus died, not to affirm and reinforce the idea that God wants blood sacrifice, but to unveil and expose the truth about sacrifice, the truth is that it is we who want sacrifice; not God. By letting us kill Him as a religious-political sacrifice, Jesus unveiled the truth about humanity and the truth about sin, and in so doing, called us to abandon our cries for sacrificial bloodshed. By letting us shed His blood, Jesus revealed that all such sacrifices have nothing whatsoever to do with God but originate instead within the hearts of mankind. Jesus fully exposed and unveiled the mystery of sacrificial bloodshed by fully submitting Himself to it. Ultimately, of course, His sacrificial death was a scapegoat sacrifice, which is the key to everything.

BLOODY SCAPEGOATING

We discussed scapegoating in Part IV of this book, but since there is a lot to remember about scapegoating, and since the concept is so critical to understand when it comes to the blood of Jesus shed on the cross, the entire scapegoat mechanism is summarized below. This seven-point summary includes a few insights into how the death of Jesus reveals the truth about scapegoating to us.

1. **Human beings are imitative.** Humans imitate what we see others doing and desiring. We desire what others desire and want what others want. This is a basic human instinctive learning pattern.
2. **Imitation leads to rivalry and violence.** Due to people desiring what others have, imitative desire can lead to competition and violence. If there is a limited supply of something, then not everyone can have it, and so we argue and fight to obtain it. Even when the supply of some item is nearly unlimited, people think that one specific item is somehow better or more desirable, and will fight over that item.
3. **Violence threatens to destroy us all.** The violence that springs from rivalry often escalates until it is out of control. If the cycle continues long enough, it threatens to consume an entire society or culture. Violence of one against one quickly escalates into violence of all against all.
4. **Violence is "cured" through the scapegoat mechanism.** Human violence of all against all can only be halted if everyone refocuses their violence on a scapegoat. If two people are in rivalry, and they want the rivalry to end, they unite together against an outside third party. Usually this third party has absolutely nothing to do with the original disagreement, yet they get blamed for the rivalry and violence anyway. This scapegoat is then cast out, exiled, condemned, or maybe even killed. This act of refocusing community violence upon an individual scapegoat creates a temporary peace within the community. This peace reinforces the belief that the scapegoat truly was guilty of the crimes for which they were condemned.
5. **Sacrifice recreates the scapegoat mechanism.** People notice the peace that comes from the killing of a scapegoat victim, and so more readily turn to the scapegoat mechanism when rivalry and violence begins to flare up in the future. This is typically a nonconscious process, but the cycles come with such regularity that the killing of a scapegoat victim soon becomes a tradition. Frequently, in an attempt to get the communal peace to last longer, or in order to ward off the escalation of violence, the killing of a scapegoat becomes a ritual sacrifice. It might be done every month or every year, but it soon becomes a regular practice within a community. This ritualized sacrifice serves as a release valve for the rivalry and violence that builds up within a society and culture.

6. **This entire system is supported by religion.** Due to the almost mystical nature of the peace that descends upon a community after a scapegoat sacrifice is killed, people attributed the entire process to the gods. They believed that the gods provided the wisdom to know who was causing the problems, the direction on how to get rid of them, and the blessing of peace that came once the scapegoat had been cast out or killed. Therefore, the entire scapegoating process became a religious ritual. It was sacred violence. The killing of others in the name of the gods was the primary way that humans created and maintained peace in a community.
7. **Jesus came to unveil this entire process and bring an end to it.** Through His life, ministry, teaching, death, and resurrection, Jesus revealed the truth about scapegoating. He never scapegoated anyone, yet became a scapegoat Himself in order to show us the truth about our scapegoat victims. We humans killed Jesus as a scapegoat in order to create peace, just as we do with all scapegoats. But the reason Jesus submitted Himself to this process was to unveil and undo it, and show us a better way toward peace.

Human history is filled with the never-ending cycle of vengeance and retaliation. We use scapegoating to create peace, but even the scapegoating process itself is violent and bloody. One person or group is sacrificed for the sake of all. Though this process "works," it is still violent. The world only knows two ways out of rivalry and violence. The first way is to allow the cycle of vengeance and retaliation to continue unabated until there is all-out war and the earth is filled with violence and bloodshed. Nobody wants this to occur, and so humans generally follow the only other way we know of to create peace: the way of the scapegoat.

Scapegoating is the most common human method for dealing with systemic violence and the escalations of conflict that threaten human society and culture. When we find ourselves in these situations, a temporary peace is achieved through finding and expelling a scapegoat victim. Though even this process is violent and bloody, people always believe that it is better for one person to die than for the whole nation to suffer. But Jesus shows us a better way to peace. Jesus shows us the way of escape.

THE WAY OF ESCAPE

In 1 Corinthians 10:13, Paul writes that no temptation has taken us except that which is common to man, but that since God is faithful, He always provides a way of escape. The primary temptation and sin that is common to man is the sin of scapegoating. All temptations lead us closer toward scapegoating. It is the foundational human sin. And though humans, from the beginning of time, have not been able to find a way out of this temptation other than through the escalation of violence or the scapegoating of others, God has now, in Jesus Christ, provided a way of escape. Jesus shows us the way out.

Jesus does not simply reveal the scapegoat mechanism to us so that He can instruct us to stop engaging in such practices. Jesus knows, as God has known all along, that without a way to create peace, human society will spiral into ever-increasing cycles of violence and bloodshed. So although the death of Jesus on the cross reveals the scapegoat mechanism to us, and although God has now called us to stop participating in this common human sin, God has not left us without an alternative way to peace. If Jesus took away our ability to scapegoat others but did not provide us with another way to create peace, nothing would stop the whole earth from being filled with violence once again, just as it was in the days of Noah.

So what is this way of escape? What is this way to peace? What do we see in Jesus through His life, ministry, teachings, death, and resurrection? We see forgiveness. Forgiveness is God's way to peace, and it is the way revealed by Jesus through everything He said and did.

The ultimate truth that Jesus revealed by becoming a scapegoat and then offering forgiveness is that forgiveness is the best, most successful, and most divine way of creating peace in times of conflict. Since most conflict is generated through an ever-increasing cycle of violence and retaliation, no party in a conflict is ever truly without fault. Except Jesus. He alone, among all human scapegoats in the history of the world, could have justifiably retaliated against humanity for the crimes committed against Him. Yet instead of retaliatory vengeance, when Jesus was on the cross, He turned to God and prayed, "Father, forgiven them; for they know not what they do." Accepting forgiveness for what we have done and extending forgiveness to others is God's only divinely-sanctioned mechanism for creating peace and restoring relationships in times of conflict. The way of Jesus, which is the way of God, is the way of peace through forgiveness.

This is indeed what we see throughout Scripture. Beginning in Genesis, God sought to teach humanity an alternative way toward peace. Though humans always turned to violence, and often blamed God for this violence, God always called humans out of violence toward love and forgiveness. While sacrifices are often viewed as a substitutional death for the one who is truly guilty, the only divinely-sanctioned substitute for sacrificial violence is forgiveness. The Bible revealed this truth only in fits and starts, as through a glass dimly, but eventually, in Jesus, God provided the perfect revelation of how to deal with violence.

Jesus reveals the best way to deal with violence. The way of Jesus is the way of love and forgiveness. When Jesus was falsely accused (as God has always been), He did not speak a word in His own defense, but let them accuse Him of horrendous crimes (as we have always done). And when we tortured and crucified Jesus on the cross, He did not lash out in retaliation, but instead offered unconditional love and complete forgiveness. In this way, the cycle of vengeance and retaliation stopped with Him. He looked at the cycle of violence and said, "Over my dead body!" And then He died, with words of love and forgiveness on His lips.

If Jesus had stayed dead, He would have gone down in history as just another sacrificial victim. But He rose from the dead, showing that He was truly innocent of any wrongdoing. Furthermore, rather than engage in retaliation and revenge against those who wrongfully accused and killed Him, Jesus forgave. In this way, He also revealed that this is what God has always been doing, when we wrongfully accuse Him for the crimes we ourselves commit. So in Jesus, we see that the way of God is not the way of sacrifice, scapegoating, and killing, but the way of forgiveness. Through His life, death, and resurrection, Jesus showed us a different way to bring peace in the midst of rivalry.

When we choose to follow Jesus in this way, we turn from the way of this world and its enslavement to the sin of sacred violence, and turn instead to the way of Jesus, which is the way of forgiveness. And forgiveness is a form of sacrifice, isn't it? Just as God has consistently sacrificed His reputation and His character by letting us blame Him for our sin, we too die to ourselves when we forgive others. Through forgiveness, we offer ourselves as a living sacrifice to others. We lay down our desires, our needs, our reputation, and even our very lives for them. The true sacrifice God wants is the sacrifice of the self in mercy, love, and forgiveness freely extended toward others. This is the sacrifice of Himself which God has always been extending toward humanity, and is also the sacrifice perfectly portrayed in the life, death, and resurrection of Jesus. This is also the sacrifice that God calls us, as His children, to practice toward others. This type of sacrifice is the only type that leads to true and lasting peace with one another, with ourselves, and with God.

Through His life and death, Jesus reveals how, and how not, to live. He shows us that we are not to make sacrificial scapegoat victims of other people, but should instead willingly lay down our lives for them. This multifaceted concept is what the Bible (and especially the New Testament) has in mind when it speaks of the blood of Jesus. The blood of Jesus reveals that true life does not come through the death of others, but through the death of self for the sake of others. While seeking life through the death of others leads only to more death, seeking life through the death of self leads to life for all. The blood of Jesus teaches that there is death through life and life through death. The blood of Jesus teaches that while humans seek death, God seeks life. So when the life of God is in us, we will finally stop seeking the death of others. All of this is seen more clearly when we look at what Scripture teaches about blood, and especially those texts that speak about the blood of Jesus.

CHAPTER 11

SCRIPTURES ON BLOOD

As we look at various texts from Scripture about blood, it is important to remember that while *blood* can refer to the red liquid substance that flows through the veins of living creatures, the concept of blood in the Bible is primarily used in a symbolic sense for violence. In other words, when we read about blood in the Bible, it most often refers to *bloodshed.* This is especially true when New Testament authors write about the blood of Jesus. Such texts have the crucifixion of Jesus in mind, and how He became the victim of violent bloodshed on the cross. He did this to both expose to humanity how this world is founded on sacrificial, scapegoating violence, and also to show us that God never engages in such things, but instead always loves and only forgives. If we are to be rescued, saved, delivered, and redeemed from the violent ways of this world, we will follow in the way of Jesus by refusing to seek peace through war and violence, and instead create peace through love and forgiveness. All of this is made clear through the texts below.

GENESIS 4:7-10

And He said, "What have you done? The voice of your brother's blood cries out to me from the ground" (Gen 4:10).

Many people believe that the first time blood is shed in the Bible is when God makes clothes for Adam and Eve at the end of Genesis 3. However, as we saw in Part III on Sacrifice, a careful reading of Genesis 3:21 reveals that no blood is shed and no animal is killed. Instead, God gave linen tunics to Adam and Eve as coverings for their nakedness. Therefore, the first reference to blood in the Bible is in the context of Cain murdering his brother Abel (cf. Matt 23:35). So the first time blood is mentioned in the Bible, it is connected with human violence and murder. And not just any murder, but fratricide, the murder of brother against brother. Since all humans are related and we're all part of the human family, this shows that all murder is fratricide. All human violence is against other members of our family. It is from this that Jesus came to deliver humanity.

We have looked at Genesis 4 several times in this book, but now the entire truth of this chapter comes into view. Sin is first mentioned in Genesis 4, and it is mentioned within the context of sibling rivalry which leads to murder. So the first time that bloodshed occurs in the Bible, it is not at the hand of God or the command of God, but is instead when one man murders his brother in direct disobedience to God (Gen 4:7). Therefore, sin and bloodshed are closely related in Scripture. The two terms are almost synonymous.

Though many people believe that blood is the solution to sin, the truth is that bloodshed is part of sin itself. In response to human rebellion, God does not demand that blood be shed, but instead warns people against the shedding of blood. Even after blood is shed when Cain kills his brother Abel, God does not then turn around and demand that Cain be killed as well. God does not demand "a life for a life." No, quite to the contrary, rather than calling for the death of the murderer, God seeks to protect Cain from retaliation and further bloodshed (cf. Gen 4:15). So even when a man spills the blood of his brother, God does not attempt to fix this by calling for more bloodshed. God does not even demand that Cain make a sin offering. In the beginning, as throughout all of human history, God does not want or demand blood sacrifice. It is humans who seek bloodshed, vengeance, and retaliation. God works to stop such things as well as bring an end to such actions.

As evidence that it is humans, not God, who want revenge and retaliation, note that after Cain kills his brother Abel, God approaches Cain and says that the "blood of Abel" cries out to Him from the ground (Gen 4:10). What do you imagine that the blood of Abel said? We are not told, but knowing what we know of human nature, it is logical to assume that the blood of Abel cried out for vengeance and retaliation. Whenever anybody is wrongfully accused or condemned, they cry out for justice and for vengeance. It is likely, then, that this is what the blood of Abel cried out for as well.

This idea is supported by Hebrews 12:24 which says that the blood of Jesus speaks a better word than that of Abel. But what word did Jesus speak from the cross? Rather than cry out for vengeance and retaliation, Jesus said, "Father, forgive them, for they know not what they do" (Luke 23:34). The opposite of vengeance is forgiveness. But humans respond to unjust violence and wrongful death by crying out for vengeance. But when Jesus is wrongfully accused and condemned to death, He cries out to God for forgiveness. This truth helps us understand what God means when He says in Deuteronomy 32:35, "Vengeance is mine; I will repay" (cf. Rom 12:19). What does God's vengeance look like? It looks exactly like forgiveness. God's vengeance and retaliation is carried out through forgiveness and reconciliation.

GENESIS 4:23-24

"I have killed a man for wounding me, even a young man for hurting me. If Cain shall be avenged sevenfold, then Lamech seventy-sevenfold" (Gen 4:23-24).

This truth about God's forgiveness in the place of human vengeance is also brought out in the end of Genesis 4, where Lamech kills a man for wounding him. Lamech's murder shows the escalation of violence, for he kills a man who simply wounded him. But beyond that, Lamech then tells his wives that if anyone tries to kill him, they have God's permission to exact seventy-sevenfold vengeance upon his murderers. God did not say anything of the sort to Lamech, but Lamech used God to justify his own retaliatory instructions to his wives. It is quite significant, then, that when Jesus teaches His disciples how they should respond to those who wrong them, He instructs them to offer seventy-sevenfold forgiveness (Matt 18:21-22). Once again, we see that while the way of humanity is an ever-increasing cycle of bloodshed and violence, the way of God is a never-ending offering of love and forgiveness.

GENESIS 9:4-6

"But you shall not eat flesh with its life, that is, its blood. ...
Whoever sheds man's blood, by man his blood shall be shed"
(Gen 9:4, 6).

Genesis 9:4-6 follows the flood account of Genesis 6–8. This is important because of what Genesis says about why the flood happened, and what the immediate aftermath of the flood involved. The flood came upon the earth, according to Genesis 6:5, 11, 13, because the earth had become filled with violence. This escalation of violence until it threatened the existence of all mankind was exactly what God was concerned about in Genesis 4 when He warned that anyone who killed Cain would see sevenfold retaliation come upon him. In Genesis 6, the sevenfold retaliation had exponentially increased so that every inclination of all humans in the entire world was nothing but continual evil and violence.

This description also included Noah and his family, and so it is not surprising to discover at the end of the flood account, when it is only Noah and his family who are alive upon the earth, that the human condition is the same after the flood as before (Gen 8:21). Noah recognizes that violence still resides in his own heart, and so in an attempt to ward off human bloodshed and violence, he offers the first animal sacrifice in Scripture (see Part III on Sacrifice).

In Genesis 9, God takes additional steps to separate humans from our violent tendencies. The first of these is that He allows humans to eat animals. The killing and eating of animals serves as a form of sacrifice, and functions as an outlet for our bloodlust. However, God prohibits the eating of the blood itself. He says that humans should not eat flesh with its blood still in it (Gen 4:4). God then goes on to warn humanity what happens if we shed the blood of others. He says that "Whoever sheds man's blood, by man his blood shall be shed" (Gen 4:6). In other words, God warns that bloodshed leads only to more bloodshed. Then as part of this warning, He takes steps to limit and restrict future bloodshed as well.

OLD TESTAMENT

Much of the rest of the Old Testament is filled with blood, whether it is the blood spilled in the sacrificial rituals of the Mosaic Law or the blood spilled during Canaanite Conquest and subsequent wars of Israel. It is not without reason that some have called the Bible the bloodiest religious book in human history. Such a charge is not unfounded, for when the actual calls for violence and bloodshed are tallied, the Bible has more bloody texts than the Muslim Qur'an or any other religious holy book. The proper response to all this bloodshed in the Bible, however, is not to try to explain it away and justify God as the bloodiest deity in the history of religion, but instead to embrace the revulsion that we feel and recognize that the reason the Bible is so bloody is not so that we emulate the behavior we read about in its pages, but instead to see these events as though they are a mirror being held up to our own faces (Jas 1:23-24). The Old Testament does not reveal God to us as much as it reveals mankind to us. The bloody passages of the Old Testament provide a better glimpse into the heart of man than they do the heart of God.

This is how to read the violent portions of the Bible. When we turn away from violent texts in revulsion, this is the good and godly response. Turning away from the bloody portions of the Bible trains us to turn away from similar violent tendencies in our own heart as well. Until we read the Bible this way, we will forever be confused about why there is so much blood and violence in the Old Testament. But once we read the Bible through this lens, we see that the Bible reveals man to us so that in Jesus Christ we receive *both* a perfect revelation of what God is like and a perfect revelation of what mankind is supposed to be like.[20] Several New Testament texts reveal this even more clearly.

MATTHEW 23:29-35

> *"[You] say, "If we had lived in the days of our fathers, we would not have been partakers with them in the blood of the prophets. ... Therefore, indeed, I send you prophets, wise men, and scribes; some of them you will kill and crucify, and some of them you will scourge in your synagogues and persecute from city to city, that on you may come all the righteous blood shed on the earth, from the blood of righteous Abel to the blood of Zechariah, son of Berechiah, whom you murdered between the temple and the altar" (Matt 23:30, 34-35).*

In this passage, Jesus clearly equates blood with murder and violence, and especially the bloodshed that is religiously motivated. By referencing the prophets, including men like Abel and Zechariah, Jesus indicates that when the Bible speaks of blood, it primarily has in mind the sacrificial and religious bloodshed which takes place when we kill and murder in God's name. But before we move on from this text, we must pause and take a careful look at what it teaches about our own hearts.

Imagine that you were living in Jerusalem during that final week of Jesus. How do you picture yourself? Are you with the crowd calling for His death, or are you with Jesus during His last days and hours? Most of us Christians tend to think that if we had lived in the days of Jesus, we would not have been among those who cried out for His arrest and crucifixion. We

[20] See my books *The Atonement of God* and *The Bible Mirror* (forthcoming) for more on this subject.

believe we would be among those who stood faithfully at His side and wept for Him as He bled and died. We Christians like to say that if we had lived in the days of Jesus, we would have sided with Him, loudly and boldly defending His innocence to the angry crowd.

Sadly, Jesus disagrees with our self-assessment. In Matthew 23:29-35, Jesus explains that religious people who claim they would not have participated in murdering the prophets are the very same people who kill the prophets of their own day. If this was true in the days of Jesus, it is likely just as true today. This is a sobering thought! Never imagine for a second that you could not ever be guilty of scapegoating or killing others in God's name, for this is the first step in doing exactly that. Worse yet, the people we scapegoat and kill in God's name are very often those whom God Himself has sent to call us back to Him. The human condition and tendency is to side with the mob in calling for the death of the innocent scapegoat victim. The religious people in Jesus' day claimed that they would not have participated in killing the prophets of old, yet it is they who led the charge in accusing, condemning, and killing Jesus.

Just as with every other violent text in Scripture, Matthew 23:29-35 is a serious call to take a careful look at the condition of our own hearts toward others. This text, like so many others, was not primarily written so that we can condemn the ignorance of those in the past, but so that we can allow this text to expose the darkness in our own hearts. Just as the people in Jesus' day were guilty of the same sins they condemned in their ancestors, so also, we are guilty of the same sins we condemn in them. We say we would not have condemned Jesus, yet it may very well be that the people we think God should kill today are the very prophets whom God has sent to us to reveal our sin. Who is it that you want to see dead? Who is it that you believe God could (and should) "righteously" kill? Could it be that you only think this about them because they are exposing your sin to you, just like the prophets of old?

MATTHEW 26:28; MARK 14:24; LUKE 22:20

"For this is My blood of the new covenant, which is shed for many for the remission of sins" (Matt 26:28).

Matthew 26:27-28 describes the words of Jesus at the Last Supper. A parallel passage is found in Luke 20:22 and Mark 14:24. This is an important text for the study of the blood of Jesus because we not only have Jesus mentioning His blood, but He also references the related key concepts of sin, forgiveness, and the new covenant, all of which are important ideas for understanding the role of the blood of Jesus. Best of all, we have an explanation from Jesus Himself about what it means for Him to shed His blood for us and for our sins.

This meal Jesus was observing with His disciples was the Jewish Passover meal, which commemorated the deliverance of the Israelites from slavery in Egypt. In a traditional Passover meal, four cups of wine are taken by the participants. The cup immediately after the supper is the third cup, and is called the Cup of Redemption. The word "redemption" means "to buy back" (usually out of slavery), and it reminded the people that they had been redeemed out of slavery in Egypt.

During this Passover meal, Jesus imbued new symbolism into the bread and wine. He said that the bread represented His body broken for them and the wine represented His blood shed for them. He then said that these things point to the new covenant in His blood, which is for the forgiveness of sins. Some seem to assume through this description of events that Jesus was teaching His disciples that His blood would purchase the new covenant and the forgiveness of sins from God. But a careful look at the context and what the rest of the New Testament teaches about blood, the new covenant, and forgiveness reveals something entirely different. To see this, let us look at the new covenant itself, and then consider what Jesus means by the phrase "the remission of sins." When we understand these two concepts, we will then understand how blood is related to both.

The New Covenant

The new covenant that Jesus refers to during the Last Supper is actually the first covenant that God always wanted with His people. As you may recall from Part II of this book when we looked at the Law, after God brought the people of Israel out of Egypt and to the foot of Mount Sinai, He initially invited them into a one-on-one relationship with them. He wanted to be their God and wanted them to be His people. He wanted to live among them as a companion and to speak to them as a man speaks to a friend. He did not want priestly mediators, laws and regulations, or temples and sacrifices to stand between Him and them.

The people of Israel, however, did not fully understand God's love for them, and were afraid of God. So they rejected God's offer of a close, loving, one-on-one relationship and instead asked that God use mediators to speak with them instead (Exod 20:19). But God still loved His people, and though they had rejected a relationship with Him, He did not reject them. Instead, God sought to protect them from the dangers of sin by giving laws, rules, commands, and regulations. God knew that such laws could never serve as a substitute for a relationship, but in the absence of a relationship, there was no other way to protect His people and provide for them. So he gave them the first covenant, the Mosaic Law.

Yet after giving the Mosaic Law, God inspired Moses to write that a time would come when they would recognize the ineffectiveness of the first covenant to guide them into the proper way of life. A time would come, God knew, when the people would realize that law and religious mediators could never serve as a substitute for a close relationship with God (Deut 30:6). When that happened, God would give the people a new covenant, which would actually be the first initial covenant the people had rejected. This new covenant is the one-on-one relationship that God always wanted with His people. It would not be based on laws and commands, but on love and a relationship. God's people would love and follow Him, not because there was a checklist of rules to follow, but simply because they love Him and saw that He loves them.

All of this was what the prophet Jeremiah declared (cf. Jer 31:31-34), and what Jesus announced at the Last Supper in Matthew 26. Yet whether we are considering the old covenant or the new covenant, both are viewed in Scripture as a Last Will and Testament of God. God made His first Will with the people at Mount Sinai. Jesus announced that God had revised and updated that Will. At the Last Supper, the old Will was revoked and the new Will went into effect.

Yet just like any Last Will and Testament, a death was required for a Will to go into effect (cf. Heb 9:15-17). For any Last Will and Testament to be enacted, the one who made it must die. Yet since both covenants were the Last Will and Testament of God, and since God cannot die, it was impossible for the Will to go into effect. The solution in both cases was to provide a substitute for the death of God.

In the case of the Mosaic covenant, Moses symbolized the death of God with "the blood of calves and goats, with water, scarlet wool, and hyssop" (Heb 9:19), so that the covenant could be put into effect. But since Jesus was against all sacrifices and violence, when He announced the enactment of the new covenant at the Last Supper, Jesus did not use a sacrificial death as a substitute for the death of God, but symbolized the death of God with a cup of wine. And since Jesus is God, the cup of wine represented His own blood. This cup of wine served as a substitute for the death of God so that this new Last Will and Testament, the new covenant, could be activated, and we, the recipients and inheritors of this covenant, might receive what was promised in it.

Note carefully that in regards to the new covenant *itself*, the death of Jesus was unnecessary. Just as God did not have to die to enact the old covenant, Jesus did not have to die to enact the new. All that was needed was a representative death, a spiritual, symbolic death. To enact the old covenant, the death of God was symbolized through the blood of bulls and goats. While these were real deaths, they were not God's death, but only served to symbolize the death of the "testator."

But Jesus pointed out in Matthew 26:27-28 that an animal death was not needed either. Instead, Jesus raised the cup of redemption and said "This is My blood of the new covenant." Jesus does not say that the cup represented the blood that He *will* shed on the cross. No, He said that the cup represented blood that *is* shed. Jesus used the deep red color of the wine *itself* to symbolize and serve as a substitute for His own blood. Jesus said that the cup of wine represented His shed blood, and by drinking the wine, He enacted the new covenant, putting it into effect. The blood of bulls and goats represented the blood of God, but this did not mean that God Himself needed to die for the enactment of the old covenant. So also, the deep red wine of the cup of redemption represented the blood of Jesus, who also did not need to actually die in order to enact the terms of the new covenant.

Of course, Jesus did actually end up dying, but this only cemented and solidified the necessity and importance of the new covenant. The death of Jesus on the cross did not enact the new covenant, for it had already been enacted at the Last Supper through the cup of wine. Instead, the death of Jesus on the cross showed in the strongest possible way the emptiness of the old covenant. The death of Jesus revealed once and for all that violence cannot cure violence, and that ritual sacrifice is not God's desire, but ours. On the cross Jesus showed us another way, the way of God, which is the way of the new covenant, which is the way of infinite love and unconditional forgiveness. Through His death, Jesus called us to follow Him in this way. This is exactly what Jesus says when he speaks about the remission of sins as the outcome of the new covenant.

The Remission of Sins

One of the central benefits of the new covenant is *the remission of sins*. But what does this mean? People read this statement and understand Jesus to be saying that the new covenant provides forgiveness for sins. Indeed, various Bible translations have the word "forgiveness" here instead of "remission," which only serves to support this misunderstanding.

The error can be cleared up by recognizing that there are two kinds of forgiveness in the Bible. There is conditional forgiveness (Gk., *aphesis*), and unconditional forgiveness (Gk., *charizomai*). *Aphesis* forgiveness is conceptually closer to deliverance, or as rescue from the damaging consequences of sin. This *aphesis* forgiveness is better understood as release, liberation, or remission, and refers to gaining freedom from the addicting and devastating power of sin in our lives. *Charizomai* forgiveness, on the other hand, is based upon grace (*charis*), and refers to God's free and gracious pardon for all sin. There are no conditions whatsoever for this second type of forgiveness, and God freely extends it to all people throughout all time for all their sin.

The type of forgiveness Jesus speaks of in Matthew 26:28 is the conditional type of forgiveness; *aphesis* forgiveness. When this is understood, we see that Jesus is not teaching His disciples that as a result of His death on the cross, God will finally be able to forgive humans for their sin because the debt has been paid. No. God has always forgiven all people of all their sin throughout all time. But just because we are freely forgiven by God, this does not mean that we have broken free from the power of sin in our lives. This is where *aphesis* forgiveness comes in. Though we all have free *charizomai* forgiveness from God, in order to actually experience freedom from sin in our lives, we must fulfil the conditions of *aphesis* forgiveness.

One of these conditions is to follow Jesus into the new covenant. In Matthew 26:28, Jesus is saying that now, because of the new covenant which is enacted or inaugurated through His blood (symbolized by the cup of wine), God was now making available a new way of dealing with the addictive and destructive power of sin in human lives. God was showing a new way forward. Through the new covenant in Jesus Christ, God revealed that violence and bloodshed never cures violence and bloodshed. Instead, what is needed is unconditional love and forgiveness, which are enabled and empowered by the indwelling Holy Spirit. All of these were gifts of the new covenant which was enacted through the blood of Jesus represented by the cup of wine.

Now although the entire life and ministry of Jesus showed His followers how to live in light of the new covenant, no human being is ready to accept the truth about our human condition unless it is clearly revealed to us. So while the death of Jesus on the cross was not necessary to inaugurate the new covenant, the death of Jesus on the cross was necessary to finally and completely reveal the stark and shocking truth about human sin. Jesus is telling His disciples that through His violent death as a sacrificial scapegoat, they will gain deliverance and release (remission) from the sin that has enslaved humanity since the foundation of the world. And this is exactly what happened. The violent death of Jesus on the cross exposed the lie of scapegoating and sacrificial violence for what it was. Those who see this lie are then able to live their lives in freedom from it. They are no longer bound by the lie of mimetic rivalry and scapegoating violence that has plagued humanity since Cain murdered Abel in Genesis 4.

So Jesus' words at the Last Supper closely mirror what we have seen about blood in Genesis 4:10 and Hebrews 12:24. The murder of Abel by Cain represents the fratricidal, murderous violence upon which all human civilization is built. In unveiling this sin, the author of Hebrews compares the word spoken by the blood of Abel with the old covenant, and then contrasts this with the word spoken by the blood of Jesus and the new covenant. Whereas the old covenant and the blood of Abel were concerned with sacrifice, vengeance, and retaliation, the new covenant based upon the blood of Jesus speaks of grace, mercy, and forgiveness. Jesus says the exact same thing to His disciples during their Last Supper.

The new covenant inaugurated in Jesus brings release from our bondage to sin. The old covenant enslaved us to sin, and thus, to sacrificial and scapegoating violence. But the new covenant in Jesus, introduced to us through His life and ministry, shows that we are completely forgiven and have always been forgiven, and that there is nothing for which God will not forgive us. Therefore, we too can forgive. Rather than lash out in violence against those who wrong us, we can, like God, simply extend love and forgiveness. By seeing God's loving, forgiving, non-retaliatory character through the death of Jesus, we are shown the way to live in loving, forgiving, non-retaliatory community with other people. Observing the Lord's

Supper, or Communion, serves as a reminder of the way we are to live with one another.

THE BOOK OF ACTS

"But you denied the Holy One and the Just, and asked for a murderer to be granted to you, and killed the Prince of life, whom God raised from the dead" (Acts 3:14-14).

Then Saul, still breathing threats and murder against the disciples of the Lord, went to the High Priest (Acts 9:1).

The spread of the church in the book of Acts is accompanied by violence and bloodshed. But ironically (and contrary to how the church has spread during much of subsequent church history), all the violence was against the church; none of it was done by the church. Furthermore, much of this violence done against the church was performed by religious people who believed they were acting in complete obedience to God and His law.

The book of Acts begins with numerous statements that Jesus was condemned and crucified by religious Jews (cf. 2:23; 3:14-15; 4:10). God's only activity in all of this was not to kill Jesus, but to raise Him from the dead (2:24; 3:15; 4:10). This truth is mentioned so frequently in the early chapters of Acts because this same pattern will be followed with the followers of Jesus as they seek to spread the good news about the kingdom of God to all the earth. Just as Jesus was condemned and killed by religious people, but God raised Him from the dead, so also, those who follow Jesus will be condemned and killed by religious people, but God will also raise them from the dead. Once again the theme to note is the close connection between bloodshed, violence, and religious law keeping.

Saul is the greatest example of how zeal for God's law leads to violent bloodshed against others. He is introduced in Acts 7 when he approves of killing Stephen (Acts 7:58), and then we see more about him in Acts 8–9 when he goes about arresting, imprisoning, and killing Christians, before he finally becomes a Christian himself on the road to Damascus. Once Saul becomes Paul and begins to follow Jesus, all his violent tendencies cease. He does not shift from seeking the blood of Christians to seeking the blood of Jews or pagans. No, in becoming a Christian, Paul the Apostle clearly saw the truth revealed in Jesus, that all blame shifting, accusation, condemnation, and violence should cease, and that we must love and forgive instead. This truth is one of the central things Paul sought to teach throughout his writings.

ROMANS 3:20-26

> *Therefore by the deeds of the law no flesh will be justified in His sight, for by the law is the knowledge of sin. But now the righteousness of God apart from the law is revealed, being witnessed by the Law and the Prophets, even the righteousness of God, through faith in Jesus Christ, to all and on all who believe. For there is no difference; for all have sinned and fallen short of the glory of God, being justified freely by His grace through the redemption that is in Christ Jesus, whom God set forth as a propitiation by His blood, through faith, to demonstrate His righteousness, because in His forbearance God had passed over the sins that were previously committed, to demonstrate at the present time His righteousness, that He might be just and the justifier of the one who has faith in Jesus.*

This passage contains some of the more difficult verses to translate in the book of Romans. Nearly every clause or phrase in these verses is surrounded by serious scholarly debate and disagreement about how it should be translated and understood. I have neither the time nor the space to delve deeply into these debates, and so all I am able to do is provide a brief summary of my own view on these texts and share with you how I believe they should be understood in light of the overall context of the book of Romans and the Bible as a whole.

Toward that end, it is best to begin with a rough paraphrase translation of Romans 3:20-26, which you can compare with the quotation from the NKJV above.

> 20 Nobody can be justified by the law, for the law only leads to more sin, for sin is created by the law.
> 21 So now God has revealed how true righteousness is achieved (as foretold by various passages from the Law and the Prophets).
> 22 The righteousness of God comes unto everyone who believes in Jesus. It doesn't matter who you are.
> 23 For all have sinned and fallen short of God's glory.
> 24 All are freely declared righteous by God's grace through the redemption that is in Jesus Christ.
> 25 Yes, God purposed to have Jesus shed His blood as a propitiary sacrifice, believing that it would prove His own righteousness. It showed that just as He had always overlooked sins in the past,
> 26 He was also doing so in the present to reveal His righteousness and to declare righteous anyone who believes in Jesus.

If you are familiar with some of the scholarly debates surrounding this passage, you might have seen by the paraphrased translation above where I fall in these debates. For example, I believe that Paul is referring both to human faith (vv 22, 26) and to divine faith (v 25). I further believe that verse 25 does refer to God's purpose and to propitiation. I do not believe, however, that God needed to be propitiated. Instead, Paul's argument seems to be that God offered Jesus as a propitiary sacrifice to expose the lie of propitiary sacrifices. What lie is that? It is the lie that God needed to be propitiated (appeased or satisfied). God allowed us to sacrifice Jesus to expose to us the shocking truth that it is we who want sacrifices; not God.

Paul's overall point is that God has never violently lashed out in the past when we humans committed sin. Instead, God has always overlooked and forgiven such sins simply because that is what a forgiving and righteous God does. So also, in the present time, God forgave and overlooked the greatest sin of all, the sin of murdering Jesus. Yes, it was necessary for Jesus to face a violent death on the cross, but this was so that Jesus would be the perfect revelation of God's righteous forgiveness. The fact that God forgives humanity for the terrible sin of killing Jesus proves that God always forgives. In this way, God is proven to be both just and the justifier of those who believe in Jesus.

The reason Paul makes this argument is because many people in his day (as in ours) believed that God was a God of vengeance and retaliation. But God's revelation in Jesus Christ showed that He is not violent or vengeful. Instead, He is forgiving and righteous. To prove this, God let us kill His own Son, Jesus, in His name, as a "scapegoat sacrifice" (thinking that by killing Him, we were propitiating God and appeasing His wrath toward sinners), and then instead of revenge or retaliation He offers forgiveness. If God was really as we thought Him to be, then He would have destroyed humanity in anger and violence for wrongfully accusing and killing His own Son. But God did not do this. Instead, He simply forgave. Why? Because this is how God always behaves toward sin. He is righteous, and His righteousness is demonstrated through His free forgiveness of the worst of human sin. This is Paul's point in Romans 3:20-26.

The context of Romans helps reinforce this perspective. The entire section of Romans 3 is about who has the best standing before God. Paul's answer is that nobody has the best standing before God because everybody has the same standing before God, which is a standing of complete acceptance and forgiveness. So there is no superior position or platform from which to boast. We are all equally sinners and we are all equally forgiven. Therefore, we can simply accept God's free gift of His righteousness by believing in Jesus for it.

In light of our present discussion of blood then, what does Paul's reference to the blood of Jesus in Romans 3:25 mean? He writes that God set forth the blood of Jesus as the propitiation for our sins. By this, Paul means that the blood of Jesus is revelatory. The blood of Jesus reveals that God does not lash out at human sin and does not retaliate or seek revenge. Though we humans do such things (and often blame our behavior on God), God always and only forgives, loves, rescues, and redeems. We thought we were pleasing and appeasing God when we killed Jesus, just as we thought that all blood sacrifices to God were given as propitiary sacrifices, but in reality, this attempt to please God turned out to be the greatest sin ever committed by humans. And even then, what did God do? He forgave this sin, just as He always does.

The argument of Romans 3:20-26 could be summarized this way: God believed that the blood of Jesus would accurately reveal the righteousness of God so that we could then believe in Jesus to receive God's righteousness. But as long as we believed that God was full of vengeance and wrath toward sin, we could never believe that we have redemption or forgiveness from God. So God sent forth Jesus, knowing that our wrongful crucifixion of Jesus would adequately reveal His own righteousness when He forgives us for this terrible sin. In this way, God remains righteous, and He is able to declare righteous those who believe in Jesus.

Romans 3:20-26 is a complex passage, but once the message is grasped, the truth which Paul unveils is beautiful to behold.

EPHESIANS 1:7

In Him we have redemption through His blood, the forgiveness of sins, according to the riches of his grace.

Ephesians is a book that has been widely misunderstood, especially in light of what it teaches about salvation. The basic message of Ephesians is that due to religion, humans have lived in rivalry and violence with each other since the foundation of the world, but now, in Jesus Christ, we have been shown a new way of living life so that all the hostilities can now cease. All of Ephesians 1–3 is about these human hostilities and how Jesus revealed them to us and showed us the way to peace and unity. Ephesians 4–6 reveals in practical terms how to accomplish unity in the church, in our families, and in our workplaces. Near the end of this letter, Paul states that while there is still a struggle, it is not against each other, but against the forces which seek to drag us back into rivalry, accusation, and scapegoating violence.

Paul introduces some of these themes with one long sentence in Ephesians 1:3-14. In the middle of this long sentence, Paul says that the blood of Jesus provides redemption and the forgiveness of sins (Eph 1:7). Redemption is when God takes something that is already His, and buys it so that it is twice His. So He redeemed us, or bought us back, through His blood. When Paul writes about Jesus redeeming us through His blood, however, we must not think that Jesus was paying off God or Satan with His blood. It is not as though there was a debt of sin to God or to Satan which could only be repaid with the blood of Jesus. This is not a biblical idea.

The redemption that Jesus accomplished through His blood was a rescue or deliverance of humanity *from humanity*. We had enslaved *ourselves* to an endless cycle of sacred violence and the spilling of blood in God's name. By dying as He did, Jesus exposed the myth of redemptive violence and the lies of sacred violence for what they were so that we can be redeemed, bought back, or rescued from this endless cycle of violence and bloodshed once and for all.

We know that this is what Paul means because he explains "redemption through His blood" with the phrase "the forgiveness of sins." As mentioned previously in this chapter under the discussion about Matthew 26:28, there are two main types of forgiveness in the Bible, one that is free and one that is conditional. The forgiveness that Paul mentions here is the conditional *aphesis* forgiveness. A good synonym for this type of forgiveness is "release." So Paul is saying that the blood of Jesus releases us from sin. And when we recall what we have learned in this book about sin (See Part I on Sin), we know that sin primarily refers to the sacred violence that has enslaved all of humanity in a never-ending cycle of rivalry, accusation, and scapegoating sacrifice. So when Paul writes about "the forgiveness of sins," he is referring to our release from the cycle of sacred violence. And since this phrase explains or defines the first phrase about the redemption through the blood of Jesus, it too can be understood similarly.

So in Ephesians 1:7, Paul is saying that Jesus redeemed us, bought us back, rescued us, or released us from the never-ending cycle of sacred violence by subjecting Himself to it. He went to the cross and shed His blood for us, not as a payment to God or to Satan, but as a revelation to humanity about the sin which has enslaved us since the foundation of the world. Now that we have this redemptive revelation through the sacrificial death of Jesus, we are able to live in a new way with other human beings. We can now live at peace, no longer subjecting ourselves to the ways of death and violence founded upon religious law, but instead follow Jesus by faith into the ways of love and grace.

If some of this sounds similar to what Paul writes in Ephesians 2, that's because it is. Paul takes this theme of how humanity has been delivered from violence and death through the blood of Jesus and expands upon it in Ephesians 2.

EPHESIANS 2:13

But now in Christ Jesus you who once were far off have been brought near by the blood of Christ.

Ephesians 2 is a powerful chapter in the Bible, but it has been terribly misunderstood and misapplied by the church today. The traditional understanding of Ephesians 2 goes something like this:

> We humans are evil sinners, under the control of the devil and our sin nature. We were dead and unable to do anything to change. Worse yet, because of sin, God's wrath burns against us, and He wants to send us all to hell (Eph 2:1-3).
>
> But God also loves us, and so set out to fix what had gone wrong. Someone had to pay the price for our sin, and since God knew we couldn't, He sent His Son Jesus to die in our place. Therefore, if we believe in Jesus, we get eternal life. But this still doesn't mean we can go sin all we want. No, God wants us to obey Him and do the good works He prepared for us to do (Eph 2:4-10).
>
> But these good works don't involve keeping the law and commandments, be-

> cause the law has been done away with. So instead, let's just live in peace and unity with each other (Eph 2:11-22).

If you have heard sermons on Ephesians 2, you know that this is how Ephesians 2 is often taught. The three-sentence summary of Ephesians 2 goes something like this: "We are sinners. If we believe in Jesus we can go to heaven when we die. But between now and then, we still need to obey God and love others."

There are many problems with this summary of Ephesians 2. For example, it does not logically follow what Paul wrote in Ephesians 1, nor does it fit well with the rest of Paul's letter to the Ephesians. Furthermore, it does great injustice to the expanded discussion about peace in Ephesians 2:11-22. Most Christian sermons and messages on this chapter focus an inordinate amount of time and space on Ephesians 2:8-9, and very little on Ephesians 2:11-22, which is where Paul places his emphasis. So what is it that Paul is teaching in Ephesians 2?

The best way to approach Ephesians 2 is to "reverse engineer" it. By beginning where Paul concludes, we can better understand how Paul starts. When we do this, we see that Ephesians 2 contains a very clear progression of thought. It follows the "Problem (2:1-3)—Solution (2:4-10)—Application (2:11-22)" format. In order to reverse engineer the chapter, we start with a careful examination of the application section in Ephesians 2:11-22, and then work backward to better understand the solution and the problem.

In Ephesians 2:11-22, Paul explains how groups of people who were formerly hostile enemies can now live together in peace and unity because of what Jesus Christ has done. Feuding groups throughout history have used race, religion, and politics (the Jew-Gentile division was a toxic combination of all three) to look down upon each other and accuse one another of being less than human and less-loved by God. But now Jesus has broken down the walls of hostility and brought everybody into one family where we live by new rules. This new way of living was revealed and explained through the life and death of Jesus Christ. When we build upon the foundation He laid, we grow into the people that God has always wanted and desired, and it is then that God is truly manifested in us, just as He was in Jesus.

So if Paul's "Application" is that people who were formerly at odds with one another (in an accusatory violent way) can now live at peace by following the example of Jesus, it only makes sense that in the "Solution" section, Paul talks about how Jesus brought the warring groups together and showed us how to live in peace. Not surprisingly, this is exactly what Paul explains in Ephesians 2:4-10. These verses, though quite popular as texts about how to receive eternal life by grace alone through faith alone, are actually about what God has done to rescue us from the condition described in Ephesians 2:1-3, so that we can become what is described in Ephesians 2:11-22.

Paul's point in Ephesians 2:4-10 is that even though we humans accuse, blame, condemn, and kill others in God's name (Eph 2:1-3), God Himself does not behave that way toward us. God does not bring an end to life, but raises us up to new life in Jesus Christ. Beyond that, He also raises us up with Jesus Christ and seats us with Him in the heavens so that we can live according to the heavenly rules, rather than the ways of this world. God acts this way toward us by grace, so that by grace, we can act this way toward others. But we can only live this way if we follow Jesus by faith. This new way of life is what we were originally made for, and what God has always modeled for us. So Ephesians 2:4-10 is not about how to go to heaven when we die, but rather about how to be delivered from our slavery to death so that we can experience the life of God in this world. The "Solution" section of Ephesians 2 shows us how Jesus is our example for how to live in peace with others.

This brings us back to the beginning of the argument in Ephesians 2:1-3 where Paul presents the human "Problem." Paul begins Ephesians 2 by teaching that we humans live in a world of sin and death, which we inflict upon ourselves by accusing, condemning, and killing one another, and justifying it all by doing these things in God's name. As you look at the terminology Paul uses, he is using the images and ideas that are found all over the place in Scripture in relation to sin and scapegoating. He writes about "desire" and "lust" which leads to wrath. He speaks of the prince of the power of the air, Satan, which is the spirit of accusation that rules the sons of disobedience. He also writes about the course of this world, which is the way of sin and death.

So the overall summary of Ephesians 2 is that while we humans tend to live in hatred and violence toward one another (thinking that this was also God's way), now Jesus has revealed a better way, and we can follow Him in this way by faith. If we do, we will live at peace with one another and in so doing, truly reflect God to a watching world.

All of this helps us come to an understanding of what Paul means in Ephesians 2:13 when he writes that we "have been brought near by the blood of Jesus." The violent death of Jesus on the cross revealed the truth about the great problem of human sin and violence. The truth is that such violence comes from us; not God. When we see this in how we killed Jesus, His violent death on the cross reveals that God never wanted or needed blood sacrifice or sacred violence of any kind in order for people to draw near to Him. All people were always welcome. We can draw near to God simply because we have no reason to stay away from Him. He has always loved us, and always forgiven us. One group is not more or less sinful than anyone else. All are invited in. All are welcome. The blood of Jesus has brought everyone near, by proving that no one was ever kept at a distance. All divisions of men are nothing more than man-made divisions, and now Jesus has torn them all down, giving us all equal access to God and equal standing before Him.

COLOSSIANS 1:20

... and by Him to reconcile all things to Himself, by Him, whether things on earth or things in heaven, having made peace through the blood of His cross.

Colossians is the sister letter to Ephesians, so Paul's argument in Colossians 1 is nearly identical to his argument in Ephesians 2. As in Ephesians 2, Paul writes to the Colossian Christians that the divisions and enmity of this world only exists between humans. It does not between God and humans. On the cross, Jesus revealed God's true nature and character toward mankind by exposing our own tendency toward accusation, scapegoating, and violence. Such things come solely from the heart of man, and having nothing whatsoever to do with God. By becoming a victim of sacred scapegoating violence, Jesus exposed such things for what they are.

Therefore, since we now know God has always loved all people exactly the same, we can now follow God's example by living in peace and reconciliation toward others as well. Jesus made peace between humans through the blood of the cross by revealing that God is at peace with us and has never taken sides in our violence. Let us therefore now live reconciled to one another (Col 1:21). The blood of the cross has made peace between us and God by showing us that God was never angry with us in the first place, but has instead always loved and only forgiven us for our sin. And the blood of the cross makes peace between humans because we see the truth about our own sin and can turn from our scapegoating ways and live instead as God lives toward us: full of love, grace, and forgiveness toward others.

HEBREWS 9:22

And according to the law almost all things are purified with blood, and without the shedding of blood there is no remission (forgiveness).

The book of Hebrews is difficult for modern Christians to understand because we are so far removed from the historical and cultural contexts in which it was written. This is especially true regarding the sections in Hebrews about sacrifice. Hebrews 9:22 may be the most misunderstood verse of all the sacrificial texts in Hebrews. The most common way of reading

Hebrews 9:22 is to see it as a proof text that a blood sacrifice is needed to gain forgiveness of sins from God. But this is a deeply distorted understanding of this text, especially in light of its overall context.[21] A careful examination of this verse allows us to see what it is really teaching, especially in regard to blood.

To begin with, it is important to note that there are two references to blood in Hebrews 9:22, each with its own significance and symbolism. The first reference to blood is in connection to the initial purification of the temple furniture and precincts through the sprinkling of blood.

As you may recall from earlier chapters, ancient people believed that sin had a substance-like quality which attached itself to people and places and made them polluted or unclean (see Parts I and III on Sin and Sacrifice). Furthermore, they believed that blood was the substance that cured or cleansed people and places from the polluting presence of sin. This idea is what Hebrews 9:13 has in view when it mentions sprinkling blood on the unclean for the purifying of the flesh. This idea is also repeated in Hebrews 9:21 where we read about Moses purifying the tabernacle and the vessels within it by the sprinkling of blood.

So since it was believed that the temple priests and precinct were contaminated with sin, blood was used to purify the temple before it could be used. This use of blood for the purification of the temple from the pollution of sin is why the author of Hebrews goes on to talk about how the temple needed to undergo continual purification every year. When sin is viewed as a polluting substance that spreads to everything it touches, nothing ultimately can be done to completely remove or obliterate sin. Instead, sacrifices must be endlessly repeated as a continual countermeasure to the relentless spread of sin (Heb 9:23–10:4).

But beyond using blood for purification of the temple, a second type of blood sacrifice is also mentioned in Hebrews 9:22. The author says that "without the shedding of blood there is no remission." Note that while

[21] Appendix 2 in my book *The Atonement of God* contains ten reasons why Hebrews 9:22 does not teach that the shedding of blood is required for the forgiveness of sins.

many English translations add the words "of sin" to the end of this verse, these words do not exist in the original Greek manuscript. Also, some English translations mention the word "forgiveness" at the end of Hebrews 9:22. But the Greek word used is not the regular word which refers to the free, unconditional forgiveness of God (*charizomai*), but is instead the word used for "release."

When all of this is understood, we see that the second reference to blood in Hebrews 9:22 is not referring to how sacrifices gained the forgiveness of sin for us from God. Instead, this second reference to blood is referring to the sacrifice that initiates the terms of a covenant. It is referring to the "release" of a covenant. This is the third type of spiritual sacrifice that was discussed in Part III under "Enacting a Will." God made a Last Will and Testament with the people, and to initiate the terms of this covenant, He symbolized His own death through the blood of calves and goats. After all, a covenant cannot go into effect without the death of the one who made it (cf. Heb 9:15-18). Heirs do not receive their inheritance unless the testator (the person who made the Last Will and Testament) dies. Since God cannot die, Moses symbolized the death of God through a sacrifice so that God's Testament could go into effect.

Therefore, when Hebrews 9:22 speaks of the shedding of blood for remission, this is not a reference to blood sacrifices being required for the forgiveness of sins, as some Bible translations mistakenly record it. Instead, the author of Hebrews is referring to the initiation of the covenant between God and Israel. Hebrews 9:22 is talking about the release of the covenant, which the author goes on to explain in Hebrews 10:5-18. The new covenant liberates and frees us by teaching us to live in a relationship with God based on love, rather than a covenant based on law (Heb 10:9, 16). Freedom from sin is found not by obeying the law, but by abandoning the law so that we might live in a relationship based on love.

So Hebrews 9:22 contains two references to blood, and in both cases, the author shows how the life and death of Jesus on the cross revealed the truth about sin and brought an end to all need for blood sacrifices. Through

His death, He did away with the issue of sin (Heb 9:26), showing that sin was never an issue with God in the first place. God never wanted or needed sacrifices, but simply wanted humans to love Him and live as He desired and intended (Heb 10:5-10). Therefore, we no longer need to approach God through the blood of sacrificial death, but can boldly approach God through a life well-lived for Him (Heb 10:19-20). The blood of Jesus reveals that sin is not an issue with God, and that the new covenant has been initiated, in which we can freely live in God's love, rather than according to a set of rules. There is much more to say about these truths (Heb 5:11), but we must move on lest this turn into a full-length commentary on Hebrews.

1 PETER 1:18-19

... knowing that you were not redeemed with corruptible things, like silver and gold, from your aimless conduct received by tradition from your fathers, but with the precious blood of Christ, as of a lamb without blemish and without spot.

Another text that praises the power of the blood of Jesus is 1 Peter 1:18-19. As Peter begins to write his letter, he exhorts his readers to turn from their former ways of living and become holy in their conduct (1 Pet 1:13-16). When Peter writes about holy conduct and becoming holy as God is holy, he does not have conformity to a divine moral law code in view. God did not make humans to be God. He alone is God. Instead, He made humans to be humans. Such a statement may seem redundant, but it is surprising how few Christians grasp this critical concept.

We are often taught and instructed in our churches that God wants us to become like Him, or that we must deny our humanity and become godly. And while there is some truth to the idea of denying human selfishness and the things that destroy our humanity, the truth of Scripture is that when we see to fulfil our God-given responsibilities on this earth, we become *more* human; not less. When we strive to become who God made us to be, we do not end up becoming like God (which was the great temptation of the serpent in Genesis 3); instead we become like ourselves. In other words, when humans become holy, we become more human. When we behave like the humans God created us to be, it is then that we are living up to God's plan and purpose for our life. It is then that we fulfil His holy plan for our lives. We live holy lives when we live human lives.

Sin, of course, is the opposite of holiness. If holiness makes us more human, sin makes us less human. Once again, as we learned previously in the chapters on sin, one of the basic consequences of sin is that it dehumanizes us and turns us into violent murderers who deface and destroy the image of God in other people. Sin seeks to destroy the inheritance that God seeks to provide to all humans, but as we learn to follow Jesus into righteousness and away from sin, it is then that we "save our souls" (save our lives from ruination) and live as God planned and intended.

All this is preliminary to Peter's point about the blood of Jesus in 1 Peter 1:18-19. Peter writes that we were not redeemed with corruptible things like gold and silver, but rather with the precious blood of Jesus. Since the word "redeemed" means "to buy back," it is important to ask what is it we were "bought back" from? From what (or whom) did Jesus buy us back? Though we often sing the hymn, "Redeemed by the Blood of the Lamb," few of us stop to wonder what we were redeemed from.

Some imagine that the blood of Jesus was so precious and valuable that it somehow "paid" off God (or maybe Satan) so that the debt of sin was therefore paid in full. But this idea is not taught in Scripture. In fact, while Scripture does reveal what we were redeemed *from*, the Bible nowhere says that Jesus actually *paid* anyone or anything for this redemption. This is okay, because a *payee* is not required for there to be a payment, especially when the payment is one's life. If a soldier "paid" the ultimate price by dying on the field of battle, or a mother "gives" her life to rescue her children from a fire, we do not then try to figure out who it was they paid. Though a costly price was paid, this does not mean that someone or something actually received the payment. Therefore, the whole question about who (or what) got paid off when Jesus died is an unnecessary and pointless question.

The real issue concerns what Jesus redeemed us or bought us back *from*. In other words, it is important to consider where we were prior to the death of Jesus, and then, as a result of His crucifixion, where we are now. The biblical answer, as well as the answer of Peter here, is that we were enslaved and have now been set free. The blood of Jesus redeemed us (bought us back) out of slavery. But what is it we were enslaved to?

The biblical answer is "sin." We were enslaved and in bondage to sin. But here again, few Christians have stopped to wonder too much about the nature of sin. Sin, as we learned in Part I on Sin, is the human tendency toward sacred violence. That is, sin is the tendency we humans have to engage in rivalry with others which leads ultimately to killing others in God's name. This is the basic human problem which has plagued all of humanity and has been passed down from generation to generation (1 Pet 1:18). This human problem of sacred violence forms the foundation of politics, religion, and economics, and is in turn supported by them.

But Jesus came to show us another way, a way of love, grace, and forgiveness, and in so doing, subjected Himself to the sin of sacred violence so that He might both expose it to us and liberate us from it. Jesus died, and He died violently, to rescue and deliver humanity from the sin and violence to which we were enslaved. He did not, however, take a bowl of His blood and pay anybody, whether it is God, Satan, or sin. He bought our redemption by giving His life over to the religious and sinful violence of making scapegoat victims out of others. By giving Himself to it, He exposed and unveiled this human practice so that we who see it might now live free of it.

This is Peter's point in 1 Peter 1:18-19, which he unfolds in more detail in the rest of his letter. We are rescued, redeemed, and delivered by the blood of Jesus from the traditions of men, which center around sacred scapegoating violence. Jesus has revealed this pattern of human behavior to us. Gold and silver did not reveal the way of being truly human (though many rich and powerful believe so). Nor did we gain freedom from sin through obedience and conformity to the religious rituals and human traditions of men (though many leaders argue to the contrary). Instead, we learned how to be truly human through the precious blood of Jesus. His violent death on the cross revealed the truth about humanity. Though He Himself was sinless, and without spot or stain, we killed Him as a scapegoat victim, and did so in the name of God. Those of us who have seen what Jesus revealed through His blood will refuse to engage in such sinful, dehumanizing practices any longer, and will instead live fully human and holy lives as God always desired and intended.

1 JOHN 1:7

But if we walk in the light as He is in the light, we have fellowship with one another, and the blood of Jesus Christ His Son cleanses us from all sin.

One famous verse about the power of the blood of Jesus is 1 John 1:7, which teaches that the blood of Jesus cleanses us from all sin. Some seem to understand this verse in light of the Old Testament way of thinking about sin, as though sin were a substance that could be washed away with blood. This idea is found in the popular refrain, "What can wash away my sin? Nothing but the blood of Jesus." But this sort of understanding creates all sorts of confusing theological ideas. For example, how does one apply the blood of Jesus to their life so that they are cleansed from sin? And if, after being cleansed, we sin again, how do we reapply the blood of Jesus to wash away the new sinful stain? You cannot literally bathe in the blood of Jesus, nor does it make much sense to spiritually apply it to your body, your soul, or your mind. These and other related questions indicate that we have misunderstood what John writes.

John's words make much more sense when we understand what sin is and how the death of Jesus exposes and reveals this sin while calling us to no longer live in such ways. As stated in this chapter and the chapters on sin (see Part I on Sin), sin is best understood as the violence we humans commit in God's name, including all the surrounding factors and circumstances that contribute to this practice. The blood of Jesus reveals the truth about sin to us, so that we no longer walk in it.

Of course, as John goes on to explain, if we deny what Jesus reveals to us through His blood, and say that we are not guilty of sacred violence toward others, then we simply have not yet seen the truth about the blood of Jesus and have not owned up to our own duplicity in human scapegoating and violence. Only once we admit it and own up to our role in making victims of others can we then be cleansed from it and work in fellowship with God and others (1 John 1:8-10). The first step toward being cleansed from sin is to admit and confess our own participation in it. As long as we deny it, we simply deceive ourselves, for we have not yet seen the truth about sin.

So the blood of Jesus cleanses us from sin by exposing sin for what it is and then calling us to no longer live in the way of sacred violence. His blood cleanses us through calling us to practice non-violence. The blood of Jesus is not a spiritual antidote to sin which somehow removes the polluting presence of sin from our lives. You do not need to bathe in blood, claim His blood, or spiritually apply His blood before you walk out the door in the morning. No, the blood of Jesus cleanses us from sin by exposing our sin to us. The blood of Jesus reveals to us our participation in sacred violence. It shows us how we make scapegoat victims out of others. And once we have seen this, the blood of Jesus then calls us to no longer engage in such practices. Though all the world functions by scapegoating others, the blood of Jesus calls us to refrain from it. When we live this way, it is then that we walk in the light of Jesus and have fellowship with Him, with God, and with one another (1 John 1:3).

THE BOOK OF REVELATION

To Him who loved us and washed us from our sins in His own blood (Rev 1:5).

Behold, the Lion of the Tribe of Judah ... And I looked, and behold, in the midst of the throne and of the four living creatures, and in the midst of the elders, stood a Lamb as though it had been slain (Rev 5:5-6).

The image of blood is a primary image in the book of Revelation. There is blood everywhere in this book. The book begins talking about blood in one of the opening verses (Rev 1:5) and then carries this image all the way through with descriptions of bloody moons (Rev 6:10-12), rivers, seas, and oceans of blood (Rev 8:7-8; 11:6; 16:3-4), monsters drunk on blood (Rev 17:6), and even a battle that fills a valley with blood (Rev 14:20).

Why is the book of Revelation so bloody? I believe it is bloody for the same reason that much of the rest of the Bible is bloody. We learned earlier in this chapter that one reason for all the bloody passages in the Old Testament is so that we become exposed to the true nature of humanity, and turn away from it in revulsion. The only way to see our own participation in the human sin of violence that forms the foundation of the world is to take a good, long look at it in all of its gory and gruesome detail. This is also why the book of Revelation is so bloody.

And in fact, I believe that this is the main point of the book. I see the book of Revelation as a sort of mini commentary on the entire Bible. The bloodiness of the book of Revelation provides numerous clues about how to understand the bloodiness of the entire Bible. In John's day, as in ours, there were two main ways of reading the Bible, specifically in relation to what it says about God. On the one hand, a person can read the Bible and come away from it with a picture of God that is bloody and vengeful. Those who have this view of God certainly find much ammunition for their view in the Bible (as well as in the book of Revelation). Conversely, it is entirely possible to read the Bible and come away with a picture of God that looks just like Jesus Christ. In this portrait of God, He is loving, gracious, kind, long-suffering, and would rather die for His enemies than put them to death. And just as it is possible to read the Bible this way, so also, it is possible to read the book of Revelation this way.

A careful reading of Revelation shows that John certainly sides with one particular view. He wants to show that though Jesus appears bloodthirsty and violent throughout Revelation, a careful reading of the text shows that He also is supremely non-violent. In the same way, while God often appears guilty of terrible violence and bloodshed in the Old Testament, a careful examination of those texts reveals that he is supremely non-violent, just like Jesus. Furthermore, just like in the rest of Scripture, the visions and lurid descriptions of violence in Revelation can be misunderstood and misinterpreted by those who want to justify their own violence.

There are several clues for how we know that this is part of John's message in Revelation. The first clue is found in Revelation 1:5, where we read that the saints are washed from their sins through the blood of Jesus. This image of being washed or cleansed from sin through the blood of Jesus brings to mind the similar terminology of 1 John 1:7-10. The blood of Jesus does not cleanse us from our sin in some mystical or magical way known only in the spiritual realm. No, the blood of Jesus cleanses us from sin when we first recognize our participation in the violent, sacrificial, and scapegoating sin of the world, and then move to follow Jesus in His repudiation of all such scapegoating violence. We are cleansed from sin when we follow Jesus away from violence to live in love and forgiveness instead. This truth from 1 John is also the central truth of Revelation, as introduced in Revelation 1:5.

Many of the letters to the seven churches in Revelation 2–3 carry some of these ideas, but the central guiding image of the book is not seen until the first glimpse of Jesus Christ in the main visionary section of the book. The main visionary section of the book begins in Revelation 4, where John is taken up into heaven and is ushered into the throne room of God, where he sees God sitting on the throne, surrounded by the twenty-four elders and the four living creatures. After this, in Revelation 5, John is informed about a scroll that no one is worthy to open. John weeps at this, because he wants to know what is written in the scroll (Rev 5:4).

The scroll represents Scripture and how to properly understand what is written in its pages. Scripture is part of the ancient debate about what God is like. Is He violent and vengeful or is He forgiving and loving? Scripture can be read either way (just like the book of Revelation), and John wants to know which way is correct, so he weeps that no one is able to open the scroll and give a definitive answer.

But the angel tells John not to weep, for the Lion of the Tribe of Judah is able to open the scroll and explain once and for all what is in the scroll, and therefore, what God is like. The Lion of the Tribe of Judah is a symbol for the Jewish Messiah, and as a lion, brings up images of fangs, claws, bloodshed, and death. So John turns to see this lion, fully expecting to see a representation of the Messiah as a bloody king who rides out to kill and destroy His enemies. Remember that this also is what the Jewish people looked for in the Messiah when He came. But when John looks, he only sees a Lamb, which appeared as though it had been slain (Rev 5:6). By describing the Lamb "as though it had been slain," John is raising the idea that the Lamb was covered in blood, for how else would a slain lamb appear? Furthermore, this image of the Messiah being covered in blood appears elsewhere in the book as well (Rev 19:13).

We later discover that this Lamb was slain since "the foundation of the world" (Rev 13:8). This does not mean that Jesus was slain when the world was created, for this would require Jesus to have died before anyone had sinned, which would in turn make sin a necessary part of God's creation. If Jesus was slain before sin entered the world, then sin would be required in order to make sense of the lamb slain. Instead, it is better to understand the phrase "the foundation of the world" as a reference to the practices and values upon which the world is founded. The foundation of the world doesn't mean the creation of the world, but the foundation of civilization, or the foundation upon which the world is built.

And what foundation is that? What is the foundation upon which this world and all civilizations are built? The foundation of the world, or the foundation of world civilization, is the practice of sacred, scapegoating violence (see Part IV on Scapegoating). It is first seen in Genesis 4 when Cain murders his brother Abel and then goes off and founds the world's first city.

This sacred, scapegoating, sacrificial violence is defined as "sin" (Gen 4:7), and is seen throughout the rest of Scripture as the method by which humans create the peace that is necessary for civilization to exist. Without the scapegoating bloodshed of sacrificial victims, all human rivalry would degenerate into a contagion of violence that threatens to destroy everybody and everything in its path.

So when John writes that the Lamb of God was slain at the foundation of the world, he is saying that by dying as a scapegoat, sacrificial victim, Jesus exposed what human civilization and culture is founded upon, identified Himself with all scapegoat victims throughout history, and showed humanity another way out from the threat of all-consuming violence. Rather than kill His enemies as a Lion would do, Jesus died for His enemies. Rather than shed the blood of His enemies, Jesus shed His own blood for His enemies. Rather than go forth to kill and destroy, Jesus went forth to love and forgive. As we follow Jesus in this way of love, forgiveness, and self-sacrificial living, it is then that we are cleansed from our participation in the sin of the world (Rev 1:5; 12:11).

This idea is introduced in Revelation 5:5-10 where the Lion of the Tribe of Judah is actually revealed to be a slain Lamb, and John shows that following the Lamb is how we are redeemed to God through the blood of Jesus (Rev 5:9-10). Though people usually kill others in order to gain power and position in this world, those who follow in the way of the Lamb are the ones who will be kings and priests on the earth. To be redeemed through the blood of Jesus, therefore, is to be bought back from our slavery to sin and death, and to be given new life, power, and liberty in this life to live as the kings and priests upon this earth that God always wanted us to be (cf. Gen 2). This is how we receive the royal and priestly robes that are dipped in blood but emerge white as snow (Rev 7:14).

Following this pattern then, one can read Revelation through the crucivision lens of Jesus, and be faced with a choice. We can either continue to walk the path of war and scapegoating violence which leads only to more and greater bloodshed as every person goes forth to slay their enemies with the name of God on their lips, or we can follow in the way of Jesus as He rides forth on a white horse in a robe dipped in his own blood (it is red with blood before the "battle" even begins), and with His only weapon being a sword that emerges from His mouth (Rev 19:11-16). Even the kings and armies who are "slain" with the sword of His mouth (Rev 19:21) later make an appearance in the Temple of the Lamb to give Him glory and honor (Rev 21:24-26). Then peace is restored, the Garden is resurrected, and the Tree of Life once again brings healing to the nations (Rev 22).

The message of the book of Revelation, and the symbolism of blood in this book all point to one central truth: If we want to overcome the world (cf. 2:7, 11, 17, 26; 3:5, 12, 21), then we do so not with the bloody ways of this world, but by following the example of Jesus in laying down our lives for others. Though this world is founded upon violence, bloodshed, and scapegoating, we who follow Jesus do not scapegoat others, but let ourselves be scapegoated. We do not accuse, but let ourselves be accused (Rev 12:10). When we follow Jesus in these ways, we will, like Him, overcome the world and its ways as we live as kings and priests within the Kingdom of God forever and ever.

THE BLOOD OF JESUS IS THE SOLUTION TO SIN

So we have finally found the answer to the problem of human sin. The solution to sin truly is the blood of Jesus. But the blood of Jesus is not the solution to sin as much of Christian theology suggests. The blood of Jesus does not purchase forgiveness for us, pay the penalty for sin, or appease the wrath of God. God didn't need the blood of Jesus as any sort of payment or appeasement. God does not desire blood and death. The blood of Jesus has nothing to do with any of those things.

No, the blood of Jesus is the solution to the problem of human sin because it both exposes the true nature of our sin to us, and then calls us to no longer participate in these practices. The blood of Jesus calls us away from scapegoating and violence, toward love and forgiveness. In this way, the blood of Jesus truly does save the world from sin. It saves us, not because it buys redemption and reconciliation from God, but because it reveals to us the truth about our sin and calls us to live toward others as God has always lived toward us: with nothing but love, grace, mercy, and forgiveness. When we live this way, all the world will know that we have been saved from sin.

CHAPTER 12

THE PRECIOUS BLOOD OF JESUS

We've been on quite a journey in this book, and there's been a lot of blood along the way. We traveled through sin, law, sacrifice, scapegoating, and blood, and in so doing, have seen something surprising about the death of Jesus. We have seen something that most have never thought or imagined. While many believe that the sacrifice of Jesus on the cross saves the world from sin because it bought God off or paid some divine debt for our transgressions, we have discovered the exact opposite. God didn't get paid off for sin, because there was no debt owed to God in the first place. Due to His great love for us, God has always and only forgiven all people for all their sins. So why then did Jesus have to die? This book has explained why. And so did Jesus.

Through His life and ministry, Jesus revealed that the true enemy of humanity is not God, but sin. Sin has enslaved humanity into a never-ending cycle of rivalry, blame, accusation, scapegoating, condemnation, and violence. Worst of all, sin has colluded with religion to blame this scapegoating cycle on God, so that we feel like God is against us and we must appease and satisfy Him in order to gain the forgiveness of sins and everlasting life.

Jesus came to expose and expel this entire way of thinking. During His life and ministry, Jesus told people through His words and actions that God is not angry, that He does not want more sacrifices or offerings, but that He loves, accepts, and freely forgives all people, no matter what. Jesus clearly and consistently proclaimed freedom from sin, and He did so, not on the basis of a religious sacrificial system (even His own sacrifice), but simply on the basis of God's limitless love, mercy, grace, and forgiveness.

What this means is that when Jesus went to the cross, He did not die for God. Jesus died for religion. He died to expose and bring to an end the sacred sin of sacrificial death and scapegoating victims. In His death, Jesus put to death the religious requirement of death. He exposed the emptiness of the sacrificial system for what it was: a form of satanic enslavement by which humans think they are appeasing God for that which He had already forgiven them. Religion says: God is angry with you, but will forgive you if you sacrifice this animal and kill that enemy. By going to the cross under the condemnation of religion, and then being raised again to new life by God, Jesus exposed the entire lie of religion, which forms the foundation of human culture and civilization. Through His death and resurrection, Jesus revealed this sin for what it truly is, and then showed us how to live free from it. Jesus showed us the way of escape. He showed us that just as sin, death, and the devil have no hold on God, when we follow the way of Jesus, such things have no hold on us either.

So if God is angry at anything, He is angry at how we have been enslaved to the lies of sin. God wants us to live free from slavery and bondage. And the greatest slaver of all is the religious lie about God's anger, and how law, sacrifice, and scapegoating others gains forgiveness for us from God. The great lie of sin is that the things which promise to release us from sin, are in fact sin themselves. Religion promises to cast out Satan, but its solution only embeds sin further into our lives. God sees this, knows this, and aches for us to be free from sin and its many lies. So He sent Jesus, to become sin for us, so that for the first time, we might see sin in all its ugly glory, and, for the first time, be invited to live free from it.

This is what we have seen in this book. It has revealed how the sacrifice of Jesus saves the world from sin. This book has shown that when Scripture talks about Jesus coming to deliver and rescue us from sin, it means that He came to reveal to us what sin *truly* is and then show us a way out of this never ending cycle of rivalry, blame, violence, murder, and scapegoating. The point of this book was not just to discuss five key terms in the Bible, but to see how we ourselves participate in the sin of violent, sacrificial scapegoating, and use the law of God as justification for doing so. This is not a book of dry and dusty theology, but is about practical day-to-day living. For if the sin of sacrificial scapegoating is at the foundation of the world, then it undergirds everything this world is founded upon, and everything that guides and directs the values and decisions of this world. But Jesus came to set us free and show us a new way to live.

He did this through His own violent and bloody death on the cross. It was not Jesus' death that was important, nor was it His blood. Instead, it was necessary that His blood be shed *violently*. Only the violent shedding of the blood of Jesus revealed the truth to us. Only the violent shedding of the blood of Jesus rescues and delivers us from sin like nothing else ever could. Only the entire bloody spectacle of the cross reveals a God who is more deeply in love with us than we ever before imagined. The reason the Bible focuses so much on bloodshed, and the reason the New Testament focuses so much on the blood of Jesus is so that we might truly see ourselves for the first time, and then follow Jesus into a life of love, forgiveness, and freedom.

So is the blood of Jesus precious? Yes. Of course! But it is more precious than most of us have ever realized. The blood of Jesus did not pay some sort of debt in the divine bank account for our sin. No, God had already taken care of that through His gracious forgiveness from all eternity. The blood of Jesus is precious because it reveals to us the most important truth of all, which is a truth we could never have seen or understood on our own. The blood of Jesus reveals to us that God does not want or demand blood sacrifice, but that we want and demand it. We require blood to alleviate our own guilt and solve our own problems. But by coming and dying as a scapegoat on the cross, and then rising again and refusing to retaliate, Jesus revealed that there is a different way. Jesus revealed the way of God, which is the way of forgiveness.

While sacrificial violence does bring a temporary peace, it comes at the price of the life of another. Forgiveness, however, brings a better and more lasting peace, and one that does not require us to take the life of another, but invites us to unite in love and harmony with one another, just as God in Christ unites with us. How thankful we can be that Jesus suffered and died at our hands and for our bloodthirsty desires, to reveal to us that we do not have to live this way any longer. Like God, we too can love; we too can forgive. Only in this way will the world finally find peace.

Nothing else reveals our sin to us like the violent death of Jesus on the cross. All other sacrificial and scapegoat victims we could justify. They deserved it. They truly were guilty. We were just treating them the way they treated us. But not so with Jesus. He was "sinless" and knew no sin, but we killed Him in God's name anyway, thereby proving that this is also what we do to others when we feel justified and righteous in killing them. Only the innocent blood of the Lamb of God could reveal this to us and also call us to put an end to it through forgiveness. For of all victims throughout history, only Jesus would have been justified in retaliation and vengeance against those who wrongfully accused and killed Him. But instead He forgave us. This shows that we too can forgive others. We can forgive as we have been forgiven. We can love as we have been loved. The way out of sin is to see how Jesus dealt with our sin against Him. Nothing and nobody else could have so clearly revealed this to us.

So let us sing that wonderful hymn again, but with slightly modified words:

What reveals to me my sin?
Nothing but the blood of Jesus;
What can make me whole again?
Nothing but the blood of Jesus.

Refrain:
Oh, precious is the flow
That unveils what His does show;
No other fount I know,
Nothing but the blood of Jesus.

DISCUSSION QUESTIONS

Below are discussion questions to help you study the concepts in this book. They also provide a good starting place for talking about this book with a small group of friends from your church, school, or town. Each set of questions is based on one of the five key terms discussed in this book: Sin, Law, Sacrifice, Scapegoat, and Blood.

QUESTIONS ABOUT SIN

1. How do most modern people define sin? What do we tend to think sin is?

2. How did many ancient people view sin? What did they tend to think sin was? Why did they think that blood could solve the problem of sin?

3. Most people today tend to view sin as breaking a law or command of God. This book proposes that such actions are little more than symptoms or signs of the greater problem identified in the Bible as "sin." What is this "sin"?

4. When humans become "holy," will we become more like God, or become more like the humans that God wants us to be? Why is this distinction important?

5. What do God's instructions to Adam and Eve in Genesis 2 reveal about the way God wants humans to live? How about God's instructions to the people of Israel in Exodus 20?

6. What do you think about the statement that sin is not necessarily breaking God's commandments, but about engaging in violence and the things that lead to violence?

7. Near the beginning of the chapter "Scriptures on Sin," what two truths are discussed about sin and God's activity in response to sin?

8. Though sin may have been introduced by Adam and Eve in Genesis 3, when did sin actually "bear fruit" and what did this look like?

9. How can Paul claim to have faultlessly kept the entire law, but also be the chief of sinners?

10. Why does God want humans to refrain from sin? Is it because He is so deeply hurt and offended by sin that He just cannot stand to be around sinners? Or is it because He loves us so much, He does not want to see *us* hurt and damaged by sin?

QUESTIONS ABOUT LAW

1. What is the law for?

2. What is lacking in the law?

3. Why are laws given? Why do laws only increase over time?

4. How can the law lead us into greater sin?

5. Why is obeying the law not the answer to our problem of sin?

6. What is it that God really wants from us?

7. Why did God give the law, when He knew it wouldn't work?

8. According to Paul, what is the purpose of the law?

9. What does the Sermon on the Mount focus our attention on?

10. Why do you think Jesus said that His disciples will be known by their love, rather than by their law keeping?

QUESTIONS ABOUT SACRIFICE

1. What are the three purposes of sacrifice? Describe the differences between the three.

2. What are humans trying to fix or correct when we offer sacrifices?

3. Regardless of our religion or heritage, who are humans trying to appease with our sacrifices?

4. If God truly did demand sacrifices from us, how is He any different from the other gods that require sacrifices? In other words, since sacrifices "work" everywhere they are performed (regardless of religion), what does this mean about the sacrificial instructions in the Bible?

5. Can God be in the presence of sin? If you answer "No," how could the killing of an animal (or a person) make a difference in God's ability to be near sinners? Also, how could Jesus be fully God and yet live here on earth?

6. If there is no sacrifice for intentional sin, how does God "take care" of these sins? Do you think God also "takes care" of unintentional sins the same way?

7. What did the chapters on sacrifice begin to reveal about why Jesus died on the cross? Was His sacrifice for the purpose of pleasing and appeasing God? Why or why not?

8. Why does the Bible contain so much information and teaching about sacrifice and violence?

9. When is the first sacrifice performed in the Bible?

10. Why are sacrifices not the solution to sin?

QUESTIONS ABOUT SCAPEGOATING

1. What are the five stages of the "scapegoat mechanism"?

2. How does rivalry lead to violence?

3. Why is a scapegoat needed to end violence?

4. If the scapegoat is relatively innocent (or at least, not completely guilty of everything for which they are charged), why does their death create peace between two warring sides?

5. What is the better way of creating peace between two parties?

6. What are the three types of scapegoat? Why do they make good scapegoats?

7. What are the three signs of scapegoating?

8. How is it that we humans "scapegoat" God?

9. What are the three ways that Jesus reveals scapegoating?

10. What does Jesus reveal about scapegoating in regard to God and in regard to humanity?

QUESTIONS ABOUT BLOOD

1. What have these chapters on blood (as well as previous chapters) revealed about the death of Jesus in relation to the wrath of God? In other words, did Jesus die to appease the wrath of God? Why or why not?

2. What does the bloody crucifixion of Jesus reveal to us?

3. Why did the crucifixion of Jesus need to be bloody and violent?

4. What does the law of God do for violence?

5. If it was not God who forced His Son to die on a cross, who (or what) put Jesus on the cross, and why?

6. The rationale behind sacrifice is that the taking of one life saves many others. Why and how is this false?

7. Why did Jesus submit Himself to the "scapegoat mechanism"? What does His death as a scapegoat victim reveal to us?

8. What is the only kind of sacrifice God calls each of us to practice?

9. God promises to always give us a way of escape from sin. How does Jesus dying on the cross reveal to us the way of escape from our own sinful scapegoating tendencies?

10. How does the violent death of Jesus on the cross save us from our sin?

SUGGESTED READING

As you were reading, you might have noticed that this book is missing a lot of the footnotes one might expect to find in a book like this. There are two reasons for this.

First, the book was written for a more "popular" audience than for an academic. In general, only academics enjoy reading footnotes.

Second, while I usually take pride in in citing my sources—and always do so to the best of my ability whenever I am aware that I am citing an idea or source that I picked up from someone else's book—the way this book was written did not allow for footnotes. Let me explain.

For most of my adult life, I have been reading, studying, and thinking about how to understand the violence in Scripture. It has always been a troublesome aspect of Scripture for me. I remember being faced with the question for the first time in college, when I was a student at Montana State University. I was told by an atheist that the Christian Bible was more violent than the Muslim Qur'an and that throughout history Christians have performed more violence in the name of Jesus than Muslims have done in the name of Allah. I vehemently rejected these charges ... until I researched them for myself and discovered that they were true. Ever since that time, I have been on a quest to discover why the Bible is so violent, and how this violence reflects the character of God.

In the twenty-five years since, I have read countless articles and scores of books. Since I learn best by writing, every time I thought I had a solution to the problem of divine violence, I set out to write a book about it. In the last two decades, I have written at least half a dozen books on the topic. None of them were ever published, because I was never satisfied with the solutions I offered.

In January of 2017, I started teaching a series to my weekly discipleship group about the 52 key words of the Gospel. The study is called "The Gospel Dictionary" and is available as an online course on my website. Since the course is patterned after a dictionary, it looks at key words of the gospel in alphabetical order. Eight weeks (and eight words) into the course, I came to the word "blood." As I was preparing to teach the students how to understand the word "blood" and its connection to the blood of Jesus, it occurred to me that I couldn't teach about the "blood" of Jesus without the students first understanding why Jesus suffered and died as an innocent scapegoat victim. So before I taught them about blood, I would have to teach them about scapegoating.

But since scapegoating began as a form of human sacrifice, this meant that before the students could understand scapegoating, they would need to understand where sacrifices came from and why humans perform sacrifices. But of course, since sacrifices are commanded by the law of Moses, then understanding sacrifices would require a proper grasp of why the law was given. And since the law is closely related to sin, and is viewed by some as the cure for sin, we couldn't really grasp the reason for the law unless we understood what sin was and where sin came from.

Once I saw this backward progression, it is then that I realized how the bloody and violent death of Jesus was the solution to the problem of sin, and especially the bloody and violent sacrificial scapegoating sin of humanity which forms the foundation of civilization and culture. So over the next five weeks, as I taught my class, I also wrote this book. Yes, this book was written in the span of five weeks, primarily as a series of lessons to a discipleship group.

Which somewhat explains the lack of footnotes. Since the book was primarily written as my teaching notes for a discipleship group, and since I wrote the entire book in the span of five weeks, I did not attempt to track down possible sources from my previous 25 years of reading and research. I wrote 95% of the book straight from my head, from the knowledge that had been deposited there over the years. And so while much of what I wrote likely depends on the ideas I picked up elsewhere, figuring out which authors were responsible for which ideas was impossible. Asking me to cite my sources would be like asking me to explain which teachers taught me to write this sentence in English. I can't remember half of my teacher's names, and even if I could, I cannot recall what each different English teacher taught. So rather than attempt to "fake it" and add a bunch of footnotes to make scholars happy and to make myself look more "academic," I left the book as I wrote it.

Nevertheless, I do wish to recognize those scholars and authors who I recall as being especially beneficial and helpful during my 25 years of study on this topic. The following list is by no means exhaustive, but these are the books I recall as being formative for the development of my thinking. If you appreciated the ideas of this book and want to learn more, I recommend the following books for further research and study.

Gil Bailie, *Violence Unveiled* (Danvers, MA: Crossroads, 1996).

Sharon Baker, *Executing God* (Louisville, KY: John Knox, 2013).

Mark E. Biddle, *Missing the Mark* (Nashville: Abingdon, 2005).

Terence Fretheim, *The Suffering of God* (Minneapolis: Fortress, 1984).

Mark S. Heim, *Saved from Sacrifice* (Grand Rapids: Eerdmans, 2006).

Jürgen Moltmann, *The Crucified God* (Minneapolis, Fortress, 1993).

Fleming Rutledge, *The Crucifixion* (Grand Rapids: Eerdmans, 2015).

John Sailhamer, *The Meaning of the Pentateuch* (Downers Grove: IVP, 2009).

Raymund Schwager, *Must There be Scapegoats?* (Leominster, UK: Gracewing, 2000).

Brian Zahnd, *A Farewell to Mars* (Colorado Springs: David C. Cook, 2014).

ABOUT JEREMY MYERS

Jeremy Myers is an author, blogger, podcaster, and Bible teacher. Much of his content can be found at RedeemingGod.com, where he seeks to help liberate people from the shackles of religion. His site also provides an online discipleship group where thousands of like-minded people discuss life and theology together in an online community, and encourage each other to follow Jesus into the world.

Jeremy lives in Oregon with his wife and three beautiful daughters. They enjoy camping, hiking, and reading.

If you appreciated the content of this book, would you consider recommending it to your friends and leaving a review on Amazon? Thanks!

JOIN JEREMY MYERS AND LEARN MORE

Take Bible and theology courses by joining Jeremy at
RedeemingGod.com/join/

Receive updates about free books, discounted books,
and new books by joining Jeremy at
RedeemingGod.com/read-books/

THE ATONEMENT OF GOD: BUILDING YOUR THEOLOGY ON A CRUCIVISION OF GOD

After reading this book, you will never read the Bible the same way again.

By reading this book, you will learn to see God in a whole new light. You will also learn to see yourself in a whole new light, and learn to live life in a whole new way.

The book begins with a short explanation of the various views of the atonement, including an explanation and defense of the "Non-Violent View" of the atonement. This view argues that God did not need or demand the death of Jesus in order to forgive sins. In fact, God has never been angry with us at all, but has always loved and always forgiven.

Following this explanation of the atonement, J. D. Myers takes you on a journey through 10 areas of theology which are radically changed and transformed by the Non-Violent view of the atonement. Read this book, and let your life and theology look more and more like Jesus Christ!

REVIEWS FROM AMAZON

> Outstanding book! Thank you for helping me understand "Crucivision" and the "Non-Violent Atonement." Together, they help it all make sense and fit so well into my personal thinking about God. I am encouraged to be truly free to love and forgive, because God has always loved and forgiven without condition, because Christ exemplified this grace on the Cross, and because the Holy Spirit is in the midst of all life, continuing to show the way through people like you. –Samuel R. Mayer

If you have the same resolve as Paul, to know nothing but Jesus and Him crucified (2 Cor 2:2), then this book is for you. I read it the first time from start to finish on Father's Day ... no coincidence. This book revealed Father God's true character; not as an angry wrathful God, but as a kind loving merciful Father to us. Share in Jeremy's revelation concerning Jesus' crucifixion, and how this "vision" of the crucifixion (hence "crucivision") will make you fall in love with Jesus all over again, in a new and deeper way than you could imagine. Buy a copy for a friend—you won't want to give up your copy because you will want to read it again and again until the Holy Spirit makes Jeremy's revelation your revelation. –Amy

This book gives another view of the doctrines we have been taught all of our lives. And this actually makes more sense than what we have heard. I myself have had some of these thoughts but couldn't quite make the sense of it all by myself. J.D. Myers helped me answer some questions and settle some confusion for my doctrinal views. This is truly a refreshing read. Jesus really is the demonstration of who God is and God is much easier to understand than being so mean and vindictive in the Old Testament. The tension between the wrath of God and His justice and the love of God are eased when reading this understanding of the atonement. Read with an open mind and enjoy! –Clare N. Bez

THE RE-JUSTIFICATION OF GOD: A STUDY OF ROMANS 9:10-24

Romans 9 has been a theological battleground for centuries. Scholars from all perspectives have debated whether Paul is teaching corporate or individual election, whether or not God truly hates Esau, and how to understand the hardening of Pharaoh's heart. Both sides have accused the other of misrepresenting God.

In this book, J. D. Myers presents a mediating position. Gleaning from both Calvinistic and Arminian insights into Romans 9, J. D. Myers presents a beautiful portrait of God as described by the pen of the Apostle Paul.

Here is a way to read Romans 9 which allows God to remain sovereign and free, but also allows our theology to avoid the deterministic tendencies which have entrapped certain systems of the past.

Read this book and—maybe for the first time—learn to see God the way Paul saw Him.

REVIEWS FROM AMAZON

> Fantastic read! Jeremy Myers has a gift for seeing things from outside of the box and making it easy to understand for the rest of us. The Re -Justification of God provides a fresh and insightful look into Romans 9:10-24 by interpreting it within the context of chapters 9-11 and then fitting it into the framework of Paul's entire epistle as well. Jeremy manages to provide a solid theological exegesis on a widely misunderstood portion of scripture without it sounding to academic. Most importantly, it provides us with a better view and understanding of who God is. If I had a list of ten books that I thought every Christian should read, this one would be on the list. –Wesley Rostoll

I feel the author has spiritual insight to scripture and helps to explain things. I would recommend any of his work! –Uriah Scott

I loved this book! It made me cry and fall in love with God all over again. Romans is one of my favorite books, but now my eyes have been opened to what Paul was really saying. I knew in my heart that God was the good guy, but J. D. Meyers provided the analysis to prove the text. I have been examining all the "proofs" about reformed theology because I was attracted to the message, but couldn't go all the way down the TULIP path, because it did not resonate in my heart that God who is Holy would love imperfectly. I believed Holy trumped Sovereignty, yet, I believe in the sin message, wrath of God, the Gospel and Jesus and decided that I was a "middle of the road" person caught between two big Theologies (the Big C and A). Now, I get it. I can with great confidence read the difficult chapters of Romans, and my furrowed brow is eased. Thank you, J. D. Myers. I love God, even more and am so grateful that his is so longsuffering in his perfect love! Well done. –Treinhart

WHY YOU HAVE NOT COMMITTED THE UNFORGIVABLE SIN: FINDING FORGIVENESS FOR THE WORST OF SINS

Are you afraid that you have committed the unforgivable sin?

In this book, you will learn what this sin is and why you have not committed it. After surveying the various views about blasphemy against the Holy Spirit and examining Matthew 12:31-32, you will learn what the sin is and how it is committed.

As a result of reading this book, you will gain freedom from the fear of committing the worst of all sins, and learn how much God loves you!

REVIEWS FROM AMAZON

> This book addressed things I have struggled and felt pandered to for years, and helped to bring wholeness to my heart again. –Natalie Fleming

> A great read, on a controversial subject; biblical, historical and contextually treated to give the greatest understanding. May be the best on this subject (and there is very few) ever written. – Tony Vance

> You must read this book. Forgiveness is necessary to see your blessings. So if you purchase this book, [you will have] no regrets. –Virtuous Woman

> Jeremy Myers covers this most difficult topic thoroughly and with great compassion. –J. Holland

> Good study. Very helpful. A must read. I like this study because it was an in depth study of the scripture. –Rose Knowles

Excellent read and helpful the reader offers hope for all who may be effected by this subject. He includes e-mails from people, [and] is very thorough. –Richie

Wonderful explication of the unpardonable sin. God loves you more than you know. May Jesus Christ be with you always. –Robert M Sawin III

Excellent book! Highly recommend for anyone who has anxiety and fear about having committed the unforgivable sin. –William Tom

As someone who is constantly worried that they have disappointed or offended God, this book was, quite literally, a "Godsend." I thought I had committed this sin as I swore against the Holy Spirit in my mind. It only started after reading the verse about it in the Bible. The swear words against Him came into my mind over and over and I couldn't seem to stop no matter how much I prayed. I was convinced I was going to hell and cried constantly. I was extremely worried and depressed. This book has allowed me to breathe again, to have hope again. Thank you, Jeremy. I will read and re-read. I believe this book was definitely God inspired. I only wish I had found it sooner. –Sue

SKELETON CHURCH: A BARE-BONES DEFINITION OF CHURCH (PREFACE TO THE CLOSE YOUR CHURCH FOR GOOD BOOK SERIES)

The church has a skeleton which is identical in all types of churches. Unity and peace can develop in Christianity if we recognize this skeleton as the simple, bare-bones definition of church. But when we focus on the outer trappings—the skin, hair, and eye color, the clothes, the muscle tone, and other outward appearances—division and strife form within the church.

Let us return to the skeleton church and grow in unity once again.

REVIEWS FROM AMAZON

> My church gathering is struggling to break away from traditions which keep us from following Jesus into the world. Jeremy's book lends encouragement and helpful information to groups like us. –Robert A. White

> I worried about buying another book that aimed at reducing things to a simple minimum, but the associations of the author along with the price gave me reason to hope and means to see. I really liked this book. First, because it wasn't identical to what other simple church people are saying. He adds unique elements that are worth reading. Second, the size is small enough to read, think, and pray about without getting lost. –Abel Barba

> In *Skeleton Church*, Jeremy Myers makes us rethink church. For Myers, the church isn't a style of worship, a row of pews, or even a building. Instead, the church is the people of God, which provides the basic skeletal structure of the church. The muscles, parts, and flesh of the church are how we carry Jesus' mission into our own neighborhoods in our own unique ways. This eBook will

make you see the church differently. –Travis Mamone

This book gets back to the basics of the New Testament church—who we are as Christians and what our perspective should be in the world we live in today. Jeremy cuts away all the institutional layers of a church and gets to the heart of our purpose as Christians in the world we live in and how to affect the people around us with God heart and view in mind. Not a physical church in mind. It was a great book and I have read it twice now. –Vaughn Bender

The Skeleton Church ... Oh. My. Word. Why aren't more people reading this!? It was well-written, explained everything beautifully, and it was one of the best explanations of how God intended for church to be. Not to mention an easy read! The author took it all apart, the church, and showed us how it should be. He made it real. If you are searching to find something or someone to show you what God intended for the church, this is the book you need to read. – Ericka

THE DEATH AND RESURRECTION OF THE CHURCH (VOLUME 1 IN THE CLOSE YOUR CHURCH FOR GOOD BOOK SERIES)

In a day when many are looking for ways to revitalize the church, Jeremy Myers argues that the church should die.

This is not only because of the universal principle that death precedes resurrection, but also because the church has adopted certain Satanic values and goals and the only way to break free from our enslavement to these values is to die.

But death will not be the end of the church, just as death was not the end of Jesus. If the church follows Jesus into death, and even to the hellish places on earth, it is only then that the church will rise again to new life and vibrancy in the Kingdom of God.

REVIEWS FROM AMAZON

> I have often thought on the church and how its acceptance of corporate methods and assimilation of cultural media mores taints its mission but Jeremy Myers eloquently captures in words the true crux of the matter—that the church is not a social club for do-gooders but to disseminate the good news to all the nooks and crannies in the world and particularly and primarily those bastions in the reign of evil. That the "gates of Hell" Jesus pronounces indicate that the church is in an offensive, not defensive, posture as gates are defensive structures.
>
> I must confess that in reading I was inclined to be in agreement as many of the same thinkers that Myers riffs upon have influenced me also—Walter Wink, Robert Farrar Capon, Greg Boyd, NT Wright, etc. So as I read, I frequently nodded my head in agreement. –GN Trifanaff

The book is well written, easy to understand, organized and consistent thoughts. It rightfully makes the reader at least think about things as … is "the way we have always done it" necessarily the Biblical or Christ-like way, or is it in fact very sinful?! I would recommend the book for pastors and church officers; those who have the most moving-and-shaking clout to implement changes, or keep things the same. –Joel M. Wilson

Absolutely phenomenal. Unless we let go of everything Adamic in our nature, we cannot embrace anything Christlike. For the church to die, we the individual temples must dig our graves. It is a must read for all who take issues about the body of Christ seriously. –Mordecai Petersburg

PUT SERVICE BACK INTO THE CHURCH SERVICE (VOLUME 2 IN THE CLOSE YOUR CHURCH FOR GOOD BOOK SERIES)

Churches around the world are trying to revitalize their church services. There is almost nothing they will not try. Some embark on multi-million dollar building campaigns while others sell their buildings to plant home churches. Some hire celebrity pastors to attract crowds of people, while others hire no clergy so that there can be open sharing in the service.

Yet despite everything churches have tried, few focus much time, money, or energy on the one thing that churches are supposed to be doing: loving and serving others like Jesus.

Put Service Back into the Church Service challenges readers to follow a few simple principles and put a few ideas into practice which will help churches of all types and sizes make serving others the primary emphasis of a church service.

REVIEWS FROM AMAZON

> Jeremy challenges church addicts, those addicted to an unending parade of church buildings, church services, Bible studies, church programs and more to follow Jesus into our communities, communities filled with lonely, hurting people and BE the church, loving the people in our world with the love of Jesus. Do we need another training program, another seminar, another church building, a remodeled church building, more staff, updated music, or does our world need us, the followers of Jesus, to BE the church in the world? The book is well-written, challenging and a book that really can make a difference not only in our churches, but also and especially in our neighborhoods and communities. –Charles Epworth

Do you ever have an unexplained frustration with your church, its service or programs? Do you ever feel like you are "spinning your wheels" when it comes to reaching others for Christ? This book helps to explain why this might be happening, and presents a convincing argument for why today's church services are mostly ineffective and inefficient. You will read concepts explained that you've not fully heard before. And you will get hints as to how it could, or should, work. –MikeM

I just finished *Put Service Back Into Church Service* by Jeremy Myers, and as with his others books I have read on the church, it was very challenging. For those who love Jesus, but are questioning the function of the traditional brick and mortar church, and their role in it, this is a must read. It may be a bit unsettling to the reader who is still entrenched in traditional "church," but it will make you think, and possibly re-evaluate your role in the church. Get this book, and all others on the church by Jeremy. –Ward Kelly

CHURCH IS MORE THAN BODIES, BUCKS, & BRICKS (VOLUME 3 IN THE CLOSE YOUR CHURCH FOR GOOD BOOK SERIES)

Many people define church as a place and time where people gather, a way for ministry money to be given and spent, and a building in which people regularly meet on Sunday mornings.

In this book, author and blogger Jeremy Myers shows that church is more than bodies, bucks, and bricks.

Church is the people of God who follow Jesus into the world, and we can be the church no matter how many people we are with, no matter the size of our church budget, and regardless of whether we have a church building or not.

By abandoning our emphasis on more people, bigger budgets, and newer buildings, we may actually liberate the church to better follow Jesus into the world.

REVIEWS FROM AMAZON

> This book does more than just identify issues that have been bothering me about church as we know it, but it goes into history and explains how we got here. In this way it is similar to Viola's *Pagan Christianity*, but I found it a much more enjoyable read. Jeremy goes into more detail on the three issues he covers as well as giving a lot of practical advice on how to remedy these situations. –Portent

> This book surprised me. I have never read anything from this author previously. The chapters on the evolution of the tithe were eye openers. This is something that has bothered me for years in the ministry. It may be truth that is too

expensive to believe when it comes to feeding the monster. –Karl Ingersoll

Since I returned from Africa 20 years ago I have struggled with going to church back in the States. This book helped me not feel guilty and has helped me process this struggle. It is challenging and overflows with practical suggestions. He loves the church despite its imperfections and suggests ways to break the bondage we find ourselves in. –Truealian

Jeremy Meyers always writes a challenging book ... It seems the American church (as a whole) is very comfortable with the way things are ... The challenge is to get out of the brick and mortar buildings and stagnant programs and minister to the needy in person with funds in hand to meet their needs especially to the widows and orphans as we are directed in the scriptures. –GGTexas

DYING TO RELIGION AND EMPIRE (VOLUME 4 IN THE CLOSE YOUR CHURCH FOR GOOD BOOK SERIES)

Could Christianity exist without religious rites or legal rights? In *Dying to Religion and Empire*, I not only answer this question with an emphatic "Yes!" but argue that if the church is going to thrive in the coming decades, we must give up our religious rites and legal rights.

Regarding religious rites, I call upon the church to abandon the quasi-magical traditions of water baptism and the Lord's Supper and transform or redeem these practices so that they reflect the symbolic meaning and intent which they had in New Testament times.

Furthermore, the church has become far too dependent upon certain legal rights for our continued existence. Ideas such as the right to life, liberty, and the pursuit of happiness are not conducive to living as the people of God who are called to follow Jesus into servanthood and death. Also, reliance upon the freedom of speech, the freedom of assembly, and other such freedoms as established by the Bill of Rights have made the church a servant of the state rather than a servant of God and the gospel. Such freedoms must be forsaken if we are going to live within the rule and reign of God on earth.

This book not only challenges religious and political liberals but conservatives as well. It is a call to leave behind the comfortable religion we know, and follow Jesus into the uncertain and wild ways of radical discipleship. To rise and live in the reality of God's Kingdom, we must first die to religion and empire.

REVIEWS FROM AMAZON

Jeremy is one of the freshest, freest authors out there— and you need to hear what he has to say. This book is startling and new in thought and conclusion. Are the "sacraments" inviolate? Why? Do you worship at a secular altar? Conservative? Liberal? Be prepared to open your eyes. Mr. Myers will not let you keep sleeping!

For all free-thinkers, for all who consider themselves "spiritual," for all who have come out or are on the way out of "Babylon," this is a new book for you! Treat yourself, buy this book and enjoy it! –Shawn P. Smith

Jeremy Myers is one or the most thought provoking authors that I read, this book has really helped me to look outside the box and start thinking how can I make more sense of my relationship with Christ and how can I show others in a way that impacts them the way that Jesus' disciples impacted their world. Great book, great author. –Brett Hotchkiss

CRUCIFORM PASTORAL LEADERSHIP (VOLUME 5 IN THE CLOSE YOUR CHURCH FOR GOOD BOOK SERIES)

This book is forthcoming in early 2017.

The final volume in the *Close Your Church for Good* book series look at issues related to pastoral leadership in the church. It discusses topics such as preaching and pastoral pay from the perspective of the cross.

The best way pastors can lead their church is by following Jesus to the cross!

This book will be published in early 2017.

ADVENTURES IN FISHING (FOR MEN)

Adventures in Fishing (for Men) is a satirical look at evangelism and church growth strategies.

Using fictional accounts from his attempts to become a world-famous fisherman, Jeremy Myers shows how many of the evangelism and church growth strategies of today do little to actually reach the world for Jesus Christ.

Adventures in Fishing (for Men) pokes fun at some of the popular evangelistic techniques and strategies endorsed and practiced by many Christians in today's churches. The stories in this book show in humorous detail how little we understand the culture that surrounds us or how to properly reach people with the gospel of Jesus Christ. The story also shows how much time, energy, and money goes into evangelism preparation and training with the end result being that churches rarely accomplish any actual evangelism.

REVIEWS FROM AMAZON

> I found *Adventures in Fishing* (*For Men*) quite funny! Jeremy Myers does a great job shining the light on some of the more common practices in Evangelism today. His allegory gently points to the foolishness that is found within a system that takes the preaching of the gospel and tries to reduce it to a simplified formula. A formula that takes what should be an organic, Spirit led experience and turns it into a gospel that is nutritionally benign.
>
> If you have ever EE'd someone you may find Myers' book offensive, but if you have come to the place where you realize that Evangelism isn't a matter of a

script and checklists, then you might benefit from this light-hearted peek at Evangelism today. –Jennifer L. Davis

Adventures in Fishing (for Men) is good book in understanding evangelism to be more than just being a set of methods or to do list to follow. –Ashok Daniel

CHRISTMAS REDEMPTION: WHY CHRISTIANS SHOULD CELEBRATE A PAGAN HOLIDAY

Christmas Redemption looks at some of the symbolism and traditions of Christmas, including gifts, the Christmas tree, and even Santa Claus and shows how all of these can be celebrated and enjoyed by Christians as a true and accurate reflection of the gospel.

Though Christmas used to be a pagan holiday, it has been redeemed by Jesus.

If you have been told that Christmas is a pagan holiday and is based on the Roman festival of Saturnalia, or if you have been told that putting up a Christmas tree is idolatrous, or if you have been told that Santa Claus is Satanic and teaches children to be greedy, then you must read this book! In it, you will learn that all of these Christmas traditions have been redeemed by Jesus and are good and healthy ways of celebrating the truth of the gospel and the grace of Jesus Christ.

REVIEWS FROM AMAZON

> Too many times we as Christians want to condemn nearly everything around us and in so doing become much like the Pharisees and religious leaders that Jesus encountered. I recommend this book to everyone who has concerns of how and why we celebrate Christmas. I recommend it to those who do not have any qualms in celebrating but may not know the history of Christmas. I recommend this book to everyone, no matter who or where you are, no matter your background or beliefs, no matter whether you are young or old. –David H.

> Very informative book dealing with the roots of our modern Christmas traditions. The Biblical teaching on redemption is excellent! Highly recommended.

–Tamara

Finally, an educated writing about Christmas traditions. I have every book Jeremy Myers has written. His writings are fresh and truthful. –Retlaw "Steadfast"

This is a wonderful book full of hope and joy. The book explains where Christmas traditions originated and how they have been changed and been adapted over the years. The hope that the grace that is hidden in the celebrations will turn more hearts to the Lord's call is very evident. Jeremy Myers has given us a lovely gift this Christmas. His insights will lift our hearts and remain with us a long time. –Janet Cardoza

I love how the author uses multiple sources to back up his opinions. He doesn't just use bible verses, he goes back into the history of the topics (pagan rituals, Santa, etc.) as well. Great book! –Jenna G.

BOOK PUBLISHING INSTRUCTIONS: A STEP-BY-STEP GUIDE TO PUBLISHING YOUR BOOK AS A PAPERBACK AND EBOOK

The dirty little secret of the publishing industry is that authors don't really need publishing companies any longer. If you want to get published, you can!

This book gives you everything you need to take your unfinished manuscript and get it into print and into the hands of readers. It shows you how to format your manuscript for printing as a paperback and preparing the files for digital eReaders like the Kindle, iPad, and Nook.

This book provides tips and suggestions for editing and typesetting your book, inserting interior images, designing a book cover, and even marketing your book so that people will buy it and read it. Detailed descriptions of what to do are accompanied by screenshots for each step. Additional tools, tips, and websites are also provided which will help get your book published.

If you have a book idea, you need to read this book.

REVIEWS FROM AMAZON

> I self-published my first book with the "assistance" of a publishing company. In the end I was extremely unhappy for various reasons … Jeremy Myers' book … does not try to impress with all kinds of "learned quotations" but gets right to the thrust of things, plain and simple. For me this book will be a constant companion as I work on a considerable list of books on Christian doctrines. Whether you are a new aspiring author or one with a book or so behind you, save yourself much effort and frustration by investing in this book.
> –Gerrie Malan

This book was incredibly helpful. I am in the process of writing my first book and the info in here has really helped me go into this process with a plan. I now realize how incredibly naive I was about what goes into publishing a book, yet instead of feeling overwhelmed, I now feel prepared for the task. Jeremy has laid out the steps to every aspect of publishing step by step as though they were recipes in a cook book. From writing with Styles and using the Style guide to incorporating images and page layouts, it is all there and will end up saving you hours of time in the editing phase. –W. Rostoll

THE LIE – A SHORT STORY

When one billion people disappear from earth, what explanation does the president provide? Is he telling the truth, or exposing an age-old lie?

This fictional short story contains his televised speech.

Have you ever wondered what the antichrist will say when a billion people disappear from planet earth at the rapture? Here is a fictional account of what he might say.

Purchase the eBook for $0.99

JOIN JEREMY MYERS AND LEARN MORE

Take Bible and theology courses by joining Jeremy at
RedeemingGod.com/join/

Receive updates about free books, discounted books,
and new books by joining Jeremy at
RedeemingGod.com/read-books/

Printed in Great Britain
by Amazon

57262673R00174